Walter Benjamin's Grave

Michael Taussig

WALTER BENJAMIN'S GRAVE

The University of Chicago Press   Chicago and London

MICHAEL TAUSSIG is professor of anthropology at Columbia University. He is the author of nine books, including *Shamanism, Colonialism, and the Wild Man; Law in a Lawless Land;* and *My Cocaine Museum,* all published by the University of Chicago Press.

The University of Chicago Press, Chicago 60637
The University of Chicago Press, Ltd., London
© 2006 by The University of Chicago
All rights reserved. Published 2006
Printed in the United States of America

15 14 13 12 11 10 09 08 07 06   1 2 3 4 5
ISBN: 0-226-79003-7   (cloth)
ISBN: 0-226-79004-5   (paper)

Library of Congress Cataloging-in-Publication Data

Taussig, Michael T.
    Walter Benjamin's Grave / Michael Taussig
        p. cm.
    Includes bibliographical references.
    ISBN 0-226-79003-7 (cloth : alk. paper) — ISBN 0-226-79004-5 (pbk. : alk. paper)
    1. Anthropology—Field work. I. Title.
    GN34.3.F53T38 2006
    301.072′3—dc22

                                                2006007289

Contents

Looking back at these essays written over the past decade I think what they share is a love of muted and even defective storytelling as a form of analysis. Strange love indeed; love of the wound, love of the last gasp, as comes on strong in the lead essay, "Walter Benjamin's Grave," where I try to let the landscape overwhelm history such that the tragedy lies bare and the words, seeking some sort of redemption, fall aside. If I can't have my stories, then at least there has to be a swerve in the writing itself because the writing is the theory and the swerve is what trips up thought in a serpentine world. They also share a love of anthropological fieldwork, a love of the classical anthropology of so-called primitive societies, and an intense curiosity as to the displacement of Marx and Freud by Nietzsche and Bataille that such old-fashioned anthropology provokes.

Thematically there is great variation; from the graveyard at Port Bou where Walter Benjamin was buried on the Spanish frontier with France, to discussions of peasant poetry in Colombia, the pact with the devil, the disappearance of the sea, the peculiarities of the shaman's body, transgression, the New York City police, and the relationship between flowers and violence.

Half the essays have been rewritten for this book and only in that process did I become aware of how much I had wanted to write from within instead of standing outside pointing. This is not so much autobiography or what is sometimes called "self-reflexiveness," though there is plenty of that and necessarily so because the anthropologist is inevitably part of the reality analyzed. It is more like having the reality depicted turn back on the writing, rather than on the writer, and ask for a fair shake. "What have you learned?" the reality asks of the writing. "What remains as an excess that can't be assimilated and what are you going to do with the gift I bestow, I who am such strange stuff?"

One way of highlighting this is to lay bare what goes on in anthropological fieldwork as a prolonged encounter with others fraught with misunderstandings that actually open up the world more than do understandings. I try to depict this in my essay "Constructing America," which concerns a peasant poet in Colombia who, in reciting his epic verses, shatters all accepted frames of historical and social analysis that I can think of. In the give-and-take there with the anthropologist, the reader can see how precarious and unstable the whole enterprise of interpretation actually is and how this instability of meaning actually thickens meaning, a result enlivened by the peculiar fiction that frames the essay, estranging the entire encounter. The scene is set by the complete disappearance of the anthropologist. It is as if he had died. What is left is a bunch of notes and audiotapes in an archive in a faraway country, which some well-intentioned researchers stumble across and, with the aid of the wise director of the archive, proceed to analyze with an engaging mix of bewilderment and keen insight.

Bataille would have called this sovereignty, meaning the mastery of nonmastery, and in this he followed Nietzsche who complained that we don't think sufficiently about the fact that when we explain the unknown we reduce it too quickly to the known. That is the first problem. We strip the unknown of all that is strange. We show it who's boss, the basic rule of a university seminar. We tolerate neither ambiguity nor that which won't conform. The second and even greater misfortune here is that we thereby forget how strange is the known. This is why I have sought not for masterful explanations but for estrangement, the gift of ethnography no less than of literature.

Along with mimesis and secrecy, transgression was an issue that greatly interested me at the time I was writing these essays. Transgression came to me by way of Bataille who got it from Nietzsche, and it appealed to me as a way of reacting to—not explaining—the presence—not the role—of the Christian devil as a peasant image of large-scale capitalist enterprise, awesomely scaled and no less awesomely endowed with the ability to destroy life as well as bestow riches. This is set forth in "The Sun Gives without Receiving," a title I took from Bataille's *Accursed Share*—the accursed share being what is offered in sacrifice.

Sacrifice, pronounced Bataille, consecrates that which it destroys. There is holiness in crossing the threshold no less than in breaking the taboo, and the holy, lest we forget, is as likely to be left-handed as not. All rites know this and are built on it. The old anthropology of "primitive" societies as much as the texts from ancient history and today's commissions of inquiry into police corruption offer a goldmine of extraordinary examples. This is what the essay "Transgression" sets out to demonstrate, not merely as an essential part of human and social life but one with consequences for the way we think about thinking. This is further elaborated in "The Language of Flowers," concerned with connections between cartoons, flowers, and mutilation of corpses.

In this I merely follow the pioneering example of Bataille's *College of Sociology* that held meetings in Paris between 1937 and 1939. Drawing upon the ethnography of "primitive" societies, Nietzsche, and Freud, the college defined its subject as that of "sacred sociology" aimed at understanding modernity as terror fell over Europe. Today the terms seem no less relevant to the United States. We could certainly do with some "sacred sociology" right now.

Nietzsche said the devil was Christianity's appropriation of that stranger god, Dionysus, spirit of ecstasy and intoxication, mimicry and dance, unproductive expenditure and too muchness—the point being that some things, the important things in a human life and history, are motivated not only by rules but by the need to break them.

Such an approach is likely to create problems for those of us who yearn to master the unknown through logical explanations of the sort that Plato's puppet known as Socrates set forth. Would that reality could be assimilated to those harmonies—of pure thought—and was not like that famous river into which you can never step twice. To step into the river means to immerse oneself in the beingness of the world, which is messy, as well as ride the incandescent wave of instability and contradiction whereby the rule is both followed and broken, which is even messier.

To step into the river . . . Every time I write I am transported to the reality depicted. When I was working in New York in the late 1990s on my book on the Pacific coast of Colombia, for example, I would say "I'm off to the Pacific coast," and I wanted the reader to do the same.[1]

This of course is mimetic magic. Drawing upon the notion of sympathetic magic as presented in *The Golden Bough*, this could be called not the magic of like-affects-like, as when you find the inspiring metaphor that connects otherwise unalike things but instead "contagious magic," involving what appears to be a physical connection in order to effect, through rite, the substance connected. Classic examples would be the use of a person's hair or fingernail cuttings or secretions to effect that person. Words can do this, too, writing no less than reading being a ritualistic practice, and thus words can be links to viscerality, into the thingness of things connected in chains of being, not chains of meaning. Sylvia Plath's poetry is famous for this. She uses her word magic to take you into plants no less than mouths. Walter Benjamin said that a mark of surrealist poetry was that its connections were physical and not due to that "penny in the slot called meaning." This is what Nietzsche was getting at when he outrageously suggested that all philosophy was, without knowing it, based on an understanding of the body—or rather on a misunderstanding.

Yet Nietzsche would be the first to point out that for all their magic in this regard, and precisely because of their magic, words are actually arbitrary cultural conventions posing as if they were not arbitrary at all. Therefore, the task of the writer, as I see it, is to play with this dual function of words; pretend they are what they refer to—that they do take you to the rain forests of the Pacific coast—and at the same time recognize the artifice. This is I call the *nervous system,* one of whose functions is to make manifest the hand of the writer so as to perturb the fiction masquerading as what we call truth, which is, of course, what we call culture too.[2]

Masquerade takes us to secrecy, one of the most persuasive ideas and feelings that fuels metaphysics, amounting to the sense that reality is constituted by a façade behind which lurk forces that form a system. Whether it be God, the psychic unconscious, the economic infrastructure, or whatever occult presence you wish to fantasize about, this two-layered model of the real consisting of a deceptive surface and a concealed deeper truth has driven religions, science, politics, and the police, as so many exemplars of "intelligent design."

Nietzsche saw this as the Great Game giving power to the depth-seekers who chase the alleged secret to its lair and emerge triumphant, clutching a system by its scrawny throat so that they can transmute disorder into order. He preferred a "gay science," which would refuse the impulse to unmask or defrock and would instead use sleight of hand to counter the sleight of hand employed by the systemizers. This gay science and the view of reality on which it is based is the same as my *Nervous System,* something I learnt about principally in the violence of Colombia from the early 1980s onwards and have dwelt upon as my practice in the essays herein, especially the one on the shaman's body, "Viscerality, Faith, and Skepticism: Another Theory of Magic," and also in "NYPD Blues."

It goes like this: reality is a shell game; our writing should be too. For a moment they interlock, but then a new pattern of ordered disorder forms, always the one before the last . . .

And when today he lights up his cigarette, he uses a flintstone and a fuse,
like everyone else. "In a boat," he says, "that is the best way. The wind blows
the matches out, but the harder the wind blows, the more the fuse glows."
—WALTER BENJAMIN, "Spain, 1932"

Walter Benjamin's Grave

A PROFANE ILLUMINATION

When she came looking for Walter Benjamin's grave a few months after he died in the Hotel de Francia in Port Bou on the border between Spain and France, Hannah Arendt found nothing. Nothing, that is, other than one of the most beautiful places she had ever seen. "It was not to be found," she wrote Gershom Scholem shortly afterwards, "his name was not written anywhere." Yet according to the records provided by the town hall of Port Bou, one of Benjamin's traveling companions, Frau Gurland, had paid out seventy-five pesetas for the rental of a "niche" for five years on September 28, 1940, two days after Benjamin died from what was diagnosed by the local doctor, Ramón Vila Moreno, as cerebral apoplexy, but is generally understood to have been suicide by a massive overdose of morphine tablets. "He had enough morphine on him to take his life several times over," writes Lisa Fittko, who took him over the mountains into Spain.

Yet name or no name, the place was overwhelming.

"The cemetery faces a small bay directly looking over the Mediterranean," wrote Arendt. "It is carved in stone in terraces; the coffins are also pushed into such stone walls. It is by far one of the most fantastic and most beautiful spots I have ever seen in my life."[1]

Scholem was not impressed. Years later he seemed downright dismissive, bringing his book-length memoir[2] of Benjamin to an end with these words: "Certainly the spot is beautiful, but the grave is apocryphal." It was an abrupt and sour note on which to end the story of a life, as if the dead man and therefore we, too, had been cheated of an ending, and what we had gotten instead was a suspension, a book whose last page was missing. For not only was there no name, as Arendt had discovered, but worse still there was a fake name or, depending on your point of view, something even worse, namely, a fake grave. Photographs clearly indicated, to Scholem at least, that a wooden enclosure with Benjamin's name scrawled on it was nothing more than what he called "an invention of the cemetery attendants, whom in consideration of the number of inquiries wanted to assure themselves of a tip." Thus ended the life of the person who would be acclaimed, by George Steiner, for example, as the greatest critic of the twentieth century. And thus ends Scholem's memoir. Even in death, Benjamin was a loser, his grave the plaything of men seeking a tip. In lieu of a real grave, we might say, Scholem buries his subject under charges of profanity.

It is as if he deliberately strives to avoid monumentalizing Benjamin, choosing instead to end on the most prosaic of notes; skullduggery in the graveyard—reminiscent of what Benjamin in his 1929 essay on surrealism called a "profane illumination." But what exactly is illuminated? In Benjamin's coining of the phrase, the illumination in a "profane illumination" bears the emphatic trace of a religious illumination it has surpassed. Furthermore, in the famous "Theses on the Philosophy of History," written shortly before his death, Benjamin had stated that "only that historian will have the gift of fanning the spark of hope in the past who is firmly convinced that *even the dead* will not be safe from the enemy if he wins."[3] What impact does Scholem's assessment of his grave have on that spark of hope?

How can Scholem state that the photographs "clearly indicate" that the grave is fake? How could any photograph clearly show such? And if the photographs do this, then why have the cemetery attendants created such a blatant fake when their machinations would surely be as obvious to visitors to the site as to Scholem studying the photographs? Surely it was not beyond the skill of these grave diggers to manufacture a wholesome replica of the real thing?

When we get right down to it, why trust that any grave contains what it's supposed to? One of the most important events in life, namely, death, is so shrouded in secrecy and fear that most of us would never dare to check. Who knows what goes on up there in the graveyard of Port Bou? Maybe none of the graves have the right body, or any at all? After all, there is a lot of movement of bodies and bones in this system: you rent a "niche" for a few years and if you fail to renew it, then the bones are disinterred and placed in the *fosa común*—the "common grave"—

Walter Benjamin's Grave

in which they lie alongside and eventually mingle and merge with who knows how many others to lose all trace of their individuality. Here they rest united in the unseemly melee that is death; friends and enemies, natives and foreigners, Republicans and *franquistas* (the followers of Franco), femurs and scapulae, jumbled together to create and recreate what Elias Canetti conceived of as the "invisible crowd of the dead" which, in his opinion, was a privileged source of religious sentiment. For if everything went according to routine then Benjamin's remains would have been removed in 1945, five years after Frau Gurland's payment of seventy-five pesetas, and placed in the *fosa común.*

But what then to make of Arendt not being able to locate his niche a few months after his death? Scholem makes sure to tell us this as it serves as a dramatic prelude to his 1975 allegation of a fake grave. "His name was not written anywhere," she said. But there is one detail that might be helpful here and that has everything to do with naming: upon his death Walter Benjamin entered the official records (supplied by the recently established Walter Benjamin Museum in Port Bou) not as a Jew but as a Roman Catholic with the name of Benjamin Walter. *Doctor* Benjamin Walter, to be precise. Hence he was buried in the cemetery reserved for Catholics and far from being nameless, he became a fake just like his grave, a fake Christian and a body with a fake name.

You see this name in the receipt made out to the dead man, the *difunto* Benjamin Walter, by the Hotel de Francia, for the four-day stay that includes five sodas with lemon, four telephone calls, dressing of the corpse, plus disinfection of his room and the washing and whitening of the mattress. You see it in the receipt made out by the physician for seventy-five pesetas for his injections and taking the blood pressure of the traveler, *el viajero,* Benjamin Walter. You see it in the death certificate—number 25—made out on September 27, 1940, for Benjamin Walter, forty-eight years old, of Berlin (Germany—as noted). You see it in the receipt tendered by the carpenter to the judge in Port Bou for making a cloth-lined coffin for the dead man, *el difunto,* Señor Benjamin Walter, a receipt that includes eight pesetas for the work of a bricklayer closing a niche in the cemetery for Benjamin Walter. And you can see it in the receipt made out by the priest dated October 1, 1940, for ninety-six pesetas, six of which were for a mass for the dead man and seventy-five for "five years' rent of a niche in the Catholic cemetery of this town in which the cadaver of B. Walter lies buried."[4]

"*Even the dead* will not be safe from the enemy if he wins," wrote Benjamin shortly before his death. This was of a piece with his philosophy of history as something in which every detail of a life counted, nothing was to be forgotten, the present had an ironclad obligation to the past, and running as a slender thread through all of this was the ever-so-faint possibility of redemption. "*Even the dead.*" It is italicized in the original to give it emphasis. *Even the dead . . .* This recalls his early work on baroque drama in which, focusing on his idiosyncratic concept of allegory, he wrote that the allegorist drains objects of their life so they become his to play with, to set into new designs and thus speak to fate. His friend Theodor Adorno had this in mind when he wrote a decade after his death that the gaze of Benjamin's philosophy was Medusan, meaning it turned to stone whatever it looked at. But, added Adorno, this was part of a larger strategy, namely, the need to become a thing in order to break the catastrophic spell of things.

It is important to recall such ideas here because with Benjamin's own death strong narratives assert themselves to wrest control of that death, narratives that have little to do with the ideas he laid down in his life's work or that subtly contradict it. Didn't Benjamin himself in his famous essay on the storyteller spend a good deal of time propounding the thesis that it is death that gives authority to the storyteller? In the shadow of 9/11 none of us need to be reminded on that score. Taken a step further we might even assert that this is what scares us about death yet tempts us as well, as if the story can be completed yet also amputated by the absence that is death, forever postponing the end to the story that was a life. We want that authority for our own story, nowhere more so than when interpreting a death and, of course, its body. A gravestone or a monument—especially the accusation of a fake one—is just such a story, just such an attempt.

"I am not making a pilgrimage," I said to myself when I visited the graveyard at Port Bou in the spring of 2002. Indeed I was not even sure I wanted to visit the graveyard. I do not think this was entirely due to fear of cemeteries on my part. Nor was it because I am also attracted to them. It was more because I feel uncomfortable about what I discern as an incipient cult around the site of Benjamin's grave, as if the drama of his death, and of the holocaust, in general, is allowed to appropriate and overshadow the enigmatic power of his writing and the meaning of his life. Put bluntly, the death comes to mean more than the life. This cult is at once too sad and too sentimental, too overdetermined an event—the border crossing that failed, the beauty of the place, the horror of the epoch. It really amounts to a type of gawking, I thought to myself, in place of informed respect, a cheap thrill with the frisson of tragedy further enlivened by the calm and stupendous beauty of the landscape. In any event, one does not worship at the grave of great thinkers. But what then is the appropriate gesture? Death is an awkward business. And so is remembrance.

There must be rules for the management of death, yet death tests the rule as well. With each death, society itself dies a little, said the anthropologist Robert Hertz in his now classic 1907 study of the collective representations of death. But what is it about society that dies? Death is especially awkward for modern intellectuals who are likely to find themselves swept over by traditions they fought and measured themselves against. To visit Benjamin's grave or even just timidly approach its outermost waves of force in the periphery of Port Bou, at the massive railway station and shunting yards surrounded by tunnels opening onto the looming mountains, to stop there and hesitate to go further, as I did, to wonder how to proceed—all this suggests a fundamental inability to deal with death and the need to reinvent procedures acknowledging it. Nietzsche pleads in vain for historians who can write histories equal to the events they relate. We need to do the same with our dead. Benjamin says something similar where he cautions that truth is not a matter of exposure that destroys the secret but a revelation that does justice to it. He was referring to the work of truth in the passage of love from the body to the soul in Plato's *Symposium*. Death poses the same issue. Exactly.

Was Benjamin the first suicide bomber? The thought crosses my mind as I read the papers in the train heading north to Port Bou with their front-page news of Israeli soldiers with their armored bulldozers and Apache helicopters invading Palestinian towns and refugee camps in response to suicide bombers. Journalists are driven back by the soldiers using stun grenades and tear gas. At least two have been shot by Israeli soldiers. A United Nations–led inquiry into war crimes in Jenin is stillborn on account of Israeli opposition. The president of the United States and the U.S. media insist the Palestinians are to blame for the violence. There is virtually no attempt to even try to understand what it is that motivates the Palestinians, no portrayal of their everyday life in refugee camps and prisons under "administrative detention" imposed without trial. Instead we get lengthy Sunday magazine articles depicting the psychic pain of Israeli elite commando snipers. Yet has there ever been a Sunday magazine devoted to the psychic pain of the apartheid-like pass system that controls the Palestinians' ability to cross the spiderweb of borders balkanizing Palestinian lands into which illegal Israeli settlements daily press? They say history is written by the victors, but this seems unprecedented. It is as if the Palestinians had no voice whatsoever. They are not only unrepresented but are unrepresentable. Or as Golda Meir once put it, they do not exist. Like Benjamin they are fated to lose. Truth itself lies on trial, and it is the border that defines and redefines it as I slowly travel north from Barcelona, north to the border at Port Bou in the local train that stops at all stops to let me down where Benjamin was stopped sixty years ago.

A young man sits on the other side of the compartment a few seats forward. He speaks no Spanish and he is worried, sick with worry. He has a large black bag made of cheap material that he keeps on the seat next to him, preventing anyone from sitting there. He looks around all the time like an animal in a cage. I first spotted him in the gloomy *Estacio Sants* in Barcelona where I waited for the train. He approached a middle-aged woman and in his gesticulations seemed to be asking her when the train to the border would come and whether the approaching train was the one he needed. In the train he came over to me with his ticket on which was printed Cerbère, the French town just across the border from Port Bou. "Francia? Francia?" he kept saying and at each, and every stop he looked imploringly at me, eyes wide open, asking if this was where he had to get off. I figured he was from North Africa and probably illegal. He smelled as if hadn't washed in a long time. A man on the run. Anti-Semitic and anti-Arab Le Pen running on an anti-immigrant platform has just beaten the socialist Jospin at the polls in France, receiving almost 18 percent of the vote. When I got off the train at Port Bou I waved and made a victory sign to the man with the black bag. He smiled wanly. Benjamin had been stopped at the border coming the other way. But of course things were different then.

You climb the hill towards the graveyard, the hill that falls green and steep into the sea. It is late April and the hillside is ablaze with yellow wildflowers. In the hollow of the deep bay just behind you lies the town. It feels cold and unfriendly. There is something wrong with it. A few tourists from France, day-trippers, walk aimlessly around looking for something to look at. The café won't let you use the bathroom, and the only café open on the waterfront is no less dark and cavernous than the station in Barcelona where I began. It is madly expensive as well. There are few young people in the town; only elderly and a few kids. The supermarket sells mainly low-priced liquor. A border town full of smugglers? But what could they be smuggling now that Spain is part of Europe? Still, why does the town seem so uptight? This is exactly how I remember it driving through from France in 1987 when we stopped for a coffee and drove on. There was no monument to Benjamin then. Just the town. The whole town was his monument as far as I was concerned—cold, nasty, and enigmatic.

Walter Benjamin's Grave

I remembered Lisa Fittko in Chicago when I first called her from a public phone in the mid-eighties having just found out from Barbara Sahlins, the wife of my anthropologist friend at the university, that the woman who took Benjamin across the border lived but a few blocks away. "Oh! You're after the briefcase!" were Lisa's first words on the phone. My heart sank. Didn't she realize that one might have perfectly innocent reasons for wanting to talk with her and that lost treasure would only get in the way? The treasure I was after was even less tangible than a missing briefcase. I only felt it dimly at that moment but looking back I'm tempted to say, to wonder, rather, if the treasure I was seeking wasn't in its inchoate way the first step of the pilgrimage that I had unconsciously begun at that very moment standing in a glass and metal phone booth on a street corner on a blustery day in south Chicago? It was the desire to absorb something of the dead man, the holy man, whatever it is that clings as living presence to the person of the woman who took him secretly over the mountain across the border so many years ago. All this flashed through my mind quicker than it takes to tell, a feeling of foreboding that no matter what I said to her I was lost. The briefcase—the idea of the briefcase, the image of the briefcase—had become a stupendous relic made all the more potent by its disappearance.

When I got to her place a little later she told me how excited Rolf Tiedemann became when she told him of Benjamin lugging a heavy black briefcase across the Pyrenees, saying it contained his most important work. "I cannot risk losing it," Benjamin had said. "It is the manuscript that *must* be saved. It is more important than I am." Tiedemann was then in charge of publishing the collected works of Benjamin in German, and he set off immediately for Port Bou and the regional capital to find the briefcase. He got the local authorities to search high and low. If memory serves me, they even went down into some catacombs under the town, but perhaps that's memory playing tricks with buried pasts. But they turned up nothing. No briefcase. No fabulous manuscript. Just like there was no body either.

It is strange, for in the documents recorded by the judge at the time of Benjamin's death that I have seen there is no mention of a manuscript, but there is noted the existence of a *cartera grande*, a large handbag, as his only baggage. Its contents were carefully itemized: a pocket watch and chain, with the watch's many inscriptions duly noted; a five-hundred-franc bill, a fifty-dollar bill, a twenty-dollar bill, (all serial numbers duly noted); a passport (numbered 224) issued by the American Foreign Service to Walter Benjamin with a Spanish visa also issued in Marseille; a certificate from the Institute of Social Research, previously of Frankfurt, now in exile in New York and affiliated in some way to Columbia

University; six photographs; an ID card issued in Paris; an X-ray; a pipe for smoking with a mouthpiece made of what looked like amber, and its case; a pair of glasses in nickel frames and its case; and several letters and newspapers. But no manuscript.

Yet Lisa Fittko remembered how heavy that bag had been. How could a watch, a pipe, some spectacles, and a few papers weigh anything? "We would have to drag that monster across the mountains," she said. Up the mountain they went, along the Route Lister, a smuggler's path set back from the sea and named after the famous Republican general of the Spanish Civil War who led his troops along this same path. In her memoir she notes that Benjamin "breathed heavily, yet he made no complaint, not even a sigh. He only kept squinting in the direction of the black bag." At one point he stooped to drink from a pool of stagnant water. It was green and slimy and it stank. She warned him not to drink. She told him he would get typhus. "True," he replied. "I might. But don't you see, the worst that can happen is that I die of typhus . . . *after* crossing the border. The Gestapo wont be able to get me, and the manuscript will be safe. I do apologize." He was always so polite.

But she also singled out his lack of "adaptability," a euphemism with her for a variety of incompetence that, so it appears, was all too common among these refugee intellectuals, lacking what today we call "survival skills" or "street smarts." This is hard to understand when one looks at academics nowadays, the majority of whom seem blessed with an abundance of such skills, if skills they be. There is even a trace of scorn in Fittko's remarks about some of the people whom she took over the border on account of their selfishness, their infantilism, and in general their inability to face up to reality and be practical. People on the run, it seems, are not necessarily at their best. But Benjamin maintained his dignity and never once complained even though he struck her as particularly pathetic; the sort of guy who, as she put it, even needed instruction on how to hold a hot cup of tea. This seems more than what we call "impractical." It encompasses a sort of helplessness and even hopelessness in being in the world for which a hot cup of tea is merely symbolic.

"One should have been able to react spontaneously?" asks her interviewer, Richard Heinemann.

"He couldn't do that," responded Fittko. "I think he could only take a hot cup in his hand when he had first developed an appropriate theory."[5]

My guess is that many of the intellectuals she escorted came from homes with servants and / or had wives who took care of business while they painted, sculpted, wrote their novels, poems, plays, reviews, and so forth. Even when poverty-stricken, as Benjamin was from the early 1930s, they may have lived in cheap hotels and depended on cafés for food and drink, aloof from the exigencies of domestic labor if not from many of the practicalities of everyday life. Who did Benjamin's typing, for instance?

"Many of these men were incapable of coping with primitive conditions," Lisa Fittko's husband, Hans, had told her after his first imprisonment in a prison camp for enemy aliens, the Stade Colombe, on the outskirts of Paris in late 1939. "How do you protect yourself from the wind and the rain, how do you dry your clothes? How do you take hold of a tin bowl of hot coffee without burning your fingers? Often someone would fall over a bench and break a bone or two."[6]

Hans Fittko met Benjamin in another prison, Versuche, near Nevers, the winter before France surrendered. He told Benjamin to contact Lisa if he ever got south to Marseille. It struck him how incapable Benjamin was at coping with prison life. A chain smoker, Benjamin abruptly gave up smoking. "Not the right time," said Hans. But Benjamin explained, "I can bear the conditions in this camp only if I'm compelled to concentrate my mental strength on one single effort. Giving up smoking costs me this effort, and thus will be my deliverance."[7]

There were other diversions, such as the literary journal Benjamin formed with a small number of other prisoners—a camp journal for intellectuals that was to show the country exactly who they had locked up "as the enemies of France."[8] The editorial board would meet by crawling into Benjamin's tent under the stairs where he slept, looked after by a young prisoner, "a holy man in his cave," comments Hans Sahl, "watched over by an angel." There they would drink contraband schnapps from thimbles the angel had acquired from the French soldiers. Other times Benjamin offered courses "for advanced students," costing three Gauloises or a button.[9] Despite these initiatives, it seems unlikely Benjamin would have lasted long without his angel. "Never have I been made so conscious of the tragic conflict between thought and action in a person," wrote Sahl thirty years later.

This conflict is all the more striking in Benjamin's case when we consider how overwhelmingly attuned his theories were to what he himself called the object world and to mimetic behavior, such behavior being in some regard the quintessence of what has come to be called "embodied knowledge" and what I think Lisa Fittko meant by "adaptability." "Faut se débrouiller," she said, "one must know how to help oneself, to clear a way out of the debacle." This translated into how to "buy counterfeit food stamps, scrounge milk for the children, obtain some—any kind—of permit—in short, manage to do or obtain what didn't officially exist . . . But Benjamin had been no débrouillard."[10] She laughed when she thought back to him trying to unsuccessfully smuggle himself aboard a freighter disguised as a French sailor, along with Doctor Fritz Frankel, notable on account of his fragile appearance and mane of gray hair. The mimetic faculty goes only so far.

Benjamin's love of modernism, and in particular of montage, allegory, and fragmentation, all would seem to strongly predispose one to "adaptability," meaning coping with new and strange circumstances. And wasn't he the theorist of "thick skin"—what Freud called the "stimulus shield"—thickened in response to the shocks of modern living? Moreover, his letters and essays written on Ibiza in 1932–33 are glowing testimony to a love of material culture and keen eye for nature. But what does all of this add up to if you can't even hold a cup of hot tea?

But of course the practicalities of suicide were not beyond reach—as if the lack of "adaptability" had a certain ethical principle behind it which was, precisely, not to adapt.

After Lisa Fittko took Benjamin over the border, she and her husband were recruited by a New York writer fluent in French and German, Varian Fry, whose mission on behalf of the U.S. "Emergency Rescue Committee" was to get intellectuals, artists, politicians, and labor leaders pursued by the Nazis out of France. About the same time Benjamin made his fatal crossing into Spain, Fry arrived in Marseille with 3,000 dollars in cash and a list of people to be rescued. On the strength of Lisa having taken Benjamin across the border, Fry recruited her and her husband into his scheme. At first they were reluctant. How competent was Fry? Didn't they themselves have to get out to freedom as soon as possible? Fry had a name for them. The smugglers' route she had used, the Lister Route, was now called the F-Route; F for Fittko.

Fry lasted thirteen months before being deported and was, by his own detailed account, pretty successful. In the first weeks, whenever a refugee came whose name was on his list, he would ask for information about the others. The news was grim. Ernst Weiss, a Czech novelist, had taken poison in his room in Paris when the Germans entered the city; Irmgard Keun, a German novelist, had also committed suicide when the Germans entered Paris; the German playwright Walter Hasenclever had killed himself with an overdose of Veronal in the concentration camp as Les Milles, not far from Marseille; Karl Einstein, partner of Georges Bataille in the famous art journal *Documents* and a specialist on primitive art, had hanged himself on the Spanish-French border when he couldn't get

across; and the body of the labor leader Willi Muenzenberg, once a German communist deputy, had been found hanging from a tree in Grenoble. "One by one I crossed these men off my list."[11] Benjamin's suicide was by no means unique, and drug overdose was a favored means.

Refugees carried vials of poison in their vest pockets "just in case . . .," according to Fry, and Arthur Koestler claims he was given large amounts of morphine by Benjamin in Marseille "just in case."[12] Most telling, I believe, are the numerous accounts of mental paralysis recorded by Fry concerning refugees who, even though they were given money and visas, were too frightened to move. "They were jittery with the idea of staying," he says, "and paralyzed with fear at the idea of leaving. You would get them prepared with their passports and all their visas in order, and a month later they would still be sitting in the Marseille cafés, waiting for the police to come and get them."[13]

You climb the hill beyond the town to the cemetery. All the bodies are buried there now. Before it was just for Catholics. The sea is on your left, several hundred feet below. The road curves as you climb. On a small plateau stands the arch through which you enter the cemetery. But about thirty feet in front of the entrance, jutting out of the ridge line like a bent elbow, on the side of the sea, there is a curious triangle of deep brown iron, at least ten feet high.

From the foot of the triangle, running all the way across the roadway, the same

rusted iron formed a five-foot-wide slab. "That's odd," I thought, marveling at the color and the perfection of this iron slab set into the road.

As I set my foot on it, walking to the cemetery, I heard Alberto, next to me, gasp. His head was turned towards the iron triangle jutting out on his left, and suddenly we saw that it formed the doorway to a chute running underground

Walter Benjamin's Grave

parallel to the slope of the hill. It was completely lined by the same brown iron, including the steps that led down almost as far as the eye could see to end in a perfect rectangle enclosing a view of the sea way below, breaking onto rocks. For a brief moment everything turned inside out. The mountain opened to create a brilliant doorway bringing the crashing sea, so it seemed, right to where we were standing. This was the monument to Benjamin that Tel Aviv artist Dani Karavan had built just outside the cemetery, completed in 1994.

Some people think of Benjamin as a Marxist or as a Marxist with a surrealist spin. Other regard him as combining Marxism with the mysticism of the Kabbalah. There is truth to these interpretations, but I myself prefer to think of him as a Proustian Marxist, an eccentric overwhelmed by the avant-garde and the fast-moving political scene of the time. As indication of his eccentricity, take "One-Way Street" where he writes: "If the theory is correct that feeling is not located in the head, that we sentiently experience a window, a cloud, a tree not in our brains but, rather, in the place where we see it, then we are, in looking at our beloved, too, outside ourselves."

That pretty well sums up what it felt like at that moment looking into the mountain opened out to the sea surging below.

We walked down the steps. Halfway down the iron ceiling gave way to the open sky, but the feeling of being in a passage running inside the earth was neverthe-

less maintained. A few steps before the end (all told, there were eighty-seven steps) there was a thick glass plate, like a door, blocking our way. Inscribed on it in German, Spanish, Catalan, French, and English was the following:

> It is more arduous to honour the memory of the nameless than that of the renowned. Historical construction is devoted to the memory of the nameless.

Underneath was written "G.S. I, 1241," which I guess referred to Benjamin's collected works in German, the *Gesammelte Schriften*, edited by Rolf Tiedemann and Hermann Schweppenhaüser.

We sat on the steps by the glass. The sea would loom through the glass. Then the inscription would loom through the sea looming through the glass. Back and forth, words on water, words on sky. We tried to make sense of the inscription.

Why this emphasis on the nameless? My thoughts drifted as if in a trance, then suddenly snapped to attention. Sandra and Cristina, like Alberto, anthropologists from Barcelona who had taken me here, were talking heatedly of the *fosa común*—the common grave where even if you were buried at first with a name you end up nameless. There by the foot of the iron stairs enclosed by iron walls enclosed by the mountain I felt we were fast on our way to entering into a *fosa común* ourselves, but the *fosa común* they were referring to was expanding before our eyes to include—in our imagination, you understand—Franco's concentration camps and mass graves where bodies of prisoners were dumped along with refugees attempting to cross the border into France. And on the French side of the border even before Vichy, there were concentration camps such as the one at Gurs in the Pyrenees just for these refugees, they assured me. This was the camp where Lisa Fittko was put, too.

Basque friend and longtime resident in the United States Begoña Aretxaga e-mailed me late in August 2001 describing

> the Pyrenees as a border between life and death where one can encounter death. That is how it was in the Basque country during the 70s and 80s and of course at the end of the civil war. I came into adolescence with that reality transformed in political mythology, a space of rumor and story and memorialization of death in its different forms of song and monument and later on film. I could tell you stories of escapes and stories of fabulated encounters with death. So Benjamin's mythology of the border articulates with other mythologies of struggle and escape.

"All Spain is full of *fosas*," I later read in Spain's leading newspaper, *El País*, "especially the ditches by the side of the roads." One *fosa* is reported to contain upwards of five hundred bodies shot by the Guardia Civil. There is a growing movement connected to the Association for the Recovery of Historical Memory to disinter the remains that, as the news item puts it, "have been sixty years awaiting this moment."

Sixty years waiting, these dead bodies. What a curious expression! Dead bodies like the princess in the fairy tale awaiting the kiss of the prince. Was this what Benjamin had in mind when he wrote that in "order for the past to be touched by the present, there must be no continuity between them." Such touching—or should I say kissing—was in his opinion the singular outcome of images that, like falling stars, would jump-start the process of redemption, wrenching history onto a new track. But these images were above all effervescent. They no sooner emerged than they disappeared. The exact opposite, one would think, of monuments.

Still later a Spanish friend who lives in Barcelona commented in September by e-mail:

> I forgot to tell you when I read your paper [on Walter Benjamin's grave], it made me think about something I read recently in Italy that several "*fosas comunes*" were being discovered in Spain. . . not in cemeteries, but in the woods, in the backlands, in places where people were slaughtered and hidden, "disappeared" . . . When I came back to Spain, nobody had heard about it. Nobody talks about these things, still nowadays, in Spain. In the meanwhile, the grand-son of one of the responsibles of the propaganda regime of Franco is the president of the government of Spain.
>
> Franco, what a character. Nobody talks about him and his crimes; and that silence seems to keep his shade alive.

The cold atmosphere of the town now made sense. Right or wrong, there was this feeling, this social fact, that secrets like nameless graves lay everywhere and that the border town had probably been the scene of much brutality and certainly of unbearable anxiety. Namelessness meant secrecy and disappearance on a mass scale, but some names were known, such as that of Benjamin Walter, or Walter Benjamin, even if the body the name belonged to was lost, while the secrecy was at the best partial—and was therefore all the more sinister. So much is this the case—what my friend described as "that silence that seems to keep his shade alive," that you must ask yourself whether such carefully crafted invisibility of the public secret is not the most significant monument imaginable. What real monument of stone or glass, people's names or lofty literary quotation, can compete with invisibility?

When we turned around to make our way back up the steps of the monument I was again taken aback. At the head of the stairs we saw what appeared to be the same rectangle of light as we had seen when we had first entered and looked down at the sea, only now, gazing up to that entrance from the inside it was of course not the sea but the clear blue sky. Inside our *fosa común*, this monument to the nameless, we were walking back from the sea into the sky.

Later in the actual cemetery we searched for some sign of Benjamin and found a rock about waist high set on the ground. It was untouched by the mason's chisel except for a plaque with yet another quotation from Benjamin's writings. His texts seem to be full of pithy statements apt for gravestones and monuments, and there is no shortage of writers who, desirous of some spectral profundity, paste in a slice or two. Poor Benjamin. To have his pearls thus cast. This one read: "There is no document of civilization that is not a document of barbarism."

At the time we thought this must be his gravestone below which lay his re-

mains. Later I realized how naïve we were; unable to conceive that such a ponderous little monument could be a fake gravestone, that there was no body below it, and that a name, even when chiseled into hard stone, can float aimlessly at the whim of time like a scrap of paper on a windy street. Yet cemeteries exist to ensure at least the appearance of a direct bond between name and body, and on this our very language rests as well, tying words to their meanings as if they were directly bound, one to the other, a form of magic, really, as Benjamin would have been among the first to appreciate.

Indeed this magic is among his most basic and fertile possessions, brought to fruition in his 1933 essay "On the Mimetic Faculty," written during his stay on the island of Ibiza, which like Port Bou is an important part of Catalan culture and history even though it lies eight hours by boat southeast across the Mediterranean from where we stood at Port Bou. Benjamin spent two summers on Ibiza, and that is where his famous essay on the storyteller germinated as well. His arrival there, destitute and homeless, on April 19, 1932, came during the spring, almost exactly the same time of the year we visited Port Bou. He was stunned by the wildflowers and the beauty of the island. For him at times it seemed like a prehistoric utopia, a leap into the remote past back to the beginnings of European civilization.

Photographs of Benjamin must be notoriously rare, which is why you keep seeing the same brooding face with or without a cigarette on all the book covers. What a surprise to come across a photo of him on the beach![14] In the summer. At Ibiza! Some of the photos have a broad frame that shows him in a group in front of a wide stretch of sea with some sand and craggy rocks. How strange, though, that while his two male companions are in white singlets enjoying the sun, Walter sits there in his deck chair so solemn in shirt and tie, chin characteristically in his right fist, and instead of looking out at the beach and the sea, he is facing into the dark interior of the house.

But then there's that sneak entry into the Benjamin photo archive that no-body—I mean nobody!—suspected. It's May 1933, and what we see are four de-liciously relaxed guys lying on their backs in the sun on a boat being steered by an equally blissful character—a local fisherman by the name of Tomás Varó ("Frasquito"). You see the edge of the straining sail and the wake bubbling. It's Walter together with the handsome, shirtless French painter Jean Selz and, lying next to Walter, the grandson of the painter Paul Gauguin. They are in all likeli-hood high on hashish.[15] What then to make of the inspired caption to this pho-tograph—"The Author as Producer"—chosen by the U.S. editors of Benjamin's selected works? I have a copy stuck on the outside of the door to my bedroom, which is also my study.

The heat of the sun shocks him. He will later write a hallucinatory essay, "In the Sun," which is also a love-letter to a dear friend in Berlin. "With astonishment he would recall that entire nations—Jews, Indians, Moors—had built their schools beneath a sun that seemed to make all thinking impossible for him."[16] This sun burns into the landscape, forging its forms like molten wax. A bumble-bee brushes his ear. The smell of resin and thyme fill the air. His mode of percep-tion is being altered as he ponders the relationships between names and things, the seventeen names for the different varieties of figs on the island, for example. Not since he wrote the gnomic "On Language as Such and on the Language of Man" in his raw youth has he returned to this issue, as when, again, he observes how things in nature keep changing but their names remain the same even when they suddenly emerge as his lips shape them, like the names of islands that rise out of the sea like marble sculptures.

The island conjures stories as well as names of things. Getting there the first time on a tramp steamer from Germany took eleven days, and this is when Ben-jamin began to construct his ideas about the tight relationship between boredom and the storyteller giving practical wisdom for living. There were so many stories, starting with the running of the ship, its machines and its maps, the history of the

Walter Benjamin's Grave

shipping company going back to the slave trade. "The conversation progressed slowly, but like a fuse," he said, "it always burned its way toward an adventure or a story."[17]

"Many of the stories I could never retell," he says, "but as I went down the steps to exchange a few words with the captain before the ship's departure, there wasn't one which failed to evoke a name or an image in my mind's eye."[18]

His writing tries to collapse the space between words and what they refer to. Theodor Adorno made a special point of this when, long after Benjamin had died, he wrote that "everything which fell under the scrutiny of his words was transformed, as though it had become radioactive." This was because "the thoughts press close to its object, seek to touch it, smell it, taste it, and so thereby transform itself."[19]

This was what was going on up at the cemetery at Port Bou, too, as names and bodies drifted apart pulling at the moorings of language, making the question of how to mark death an increasingly urgent question, parallel to Benjamin's theories of language. In his memoir of his childhood, "A Berlin Chronicle," part of which was also written in Ibiza in 1932, Benjamin wrote: "Language shows clearly that memory is not an instrument for exploring the past but its theater. It is the medium of past experience, as the ground is the medium in which dead cities lie interred." One digs and digs in this ground, scattering the earth searching meticulously for its real treasure; "the images, severed from all earlier associations, that stand—like precious fragments or torsos in a collector's gallery—in the prosaic rooms of our later understanding."[20] He could have been referring to the *fosa común* as well.

Enclosed by a high white wall, the cemetery itself is terraced to fit the contours of the slope. Along these contours, which parallel the coastline, run white banks of tombs, the so-called niches, about twelve feet tall. At the highest point of the cemetery there is a small white chapel with a peaked roof and green wooden doors. Down the middle of the cemetery there are brick steps, dividing the cemetery into two halves. As you ascend the steps, the banks of niches run right and left of you but I could not enter the chapel because, in contrast to the open entrance to the ironclad chute of the monument to Benjamin just outside the cemetery, its doors were locked, a sign of its sacred status.

As I walked back down the brick steps and stopped at the lowest point, where a bank of niches formed the bottom wall of the cemetery, I turned around and glanced up the stairs to see the peaked green doors of the chapel at the very top of the stairs. Suddenly I felt I was back on the steps in the Benjamin monument.

It was exactly the same idea. Virtually the same steps. In the cemetery they led up from the graves to the chapel, while the monument's steps guided one from the breaking waves to the open sky.

Exactly the same? Well, not really. For what the monument expressed in uttermost perfection was Benjamin's surrealist conception of the "profane illumination." The forms were similar, practically identical, but in the monument the conventionally sacred illumination to be found in the cemetery was mimicked by this quite other illumination of sea and sky. In the cemetery the niches bear the name of the dead person within. If the remains of the corpse are later removed, they are then concealed under a small iron trapdoor in the *fosa común* where they join the nameless multitude. But the profane illumination gathers its strength through the open expression of namelessness as empty space, sea, and sky. It truly is an emphatic statement on the weighting of the world by its nameless dead.

Scholem may have been right about the fake grave, but the evidence he presents is weak and, what is more, seems to ignore the burial system in Port Bou according to which remains of bodies are moved from niches to the *fosa común*. If the grave diggers then erected their own memorial, in response to visitors asking to see the grave, who is to say this is any less respectful of the dead or any less fitting a way to register the claims of memory and history? Who is to blame here, if blame there be, the grave diggers or the visitors who don't share the same culture and don't understand the system of reburial whereby the bones of the individual rejoin the mass of generations after generations of dead, what Canetti called the invisible crowd of the dead? Scholem wants an honest grave uniting body with name in the soil of the graveyard, which seems to me a far cry from Benjamin's passion for allegory—his sense both philosophical and aesthetic that we find meaning in the world not only from smoothly functioning symbols, as if reading signs in a dictionary, but also from an awkwardness of fit between signs and what they refer to, most especially when those signs cluster around death.

Benjamin's life after death was his final essay in this regard. There are no bones we can point to, no honest gravestone, no embalmed corpse, nor locks of hair.

His name was reversed, as was his religious affiliation. We carry few visual images of him after his death for there are few photographs of him when he was alive, which is one reason why the postmortem list of his personal possessions is so valuable. We note the presence of a pocket watch and chain, his nickel-framed glasses and his pipe with its amber mouthpiece. But what about the actual things, especially that mysterious and irritating briefcase that seems not only more important than his dead body but also a substitute for it, circulating lost in some mysterious mistake of memory or in an underground archive in Port Bou or the regional capital? We cling to the written list as if to those actual physical things, when all around us we have something infinitely more worthwhile; his wonderful essays and the essays those essays have generated. He is more spirit than body and as such the site as much as the manner of his death connects us with the most profound form of spiritual warfare, that of state disappearance of people, their torture, and their mass, secret, execution—for which the Spanish border where he killed himself is such a potent reminder, not to mention the camps in Germany and Poland and what is happening with frightening velocity with the new state of emergency we are experiencing with the terror of the War against Terror

Walter Benjamin's Grave

Attendant pointing to trapdoor to the fosa común.

as I write this essay, mindful of Guantánamo Bay, the ghost prisoners held by the United States in Abu Ghraib prison, as well as with prisoners "outsourced" by the United States for torture in countries such as Egypt and Syria.[21]

Benjamin's name was not written anywhere, Arendt had informed Scholem. Yet name or no name, she found the place where he was supposed to have been buried to be overwhelming: "It is by far one of the most fantastic and most beautiful spots I have ever seen in my life."

I take this heightened sense of place and space to be *allegorical* in some special way. I have already quoted Begoña Aretxaga on the political mythology of the Pyrenees that she grew up with in Basque country in the 1970s–1980s—"a space of rumor and story and memorialization of death in its different forms of song and monument"—and I want to fuse that with the exquisite sense of beauty, too exquisite, really, that Arendt records in the 1940s. What is more, I want to draw your attention to that rendition of startling, natural beauty combined with an absence—the absence of a name, Benjamin's name.

It is then to this sense of space and place as a mix of beauty and death and namelessness that I want to draw in the notion of *allegory* as used by Benjamin for that art of understanding in which, under the spell of death and terror, the human world was frozen and naturalized in what we call a *still life* or *landscape*. Years later at the very end of his life in his famously difficult and strange "Theses on the Philosophy of History," he applied this idea to what he called the *state of emergency*, which he saw as no longer the exception but the rule.[22] It was as if because of the terrible turmoil and galloping dynamic given to history, suddenly everything becomes stock-still and frozen in time as a deathly silence holds history in thrall as we await the Last Judgment and the coming of the Messiah. In this situation, the one permanently before the last—as in the culture of terror produced by our leaders in their War against Terror—our modes of reading or interpretation of reality shift in a fundamental manner. They become cinematic, as when Benjamin asserts that the "true picture of the past flits by. The past can be seized only as an image which flashes up at the instant when it can be recognized and is never seen again." It is danger that provokes these fugitive images that hold both the past and the future in abeyance as the catastrophe mounts, yet it is this same danger that coagulates the turmoil into a still life. How strange: fleeting images, on the one hand, stock-still landscape, on the other.

Long after Benjamin died, his friend Theodor Adorno would remind us of the intellectual and spiritual need in our time in history for us to follow or at least be aware of Benjamin's critical practice of the need for everything to "metamorphose into a thing in order to break the catastrophic spell of things."[23] "He is driven," wrote Adorno, "not merely to awaken life in petrified objects—as in allegory—but also to scrutinize living things so that they present themselves as being ancient, 'ur-historical' and abruptly release their significance."[24] And this is why we cannot take our leave of Benjamin's grave without taking leave of the still life, the *nature-mort*, the landscape, in which the grave—or should we say "grave" as in fake grave—is set, paying special attention to Adorno's nod to the "spell" as in a magic spell.

If death is what gives the storyteller authority, as Benjamin suggested, then it is also subject to retellings and speculations as with the stories of his own death. A conversation begins and follows the trails back and forth, as I have done here and as Lisa and Hans Fittko undertook back and forth guiding refugees across the border. For a while a monument such as the one to Benjamin may center and fix this landscape, but that spell is broken by the even greater spell of the landscape.

For beautiful it certainly is, this landscape. More than beautiful it is majestic, even transcendent and sacred. Hannah Arendt gave us a version of that. And before her, Lisa Fittko: when the socialist mayor of the village of Banyuls, on the French side of the border, took her in shortly after she arrived there after being a prisoner in the concentration camp of Gurs, he gave her food for her sister-in-law, Eva, and Eva's small child. The kindness and sense of security had its effect. Lisa looked up from the path and saw the region, she says, *as if for the first time*—"the incredibly blue seas and the mountain chain, on its slopes green vineyards with a hint of gold between them, and a sky as blue as the sea."

"One cannot describe it," she wrote, "one had to have been there to see it."[25]

When she dragged Benjamin plus his briefcase up through what seemed like an almost vertical vineyard with the help of Frau Gurland's son, the vines were heavy with the nearly ripe Banyuls grapes. They were sweet and dark. It was the first time she had made the trip. Benjamin was her first refugee. Together they established the route, what Varian Fry came to call the F-Route, meaning the Fittko Route, along which so many more refugees would be taken. She got lost. They backtracked. Then they found the way to the summit: "The spectacular scene appeared so unexpectedly that for a moment I thought I was seeing a mirage . . . the *Vermillion Coast,* an autumn landscape with innumerable hues of reds and yellow-gold. I gasped for breath—I had never seen such beauty before."[26]

Her husband, Hans, with his Basque cap and sandals, came to look like a local peasant. It was best that way. You could mix with the workers before the sun rose and take refugees past the officials. Later he would sit for hours on a cliff projecting into the sea. The waves carried away his tension. In her diary for November 1, 1940, Lisa Fittko noted: "In truth he no longer makes long speeches in his sleep as he once used to do."[27]

Perhaps this is one of those images Benjamin was talking about, those fleeting images conjured up at a moment of danger, a dialectical image, one minute aching danger and turmoil, another minute, repose on rocks above the waves rolling in from the sea. To sit on a ledge by the sea and watch the waves is to invite us, for a moment, at least, to slow down and think, to join with the man sitting on the ledge and the young woman writing about that in her diary. That is a memorial, too, a type of monument, to slow down and think. They were very young, these Fittkos. They had risked their lives and torture on innumerable occasions fighting the terror across the face of Europe, from Berlin to Prague to Paris and now the Spanish-French border helping others escape.

It is this crisscrossed landscape of the border that exists in nature and in stories that I regard as the most fitting monument to Benjamin *and* to the anonymous victims of history invoked on the glass slab cut into the slope by the graveyard at Port Bou. This is the monument, if that word be used, that testifies to Benjamin's aching curiosity and fervent efforts to create what he called "dialectical images" in which human history surfaced as prehistory.

The wind howls up there. It has its own name, the *transmontaña,* its own personality, its mysterious origins and reasons for being. In the Spring and again in Autumn it is so strong it bowls you over. Makes you crazy, they say. Can we imagine a state, a religion, or a community bound to remembrance, which would have the courage or craziness to call a wind a monument? And why not, provided we humans with our superior, language-ordained, consciousnesses, have to give it a name and bring it into our reason and our memorization lest it bowl us over and drive us nuts. After all it has a name and like Hans Fittko it mimics the people of the land and sea even if, as is history's want, it howls in its sleep.

And when today he lights up his cigarette, he uses a flintstone and a fuse, like everyone else. "In a boat," he says, "that is the best way. The wind blows the matches out, but the harder the wind blows, the more the fuse glows.[28]

Over the long haul, he said, history is subject to the conflict of writing.
—TOMÁS ZAPATA

It will speak a secret language and leave behind documents
not of edification but of paradox.
—HUGO BALL, *Flight out of Time*

Constructing America

In response to the 1992 quincentenary of the European invasion of America, the Colombian Anthropology Association has invited us to Bogotá today to discuss "the construction of America." This is a good choice of topic, it seems to me, because it grasps the opportunity of the quincentenary ritual to stand aside from our usual practice and reflect upon what we are doing and why we do it, to what degree and in what manner of ways we are constructing America, and to what degree America constructs us—our identities, in all their multifaceted incarnations, as much as our ways of perceiving and interpreting the world and producing knowledge. Herein, of course, lies a fundamental quandary: how do we make sense of the construction that constructs us? In particular, bearing in mind the stuff of which this quincentenary event is made, what is the role of memory and of rituals of memorization in such constructions?

As I see it there are two great narrative forces in the construction of America, forces that have preoccupied us in our examination of the anthropology of the

A Spanish version of this Columbus quincentenary talk given to some two hundred conferees in Bogotá was published as "La construcción de las Americas: El antropólogo como Colon," in *Cultura y salud en la construcción de las Americas: Reflexiones sobre el sujeto social. Primer simposio internacional de cultura y salud: La cultura de la salud en la construcción de las Américas / VI Congreso de Antropología en Colombia*, edited by Carlos Ernesto Pinzón Castaño, Rosa Suárez Prieto, and Gloria A. Garay (Bogotá: Universidad de los Andes, 1993), 175–202. Many thanks to anthropologist Clara Llano, who performed this piece with me, especially for her strikingly capable rendition of the poetry.

southwest of Colombia, from the Pacific coast over the *cordilleras,* or ranges, of the Andes to the eastern foothills of the Amazon basin. These narrational configurations are centered on the Indian, on the one hand, and the Negro, on the other, which owe much, of course, to the needs and fantasies of the European imagination as transplanted in America.

There are many threads to follow and sort out here, but there is one that is strikingly dominant. For while the Indian has been recruited to the task of carrying the originary America and thus the seed of the great American story and its authenticating seal (perhaps no time more than now of burgeoning Indian movements and worldwide concern for the rain forest), the Negro has been recruited as the carrier of disturbance and fragmentation in that great American story, even threatening it with destruction.

One has only to look at anthropology itself, the basic professional instrument for the fetishization of the Indian. With its aura of scientific expertise combined with the romance of fieldwork, anthropology has seized on the Indian to create a vision of society no less than of history as coherent intelligible structures—structures of so-called mythology, structures of so-called kinship, structures of ecology, structures of annihilation and nostalgia—a veritable structure of structure itself, the new world order and a master narrative if ever there was one.

Compared with this, anthropology's interest in the Negro in the New World has been diminutive, and what anthropological work has been done has certainly provided discomfort for the claims of structure and structure's claims for the project of making sense of the world. Take the endless anthropological attempts at juggling an endless parade of statistics on household "structure" in the Caribbean, for instance, as an ever-intensifying obsession because of the lack of recognizable, ordered kinship and, in many but not all places, the absence of a mythic or even a religious "order." I recall a French student of Lévi-Strauss who had previously worked in West Africa and setting out in 1970 or 1971 for the Pacific coast of Colombia only to return to Bogotá complaining that "Those blacks have no myths!" So she decided to study Indians because they were bound to have myths. This story has the added virtue of reminding us of those studies and contemporary social movements devoted to the attempt to locate African vestiges in the Negro communities in the New World because, in that way, the threat of dislocation, fragmentation, and ultimate senselessness can be mollified if not thwarted by the soothing flow of narrativity.

For whatever complicated historical reasons and by whatever complicated and always already stupendously politically saturated logic of representation, the fact is that the Negro in the New World acquired up to today both the burden and the advantage of the power to persistently disturb the patterns of contrast to which white and Indian had been harnessed, to harass them, to overturn them, to make fun of them, but to never let those contrasts rest in peace. This I might call, then, the deconstruction of America, and it is surely no less American for so being.

The Prague Archive

In light of these remarks and bearing in mind that we are gathered together to-day in a scholarly ritual of memorialization by virtue of the quincentenarializing project, I would like to draw your attention to the theory and practice of histori-ography of a very old, very black blind man, Tomás Zapata, who appears in the diaries, papers, photographs, and tape recordings discovered in the belongings of an unidentified young white man traveling from England and Australia. This man's name in the recordings appears simply as Miguel, and it appears that he went to live in the small town of Puerto Tejada, Cauca, in the southwest of Colom-bia in late 1969, two years before Tomás Zapata died. From these papers it seem that although this Miguel's initial impulse was to write a history of the *Violencia*, the reason why this traveler stayed almost two years (and apparently visited fre-quently thereafter) was because he got interested in the local history of manu-mission and its aftermath. Because he has disappeared and because his records are of such interest, I refer to him as the Recorder.

Although there are many unanswered questions about these papers, the bulk of which are typed with effusive energy and many typographical errors, they are of obvious anthropological interest and, in the right hands, the tape recordings would seem especially valuable, stretching back, as they do, some twenty-two years to preserve the voices of the town's inhabitants. These materials were dis-covered four years ago in an obscure archive of Latin American studies in Prague and have been kindly made available by the Director of the archive, despite finan-cial and administrative difficulties hardly worth going into here.

The Town

From government censuses and the Recorder's notes it appears that in 1970 Puerto Tejada was a town largely of poor wage laborers working in the fields of the nearby sugar plantations, which had taken over most of the peasant farms. A generation or so before, however, it is said to have been the center of a thriving economy of smallholders cultivating cacao, coffee, and plantains. As many as one-third of the peasant households were headed by women, who were no less capable of running the farms than men, and the farms were analogues of the rain forest with large red-flowering cachimbo trees shading the cacao trees that, together with the broad-leafed plantain trees, in turn shaded the coffee. These "forest farms" were created in the mid-nineteenth century when the ex-slaves took up independent farming in the *monte oscuro,* the dark forest, as it was called, along the Palo and Paila rivers running through the former slave estates. The coffee got added later, in the early twentieth century. This rain forest type of agriculture was a kindly one, inhibiting weed growth, hence labor, and flattening out the swings of heat and rain. The arboreal net diminished the harsh sun, while at the same time it conserved throughout the summers the water from the downpours of the rainy season. The plantains—which are self-reproducing—bore fruit every year after planting, and the cash crops were harvested every two weeks throughout the whole year; when the coffee was abundant, the cacao was minimal, and vice versa. Because there was always at least some produce to gather, and because the trees were in place, the farmers could avoid large labor, capital, or energy inputs; bank loans; or long periods of inactivity.

But with the arrival of agribusiness, first with the sugar cane plantations in the 1950s, and then in the late 1960s with the state-sponsored, U.S.–inspired "green revolution" of chemicals and machines, the opposite occurred. In the Recorder's notes we see that the little red-and-white chequerboard logo of Ralston-Purina (of St. Louis, Missouri), the flagship of U.S. corporate farming, sprouted forth on mud walls of stores in the humblest villages. "They're going to get hens to lay square eggs," the *paisa* said after he and his portly brother won a free trip to the company's headquarters in St. Louis, having sold more fertilizer, hormones, and herbicides to peasant farmers than any other agent in the area that year. A few months later he was shot dead in his store in a dispute over a debt. "It could have happened to anyone," noted the Recorder, "but it seems somehow prophetic of a new type of violence, that of chemicals and an imported technology developed for rich farmers in totally different climate and ecological settings." Meanwhile a whole culture of agriculture was being demolished. What peasant lands did not fall into the hands of the sugar estates were denuded and exposed to sun and floods as the peasant men themselves felled the cacao and coffee trees on their own small farms. Weeds shot up within weeks of clearing and expensive and dangerous pesticides and herbicides were used, contaminating water supplies and altering the insect and plant disease balance. Long periods of waiting and dependence on wage labor and banks took the place of biweekly harvesting. In general women peasants resisted the change, refusing to grant their sons permission to fell the trees. "It gives me little, but it gives," they would say about their farms. As the peasant farms were destroyed by plagues and inability to manage the new technoeconomy, so they were acquired by the expanding sugar plantations. A new world came into being. A familiar story, perhaps more stark than usual, and just beginning when the Recorder first set foot in the town. Be it noted that the environmental critiques so common today were absent when he began his work there and that his observations as to the wisdom of the forest farms were quite novel, flying in the face of agricultural science, state-sponsored farming programs, and of course the self-congratulatory attitude of the well-organized plantation sector dedicated to cutting down the forest with the goal of installing an open-field system like that in Europe and North America. It is hard to see many John Deere tractors or Caterpillar and Volvo backhoes being sold in Colombia if the peasant system of tree farming amidst the tropical rain forest was maintained.

In 1970 Puerto Tejada had a population of around 11,000, and from the Prague archive it seems that most of the inhabitants—maybe 95 percent—were descendants of African slaves. Many of them, from the eighteenth century until the abolition of slavery in 1851, had worked in the alluvial gold mines and on the Japio, La Bolsa, and Quintero haciendas owned by the Arboleda family in that stunningly beautiful region of plains and woods bounded east and west by the ranges of the Andes, twenty-five miles apart, rising dark blue to disappear in mysterious clouds. By 1970 many other people of African descent had recently migrated to the town from the far-off and isolated Pacific coast to find work in the cane fields or as servants in the city nearby.

The Recorder and the Madness of History

I gather that the person who assiduously tape-recorded and noted things down, the Recorder, had been only two months in Latin America when he began his interviews with Tomás Zapata, that his ability to converse in Spanish was rudimentary, and that his knowledge of local life and history was negligible. His interviewing style was impatient. Instead of letting his subjects speak at will, when they appeared to be meandering he would interrupt and choke off what to us, many years later, sometimes seem like astonishing lines of thought. He seemed inclined to cancel out the woolly associations, stutterings of thought, and illogically organized reminiscences. Now, while I realize that people, especially old people, may talk in meandering ways, this has made me wonder how other Recorders obtain texts that are concise and harmonious, and beyond that, I feel impelled to ask what it implies for representation in general and the writing of history, in particular, if the texts of lived speech of reminiscence are strewn with leaps and swerves, let alone with the debris of false starts and detours?

I also wonder whether the Recorder was trying to have the spontaneity of conversation and the rolling weight of the human voice echoing the past, making it really real as salvaged material, while at the same time having the carefully wrought order of a prepared text. As you shall see, this takes one to the heart of the problem of history—cleaning out the opaque density and minutiae of the past to get to its secret? its meaning? its power to unseat bad history? the lineaments of the well told tale? . . . Oh! Oh! Now look who's meandering! Perhaps the problem here lies in assuming that one can be sufficiently outside of history to be able to ask the sorts of questions implied by these dubious answers—while a more accurate response would be to give history and not the Recorder primacy of place, to see the historian as constructed by history and to see ourselves no less than the professional historian as embodiments enslaved by past obsessions to which we usually succumb, other times struggle with, and from which, by and large, we rarely escape. The reason for doing history, then, would be because one can do naught else but try to breathe in this turmoil and if possible escape from it.

What is today understood by History is the attempt to dignify this obsessive madness with fine-sounding goals such as the search for "meaning" or design—goals whose primary function is to ensure the empowering illusion of standing freely above history, now the object of study. To the contrary, the end point of the madness that is history would be that the patient is able to get off the psychoanalyst's couch for the final time because the transference with the present had achieved a functioning praxis.

Of course I know how easy it is to be critical of the Recorder after the event. Indeed the Director of the Prague archive has urged me to exercise restraint lest I merely repeat the Recorder's anxious impatience and lose sight of the history of the erasure of history.

The Philosopher

Early on the Recorder found his way to the poorest section of that poor town where an elderly cigar maker, Eusebio Cambindo, introduced him to his neighbor, Tomás Zapata who, from the notes typed up that night, is said to have been a massive and gentle blind man eighty years of age seated in the sun in the corner of a tiny cemented-over patio, his trembling hands resting on a walking stick. He spoke in a high-pitched, quavering, singsong voice as his daughter and some great-grandchildren cleared a space for their unusual guest.

"He's a philosopher," Eusebio Cambindo is recorded as saying with admiration, although later he displayed exasperation—like when the Recorder was asking Don Tomás about the legendary bandit, Cenecio Mina, who had been, he said, a colonel in the War of One Thousand Days and active in this area in the early twentieth century when the large landowners, rich, white men and women from Bogotá and Boyacá, returned after the Conservative Party victory to force the black "squatters" off what the large landowners considered to be their land or else make them pay rent. These landowners belonged to the Conservative Party and came from the families that had owned many slaves in these parts. But the blacks had long been supporters of the Liberal Party. It was the Liberal Party that had freed the slaves in 1851 and the blacks had at times shed blood for it, there being apprehension among them throughout the second half of the nineteenth century that the landowners intended to restore slavery. And if the blacks were worried, we should not forget that during much of the second half of the nineteenth century, travelers recorded that whites said they greatly feared that as in Haiti, the "black horde" would sweep out of the dark woods to engulf the towns and haciendas of the Cauca Valley . . .

Speaking about Cenecio Mina, Don Tomás said: "This was in one sense a superman, in one sense, and in another sense was . . . a reproductor because he had the capacity to make his writing, to send his writings all over, and being a superman he was thus able to outwit the law, he juggled the law, and this man had everything, had everything, because amongst the people of our time and further back, all have contained people of different measure and capacities, as you can see in the work of . . . [he pauses] Pythagoras."

"Good! But, pardon, pardon me a small intervention," broke in Eusebio. "Let's not put in Plato or Pythagoras or other great sages that history tells us about . . . let's work with nothing more than the facts involving this man, what sort of a person he was, his intelligence, his cunning,. . . and his political deliberations that you knew."

But at least on that day Don Tomás's mind was elsewhere as he pondered the differences between common men, supermen, and God. He would swerve between sources plucked from the Western canon, such as Pythagoras, on the one hand, and complicated accounts of local history, on the other. That's how the Recorder saw this, as an unpredictable back and forth between these poles of cultural reckoning, yet in the process those poles dissolved. Mix and motion became stronger than boundary. In his notes the Recorder seems to have been confused at this process of what he called "flow and mix" and "flow and swerve." The Director, known for his heavy-handed humor, pointed out that when you look at the Recorder's own writing, however, it is also prone to this process of flow and mix, swerve and flow. At this point I too became somewhat confused.

As the discussion lingered for a moment on the bandit's magical capacity to transform himself, Don Tomás went on, "An example: . . . to study the word of God one has to go back, to the beginning . . . and Greek mythology tells us that gallant Zeus, in love with Leda, being on the other side of the lake, converted himself into a swan . . . Zeus is the sun, Leda, the earth; space is . . . how can I explain this? Eventually in this sacred euphoria he lay with Leda and from this came many gods." His voice trailed off. "For instance," he went on, "I was having a conversation with a man who just wouldn't believe anything. Nothing! Sometimes he'd understand but other times he'd just close up, saying there was only one heaven. And I told him No! Just one heaven! No!"

"Pardon, Don Tomás, are you speaking of Greek mythology?" asked Eusebio.

"Sí, señor. Sí, señor," replied Tomás.

"Well! It's clear that Greek mythology can never be anything but myth, and that myth is nothing but farce," said Eusebio, who went on to rebuke Tomás for his failure to talk of what he had been personally acquainted with. "Just try to remember," he urged, "just try a little. Miguelito [the Recorder] wants to know what sort of person Mina was; more or less smart, astute, cruel, magnanimous? What did he have inside? Did he fight honestly on the battlefield or was he a man who changed his party, being somewhat dishonest? This is what Miguelito wants you to analyze, because being older than me, you lived closer to those events."

In this way the discussion turned to how Mina played one political party off against the other to his personal benefit and how he was able to transform himself into animals and plants to avoid his enemies—all communicated in a matter-of-fact, unromantic way, so unlike the attempts begun by intellectuals and students in the 1980s to apotheosize Mina as a symbol of resistance — and always with this swerve and flow process intermingling what Eusebio, to his despair, saw as farce with fact, mythology with reportage.

Old Age and the Ancients

It early on occurred to me listening to the tapes that this process of swerve and flow was largely on account of Don Tomás Zapata's venerable age and the tricks aging plays with memory. He himself would stop and say with some remorse that his memory was shot. But then, as you shall see later, his memory for ritualized speech, for his poetry, was well-nigh perfect. What's more, I had to consider whether these very "tricks" that oldness plays with memory might not be as revelatory as the absence of tricks. Doing tricks could be just what the obsessions of the past need to get the juice flowing.

It also occurred to us that in "accessing" the elite Western tradition the old man was trying to impress the Recorder, the educated foreigner, the *inglés*—the Englishman—as he came to be known. By peppering his remarks with ancient Greek philosophers, for instance, was not the old peasant merely showing off and hence betraying philosophy with sycophancy? Was he not merely aping the intelligentsia of the cities, the upper classes, and old Europe?

To be sure, this suspicion was tempered when one realizes the great and genuine respect, together with a measure of fond familiarity, with which Tomás held the ancients. But when one thinks about the implications of the aping argument, you realize that, first, there is a sense in which *all* thought is derivative, and second, that it was not all that uncommon at that time in Puerto Tejada—according to the Recorder's notes—to every now and again come across in the late afternoons, lounging on street corners, middle-aged or elderly men (who surely had spent very few years in school) arguing about Socrates or Plato, as if they lived just around the corner. Then again, the authority of the ancients can be used in wildly different ways. To invoke the ancients is not necessarily to imply conformity with the present setup. The great revolutionary theorist Karl Marx, for instance, owed some of his key economic distinctions, such as the distinction between use value and exchange value, to Aristotle, and peppered his *Capital* with quotations from the ancients, while Bertolt Brecht based his fundamental distinction between epic and dramatic theater on Aristotle's *Poetics*. And these were modern European theorists with an eye not on the past but on the future.

One also had to consider that the aping argument really doesn't tell you all that much because neither the intelligentsia nor the upper classes are all that uniform and therefore don't provide just one model or one cannon to ape but several, often antagonistic, ones. And then what is one to make of the strikingly different style of thought exhibited by Eusebio Cambindo as compared with Tomás Zapata? Here was a man, perhaps also trying to impress the *inglés,* yet far from adulating the ancients, he was impatient with Don Tomás for failing to keep to what he conceived of as the historical record. So how does one explain two very different styles of thought as the one reaction to the Recorder's presence? But then what was that presence?

Storyteller, Historian, Columbus

In a famous essay Walter Benjamin says the storyteller can be understood as located at the junction where the traveler returns to those who never left.[1] This puts emphasis on situation as much as storyteller, the story emerging from a meeting of persons on different trajectories, bringing the faraway to the here and now. I assume that the Recorder's presence was bound to and defined by this nexus, complicated by the fact that this must have been to some extent also an encounter with History in the figure of the old, blind man, iconic of the wisdom stored in the opacity of the past's pastness. In listening to the tapes and studying the notes I remembered the Director's puzzlement as to how the old man might have felt at being in this position. (Was this because we were putting the Director in a similar situation?)

This was made vivid at one point early on in the tapes where Tomás said to the Recorder and Eusebio Cambindo, "Good! Before anything else I want to clear up for you the history of Columbus. I could see that you didn't understand me, and this is what I wanted to tell you: this existed, but in private. When Columbus came it then passed into history. No longer did it remain in private. Now it had passed into history. This is what Miguel [the Recorder] is coming to do, too; getting hold of things that were in private, in order to take them to history. That's what I wanted to tell you about Columbus."[2]

"There's so many things forgotten," commented Eusebio. "That's why one goes to an old person who can give a summary of more or less how things were."

"Sí, señor. Because before things were written down in books like the Sacred Scripture, it came by tradition, what they called the tradition of the ancients, with one old person telling another . . . and it's this tradition that Miguel is acquiring for history."

Eusebio said it would be too tiring to get through everything in one day and that he and the Recorder would return later. "Let me make it clear," Eusebio said, "that there's no danger whatsoever, no social danger at all."

"No! I understand what sort of person he is."

"These are affairs that . . . Clearly, Miguel is making a computation of the anterior life of the country, maximally of the Negroes . . . what sort of treatment they received from their masters in the epoch of slavery, if your father or grandparents were slaves . . ."

"Exactly" affirmed Tomás. "He's an investigator. Precisely. For instance, you can't lie to an investigator. You have to tell the truth."

In Accord with What's Written

According to the field notes supplied by the Director, the Recorder returned on his own many times and tape-recorded his conversations with Don Tomás about slavery and abolition. The Recorder seems to have assumed that the old man was privy to a chain of oral tradition. The recording would thus be a continuation, a plumb line of magnetic tape hurled into the abyss of history, then hauled out, wet with the sticky weight of dripping speech. As Don Tomás himself said, what the Recorder was doing was recovering "the tradition of the ancients" just like in the times before books like the Sacred Scripture came into being.

But Tomás would confound this expectation by stating he was working from books and not from oral tradition. It was the ultimate double bind: the authority of the oral tradition privileging the authority of the text.

"I'll tell you according to what's written," he would say. "I'm going to tell you what I understand in accord with what's written. After the War of Independence they got together and made themselves owners of the land, but during the war the three parties fought united—Conservative, Liberal, and the priests—against the Spanish. But once they'd achieved victory they left the poor in the cold and the land was partitioned amongst the heavyweights, the rich. They partitioned it amongst the rich Conservatives, the rich Liberals, and the rich priests. And the poor? They abandoned the poor! Nothing! Thus the poor began to rebel and join with someone called José Hilario López, and when the rich got wind of the fact that the poor were after land, then they imposed politics—*la política*—so there would be no unity among the poor. Thus came politics and thus came hatred of the one against the other so that nobody ever got any land!"

"After independence there arose a man called, whom I have studied . . . Are you listening?"

"Yes."

"To support José Hilario López and the rights of the poor."

"Without land?"

"Sí, señor. There arose Napoleon Bonaparte. This man fought the good fight."

"Here in Colombia?" asked the Recorder.

"Yes. He fought good."

"Here?"

"Yes."

"Or in Europe?"

"Here in Colombia. At that time there existed the Concordat. The Concordat consists in that the priest has the same power as the mayor, and thus the law of the Church had more power than civil law and had many people placed in the Inquisition. And Napoleon Bonaparte succeeded—this was in Spain—succeeded destroying one of these prison houses. In these houses they had a Virgin Mary together with the judges. They would take everything a person owned and the person would wither away because these prisons were underground. They would order you to kiss the Virgin and as you stepped out towards her along a pavement so she moved and opened her eyes and when you went to kiss her she opened her arms and you were cut to pieces that fell to the ground because those arms were knives. So when Napoleon triumphed he made those judges go and kiss the Virgin. They screamed they couldn't go but he forced them and then he placed a stick of dynamite and blew up that house of Inquisition because Napoleon was fighting to destroy the Concordat. Concordat comes from concordance, two different people agreeing on a single thing. But he was not able although he diminished it greatly. You can't destroy it because it's so well put together . . ."

The Director and I chuckled over this astute but, to me, geographically disorienting history of Napoleon as we sat in the mottled light drifting through the unwashed windows of the Prague archive. Did we not feel a little uncomfortable, wondering if maybe the laugh wasn't on us, that we who were sitting in judgment were, in that laughter, having our own bases of judgment judged?

Don Tomás's world was one in which the art of storytelling was very much alive, while at the same time the written text was accorded great prestige. Could it be that his ability to evoke the past, condensing it into brilliant and eccentric image-fragments of commentary and counsel, was predicated on just this overlap of storyteller and book?

Poet or Historian?

The old man often answered questions about the past by reciting verse. So natural was this disposition, so in keeping with his formal mode of address, that the Recorder at first failed to realize that he was being answered in verse. The tape on which we first picked this up began typically enough with the Recorder's persistent questions about land tenure and marriage after the abolition of slavery. "Free unions were more common than marriage," Tomás was saying. "But then came the war."

"What war?"

"The War of One Thousand Days.[3] After the war was over it was said that men were scarce and that therefore anybody living in a free union had [by orders of President Reyes] to get married."

> Están los enamorados muy enojados con Reyes
> Que con sus rígidas leyes
> Les obliga a ser casados
> Si no arreglan su conciencia de aquí a fines de mayo
> Sean liberals o godos
> Los manda p'al Putumayo
>
> [Lovers are mad at Reyes
> On account of his inflexible laws
> Forcing them to get married
> If you've not squared your conscience by the end of May
> Whether Liberal or Conservative
> You'll be sent to (the penal colony of) the Putumayo]

"Sí, señor. The Putumayo was a jungle. It was serious. Anyone who resisted marriage got sent to the Putumayo."

It was snowing in Prague. The archive was miserably cold. The Director and I tried to imagine Tomás and the Recorder sitting there in the heat of that dusty plantation town with its open sewers, the old man tremulous, the Recorder anxiously awaiting the response to his next question.

"Don Tomás, do you remember well what happened the ninth of April?"

Tomás must have been talking about the War of One Thousand Days, because the "ninth of April" is code for the notorious *Violencia,* which began at noon that infamous day in 1948 with the assassination of the populist, Liberal Party leader Jorge Eliécer Gaitán, leading to peasants from the two political parties killing each other for over a decade. The Conservative Party held control of the state, the army, and the police.

Don Tomás curtly answered, "Sí, señor!"

"Can you tell me about it?"

"Sí, señor."

And I here translate this poem, but without its strong rhythmic beat or rhyme.

Blessed God, what is to be done with Zambrano's government?

Already we are like two beasts with brother killing brother.

When Zambrano came, the town began to shiver and shake

They stripped us naked, not even a needle remained

Defenseless, because on the ninth of April,

The knives had marched off behind the gun.

Oh My! What a time for the black folk!

With a gun at the door:

"Hands up, you fuckers!

Cowards.

Your courage flees, you're too scared to fight!

Screw the damn blacks and the Liberal Party, too.

Long live Doctor Laureano Gómez!

Elected president of Colombia!

We are going to wipe out even your shadow."

Strutting in tranquility, the *chulavitas*[4] took over with the Military Police

Breaking doors and signs, whooping their battle cries

When they bumped into people on the street,

With the flat of the machete they tenderized them, just short of killing.

To Don Anselmo Cetro, it happened; at five in the morning on his way to
    work they got him good

To Dionisio Mercado—to disarm him of his machete

They shot and left him; mouth shut tight, body fried.

    As for Don Manuel Pizarro, the MPs took his 400 pesos

And when the man saw himself lost

He went directly to the town mayor [Zambrano] and the mayor said to him:

"Get out of here, you bum, before I have you shot!"

When the man understood he'd lost his entire economy

All he could do was keep saying, "God bless the Virgin Mary!"

To Felix María Acotsa, the MPs paid a visit,

and the money in his trunk disappeared in an instant.

One night they set off, Oh! So joyous in their truck!

But it got stuck at the corner and so they went to worry the daughters of
  Ospina

Since that at first didn't work out, they rolled down the ditch to relax at
  Josefa's,

That house of ill repute.

Raving like madmen they got Ospina's daughters and filled their mouths
  with shit.

To Manuel Bedoya they came saying, "A thief got in here and we're after
  him."

On hearing these words, Bedoya replied, "Nobody has come. I'm the only
  one who dwells within."

"Don't deny that a gangster's inside. If you don't let us in then we'll spray
  you, by God!"

"I won't open my door because this store's mine!"

"Whomsoever touches my door I'll gut with lead!"

After a hail of shots, well, they got what they wanted.

Bedoya was alone and they numbered forty.

They subdued him, made him prisoner, and took him to Zambrano.

"You have to pay me two thousand and if not, then right here we'll kill you."

So to set himself free he put his hand to his pocket.

"Here! Take it, and don't make such a fuss."

Then they were on their way to Jesús Giraldo's.

"We've come for two friends, on account of Don Zambrano."

"Why are you taking me away? I've got no debts. I'm here in my agency
  awaiting my people."

"You come right along, but not with any ambassadors.

If you try to be brave, we'll kick you along."

And off he went propelled by the flat of the machete
To be dumped with rifle butts inside the jail.
"You've got to pay two thousand pesos to get yourself free.
And if you don't, you'll go to eternity!"
And so, to free him of his doleful song,
From this poor citizen, too, they got their due.
And, speaking of valor, Zambrano came up with an idea.
"I'm off to Villa Rica with all my means of State.

So spoke the Means of State.

"If you go to Villa Rica then we'll come, Sire,
And if those blacks try anything, we'll finish them with fire."
Into their jeep they clambered and took off for Villa Rica
Saying to each other, "Oh! We'll be bringing back the dough!"
But it didn't work out like that, because,
On seeing the soldiers in droves
The black folk slipped like ghosts into their cocoa groves,
Until the jeep hit a ditch and hurled out its passengers.
"And now those blacks are firing on me like I'm a wounded bear."
"Run! Run! Compañeros! This black fellow is gonna kill me."
"Jump! Fly into the jeep! Oh the pain! Already I've been shot.
Look here at this wound! If we don't get outa here real quick, the game
    is up."
So the pale heroes came back to Puerto Tejada.
At the hands of the sweet black folk, how many came wounded!
"I tell you, Zambrano, old buddy of mine,
Never, never, never, can I go off with you again.
I have traveled too far and life's just too precious

Now surely they will kill me because I always tell the truth
Because my pen keeps writing even when I stop to think of proof.
And if, through my writing, enemies come a' swarming
I feel fortified; and not only on account of this warning.
By the way, I must inform you, I never had a teacher
Yet, just as the tiger is known by its stripes,
So you get to know a person by the shape their writing takes,
Here stop the verses written by my hand.
Thus came and went the government of Marco Polo Zambrano.

He stopped here. Only later, after hearing different tapes, did I realize that this poem has other stanzas for each of the military mayors imposed on the town at that time. And I am crestfallen at the size and shape of my failure, at my inability to render either the rhyme or the rhythm in the English language. The intelligence and skill of the poet cannot survive my translation—and this sober reckoning surely makes one pay keener attention to the task of the anthropologist in the figure of the Recorder. Poor soul, doomed to failure in a practice given over to the contrast of difference, desperate for a language of mediation.

As the weeks went by, the old man increasingly responded in verse to the Recorder's questions about the past. From questions *about* the past to speaking *of* the past and then *speaking the past* is but a series of fine lines, yet how different the end point is compared with the beginning! While *questions about the past* smack of an interrogation of the past as much as of an informant and rather magically assume the necessity no less than the capacity for distancing the subject from the object of inquiry, and hence the existence of an objectified knowing, *speaking the past* detours amiably around these wishful assumptions. It was poetry, for some reason, which provided just this epistemological ease, and once loosed, it flooded. Oh! There were so many poems! Poems for the mother, for the wife who had just died, poems about land disputes in the 1930s.

Tengan presente señores lo que les voy a contar
Los enemigos de los pobres no les deben olvidar.
El asutno es bastante grave que mucho admirán
Los amigos de Don Lisandro, más tarde reclamarán.

[Listen hard my friends, to what I'm about to recite.
The enemies of the poor, you must never put out of sight.
The case is a serious one of interest to many people,
Not least the friends of Don Lisandro, who will later says it's feeble.]

And so it continues with precise accounting of boundary lines, names of judges, defendants, plaintiffs, witnesses, each speaking in their own voice. The poet sets scenes to such an extent that the poem appears like a dramatic script moving from the courts to the land to prison, encompassing the corruption of the state-legal apparatus.

"Seeing as you've brought the tape recorder," said Tomás, "I'd like to recite a history, a farewell by Doctor Laureano Gómez.[5] I'm going to recite this composition so that we might understand that not everything written is certain. In studying universal history I came across a man who said that this or that part had been corrected . . . that he had to correct this and that because it was badly put. He said that over the long haul history is subject to the conflict of writing." He paused. "I never knew Doctor Laureano Gómez personally," he continued. "I knew him from his picture."

He then recited his farewell—*Adiós, Colombia, the Benighted*—which recorded the history of the expulsion of the deposed leader, the rise of Ospina Pérez, the coup led by General Rojas Pinilla, and the implications of this coup for re-strengthening the Liberal Party. Each personage would speak in their own voice. The ending was ominous on account of Laureano Gómez declaiming, "Well, now I leave Colombia, but I have to come back, I'll return as president to occupy power forever." But this poem was immediately followed by "The Death of the Conservative Party," which worked around the image of the burial of a corpse, the corpse of the Conservative Party, officiated by leading politicians carrying out their ritual duties. "Yes it's dead, the Conservative Party, and now it's being buried / And those who read these verses must never, never forget," is how this poem, begins. It ends with the announcement of a birth—the birth of the newly invigorated Liberal Party.

The child is very beautiful, a marvel to behold
So was born the Liberal Party, in the hands of Rojas Pinilla

These verses are those of a humble poet
Written while the Liberal Party was but a suckling child.

[El niño es muy hermoso, se parece una maravilla.
El Liberalismo nació en manos de Rojas Pinilla.

Estos versos así escritos son de un humilde poeta
El niño del Liberalismo estuvo mamando teta.]

There was a lot of laughter when he finished, the Liberal poet poking fun at *Liberalismo* and at himself, too, resurrecting new life from the death of the enemy, the Conservative Party, yet avoiding histrionics.

Asked by the Recorder the meaning of P.M. in this poem, Don Tomás replied, "The police, the military police," and without pause continued with another of his verses, not about the police but, in mock serious terms, Biblical and colloquial, he spoke of the vulnerability of the poor to theft, the necessity for the poor of all races to unite, and the power for justice that he, Don Tomás Zapata, a black man, wields with his poetic pen. And so it goes until the end, which is as follows:

Many are those startled by my pen
and wish to know my name
I am Tomás Zapata Gómez.
If you wish to answer me
you have to understand that this is not something I learned
but something I acquired in the cradle . . .
There they go saying "What a devil, this black man!
If only we'd known how he writes we would never have committed our crimes
Colombia has always known countless men without a conscience
who rob whatever they can
and I say this from experience
so let us unite, us poor, without distinguishing our color
that way we'll free ourselves from attack
it's always the poor that suffers
Tomás Zapata Gómez.

As an admirer of Bertolt Brecht, the Director liked this verse and pulled out a copy of John Willett's *Brecht in Context,* from which he began to read an essay showing the influence of Kipling on Brecht. Both poets were steeped in the language of the Bible and the hymnbook, notes Willett, as well as that of Horace and other Latin poets. Both "were basically un-literary" in a way that other "socialist" poets such as Aragon, Becher, and Neruda, were not, with a respect—writes Willett—for the direction of a person's actions rather than the quality of their feelings. Intended for action, the work of both Kipling and Brecht is marked by its "popular forms, clear language, rough rhythms, and 'gestic' or syncopated line-breaks."[6]

The Director continued reading where Willet quotes Kipling:

But it will take a more mighty intellect to write the Songs of the People. Some day a man will rise up from Bermondsey or Bow and he will be coarse but clear-sighted, hard but infinitely and tenderly humorous, speaking the people's tongue, steeped in their lives and telling them in swinging, urging, dinging verse what it is that their inarticulate lips would express. He will make them songs. Such songs! And all the little poets who pretend to sing to the people will scuttle away like rabbits.[7]

And Willet sees this as a prescription close to Brecht's later aims.

But as the Director pointed out, in his spoilsport way, Don Tomás would never compose a poem like Kipling's "When 'Omer smote his bloomin lyre" because that would be disrespectful of Homer and the ancients. It would take a poet from the educated classes to put that into the mouth of the uneducated Poet of the People. What Brecht and Kipling found in "ordinary speech" was a language they in part invented, a vigorous Creole language mediating class mixture that could be turned against the quite different pretensions of literary languages.

The Voice of the People

Coming from an as yet unexamined intellectual and poetic location on the poverty-stricken margins of burgeoning agribusiness, these verses invite one to do more than identify them as the soul of the people. Indeed, what the Recorder called "flow and mix, flow and swerve," juxtaposing local history with authors canonical to the Western tradition such as Plato and Pythagoras, and with mythological figures such as Leda and Zeus, should be sufficient to check knee-jerk nostalgia and authenticity projected onto the "Latin American peasant," the "descendants of the African slaves," and so forth. Far from reflecting a continuous tradition or even creating one, mix and swerve suggests an art of interruptions, of cultural and temporal montage.

I would like to somehow get around the seductive power of nostalgia and authenticity by speculating on our need for them and why they should be so intimately part of our being in the world. I would like to point out that this voice of Don Tomás Zapata is a very powerful contribution to the construction of America precisely because, being of "the people," it is also a reworking of the Western canon that, in its own way, it holds in great esteem and on which it so dependent. Not least noteworthy in this reworking is a stress, at once dignified and ironic, heartfelt yet mischievous, on the need of the poor to organize against the classes that are supposed to identify most closely with that very cannon and be its living embodiment into the future. (Not for nothing was Bogotá called "the Athens of America.")

Yet at the same time there are significant parallels, perhaps complicities, between this economically poor Colombian peasant, descendant of slaves from Africa, and the Western cannon. Apart from his obvious respect for the ancient

Constructing America

philosophers and Greek mythology, and so forth, and the enjoyment his understanding of them affords him, there is the fact that his personal style—his dignity and humor, his confidence and directness—has an aristocratic, yet nonauthoritarian resonance—the sort of character we might mean when we talk of nobility of character, humble yet assured, down-to-earth and direct, more concerned with ends than with utility—what Georges Bataille philosophizes as *sovereignity* as opposed to *mastery,* which I understand as the mastery of nonmastery.[8] Perhaps, then, this can be usefully rephrased; that the old man uses an aristocratic style associated with the learned elite of yesteryear so as to critique the elite and the system of laws and property on which it rests.

When one sees the nature of the impact that commercialized mass culture now exerts in Latin America, no less than in the so-called developed world, to the extent that extraordinarily violent and sexist movies are shown routinely to captive audiences via video monitors in city buses, and to the extent that heavy-metal music subculture defines the ideals of young men in the drug-saturated and homicidal barrios of Medellín, cocaine capital of the world—then we can gauge the degree to which Don Tomás's way of thinking, style of being, clothing, forms of address, bearing, and body movement have not only been left long behind but to what degree they might seem to share far more with the culture of the elite of yesteryear than with the poor, both rural and urban, of today.

But there is more to it than this, for what the old man speaks from is not so much an elite culture that he imitates as a peasant culture of great formality and measured, rhythmical speech in which persons are acutely sensitive to inequality of moral standing and to sleights of honor. The moral world in Don Tomás Zapata's verses is this world of great formality and sensitivity to the person. It is an ideal that lived in speech, especially what I would call the speech of address, the manner of holding the other in the scaffolding of words as greeting, as framing, as the basis for statement and response which is what the poet strives for as the implicit power carrying the line. In some ways its time is now gone even though the memory may be strong as carried in the form. Yet it may not be too far-fetched to suggest that something of it lives on in the warrior ethos of the youth gangs that are responsible for some 85 percent of Colombia's homicides today.

The Voice of the Past

The Director and I were struck by the old man's ability to remember his verses, which could go on for maybe twenty minutes at a time. Because the Recorder's notes indicate that what we might call collective memory in this town was of a very short span indeed, we wondered whether in fact history would be kept alive without these epics—assuming that the poet had some sort of real audience. Otherwise people seemed to live immersed in the present, a fact that never ceased to surprise the Recorder who had naively assumed that history was necessary to human life and that a peasant village in Latin America—shades of one hundred years of solitude—being "of the past" would hence have a high degree of consciousness to the past. We could sense the terrible shock in his later notes when we came across the huge scrawl, in *Nietzsche*, "*life in any true sense is impossible without forgetfulness.*"[9]

I then wondered if the old man frequently recited his poems or whether he was isolated and lost until that remarkable day when fate brought him and the Recorder together. I began to suspect that were it not for the Recorder coming to town, the poet could well have remained silent in his last year of life, politely ignored by his neighbors. What a sight that must have been, the two lonely historians face-to-face in the sun-drenched, cement-covered patio with old burlap bags and the excreta of chickens, the old black blind man, a year before his death, and the young white "Englishman" with his tape recorder. Was the old man, then, living in some sort of time warp, alone with his verses rattling inside his head?

In this vein I also wondered, after discussion with the Director, whether the Recorder and Zapata jointly created a sort of "playground"—"between illness and real life," as Freud referred to the transference scenario in his 1914 paper "Remembering, Repeating and Working Through"—a playground in which repetition is allowed to expand in almost complete freedom such that remembering can eventually become a force for understanding and even change.

Could the Poet and the Recorder have *jointly* created something rather special, an *intercultural transference* space made out of poetry as a playground of memory and language, bound to the repetition of formal rhyme and meter? It was my hunch that in its very repetition and character as ritual, the poetry provided a type of repetition which, instead of blocking, facilitated remembrance.

Far from being a neurotic repetition due to resistances that could be exposed through the transference space, and far from being the practice of an analyst listening to a madman, this "playground" was a two-way street with two analysts or two madmen, simultaneously existent or changing places, whichever way you care to take it, creating a transference space not so much of two individuals as of two world histories brought into a serendipitous overlap for a certain, small period of time. Surfacing in this intercultural space provided by the accident of the

Recorder's arrival, it was the very repetition of the poetry, its aesthetic of repetition, which provided the constant that is one way of trying to live with, if not temporarily outwit, the nervousness of the cultured being that is the nervous system of violence, upheaval, and phantasmagoria of twentieth-century Colombian rural existence.

Blindness and Writing

I couldn't stop thinking of the Poet's blindness, apparently caused by cataracts late in life. Perversely romantic as it may seem, I wondered whether blindness in some way magnified either his powers of memory or need to remember, plunging him into an interior world of the past, remembrance becoming a sort of hypertrophied sensory or emotional tool compensating for the atrophy of sight. I started to realize, however, that instead of emphasizing the vision turned inwards, the more important issue was the need for expression of that thwarted vision and the means chosen, such as the poems.

What concerned the Recorder in this regard, if I am interpreting his notes correctly, was the confusion in his own mind about the poet's continual emphasis on writing and reading. Here he was, the epitome of the "oral tradition" reciting poem after poem, yet it was writing—his own writing—and books—history books and the Bible— that he underlined as the source of inspiration and legitimation. "Según las letras . . ." (According to the printed word) is how he'd begin. And then he would follow with all those references to the weight of his pen and how he had no option but to keep on writing, and so forth.

It is surprising that the Recorder never seems to have recorded whether the old man did indeed at one time write down his verses. I concluded that fieldwork is prone to blindness, too. But I did figure out that the old man had learned to read although he never spent a day in school. I wondered if he'd ever come across those amazing newspapers that the Recorder had found in the National Library of Colombia, in Bogotá. Dated 1916 (when Tomás Zapata was twenty-six years old), both newspapers claim to be from Puerto Tejada. There was the *Cinta Blanca* (White Ribbon), a "fortnightly organ of general interest," and what looks like its opposition, *El Latigo* (The Whip), an "epidemic publication, not familiarized with the endemic of the nation, arriving when you spy it."

This was at a time when the population of the town could hardly have been more than 2,000 adults, with links to the nearest city, Cali, being via a dirt track or bamboo rafts, and probably a large proportion of the population illiterate.[10]

What is even more astonishing than the fact that two newspapers could be published in such a small town at that time—making us revise all our preconceptions of the development of print and culture in the Latin American countryside—are the covers of *El Latigo,* stark woodcuts displaying virulently anticlerical cartoons, *underlain by rhyming verse!*

As a child Tomás had badly wanted to read. He told the Recorder how one day he'd asked his stepfather for three reales to buy a book but his stepfather whipped him instead, saying reading was for girls. He then secretly saved the money and went to the weekly market in Santander and found a man selling books.

"Have you got the book *Mantillo,* number 1?" I asked.

"Yes.

"How much?"

"Three reales."

"Sell me one and teach me the first lesson."

"I gave him the three reales, and he gave me the book and he taught me the abc's for the first time in my life, then a second time, then a third time, then a fourth time, and then he left me there and wandered away selling his stuff. So I

struggled, and when I forgot a letter I would go back to the marketplace and he would teach me that letter."

I could not but be reminded of this feat when we came across the old man's poem that we found towards the end of a tape marked "January 1970." It is what he called "a composition I made for a young girl going for the first time to school":

Adiós, querida niña, te alejas de este hogar
Manaña cuando partas, no vayas a llorar
Te espera un nuevo ambiente, la puerta del saber
Que elevera tu alma a un más alto nivel

Y tu hermanita Adela se queda sin consuelo
Que por ti pide bendiciónes al Santo Dios del Cielo.

Manaña cuando vuelvas a este querido hogar
Trayendo la semilla que ya debes sembrar
Pues tu hermanita Adela te ha de acompañar
Por llanos y montañas que han de trabajar
Jesucristo fue maestro en las tribus de Judá
Y el que tenga vocación, esto debe sembrar.

[Farewell dear child, leaving home
Tomorrow when you go, don't cry.
For there's a new world awaiting through the gates of knowledge.
And while your soul will be uplifted
Your little sister Adela remains without comfort
Asking benediction for you from the Lord above.
Tomorrow when you return to this dear home
Bringing with you the seed you need to sow
Your sister, Adela, will be there to help you
Through the valleys and mountains we have to make our way
Jesus Christ was teacher amongst the tribes of Judah
Whoever has the vocation, this is what has to be sown.]

Sentimental, for sure. But also an accurate statement as the value accorded formal education in the Colombian countryside today, despite what Don Tomás says about his father. With its promise of education, the school elevates the soul. Such a generous view is only likely to come, we are tempted to say, from a person who'd never been to school—and surely it is a view deeply shared by Colombia's peasant farmers whose respect for the local school is boundless. More than that, the Director and I found ourselves wondering if the poet's attitude towards the world of letters and poetic forms was the result of just this misrecognition, just this generosity and idealism.

Peasant Farming and Epic Poetry

Indeed, might not his position as a reader who never went to school, a peasant farmer with one foot in the market economy and the other foot in a self-subsistent agriculture, might not this marginality vis-à-vis formal institutions of state, economy, and culture, be the "structural condition" of his mix and swerve, flow and mix, of high culture and popular? Might not this marginality with respect to the state and the market, this marginality trembling with ambivalence with its mix of pain and desire, blindness and insight, be precisely the spiritual source of the epic, a poetic form bearing witness to *the lived effects of formalization*—of the rationalization of the mind, of the body, of social and economic life?

Perforce the poetry that fills this conflictual locus will also bear the brand of law, the state's mighty instrument of formalization, as we see clearly in Tomás Zapata's poetic output with its endless civil suits over jurisdiction of land, police who take the law into their own hands, town mayors who resort to violence, and presidents who make laws to force marriage instead of free unions. Certainly we can read the *Odyssey* as Robert Fitzgerald so pithily describes it—as "about a man who cared for his wife and wanted to rejoin her."[11] But a more historically pungent reading embeds it in philosophical problems of representation and the mythological basis of modern reason. We can see the *Odyssey* as the pre-Socratic primal tale of mimetic forms of knowing succumbing to the impersonality of capital and the modern state, the epic rendition of how yielding to the particulate sensuousness of worldly detail through imitation is turned against itself in the vast story of worldly progress known as the domination of nature (and no doubt this vast story is still Fitzgerald's story of a man who cared for his wife and wants to rejoin her).

This is how Horkheimer and Adorno read Homer in their *Dialectic of Enlightenment,* a book of special interest for peasant poetry if we care to define the poetic as that art of mimetic signification that delights in taking relations of sound and sense, nature and culture, to their outermost limits where signs hover in the fragility and power of artifice exposed. That is one reason why the rhyme is enjoyed, something hard to convey in our translations, for rhyming shows language, and hence our ways of apprehending reality, as man-made approximations. And just as poetry is language at one remove, is it not also a form of sympathetic magic, of like affecting like, of contagion along the sympathetic chain where ideas become forceful presence using correspondences in order to outwit and even dominate reality?

Here the Director reminded me of one of his favorite critics, Walter Benjamin, who concluded from his study of the lyric poetry of Charles Baudelaire that the *correspondances* are scored in that poet's work as an attempt to preserve experience in a crisis-proof form but that nevertheless the poetry is formed by a ready acceptance of failure, in the face of the shock-force of modernity, to maintain this crisis-proofing.[12] With particular poignancy these observations touch upon the issue of peasant memory and the forward march of machine and chemical-based agribusiness in Latin America, environmental pillage, mass unemployment, breakdown in the courts and police, forced migration to the cities, and the phenomenal rise of violent gangs of young men and women.

History as Epic

By opening up the range of possibilities for doing history, these verses threaten one with unnamable dangers. By the same token they elicit excitement, for if the historian gains power by standing apart, this epic poet gains power from embodiment within—an embodiment that, precisely because it is *poetic* and hence self-consciously performative, precisely because it lies so close to the fault lines of language and the evocative power of speech, turns out to be a mobile location within and outside of time. One can also see how this creates a curious reverse movement; by laying claim to a profound kinship with a particular moment to which it gives voice, the verse is able to stand apart from that moment and erode its momentousness.

I assume that for *professional historians*—an ominous appellation—these verses would be dismissed as history, in the sense of historiography, and be cautiously embraced as history in the sense of raw material from the past which the modern historian has a license to store and analyze, plunder and appropriate for the "telling detail," the "voice of the past," the "authenticating seal," even "false consciousness." Yet in categorizing it as booty (also known as "data"), surely the professional historian is desperately trying to deny the way such verse defamiliarizes the historian's task and therefore has to be classified as art, not science. Nietzsche's words come to mind here where he addresses the curious cultural power that flows towards those whose job it is to judge the past. In *The Use and Abuse of History,* he writes "As judges you must stand higher than that which is to be judged; as it is you have only come later."[13] He goes on to say, "The guests that come last to the table should rightly take the last places; and will you take the first? Then do some great and mighty deed—the place may he [be] prepared for you then, even though you do come last."[14] Speaking of great deeds, what fun it would be if our historians were quick-witted enough, were sufficiently brave and adept with language and image, so that they, too, instead of perfecting the culturally contrived performance of objectivity could sing us their verses—verses that gambol with truth's pretensions.

With reference to the great historians of the nineteenth century and, by implication, all subsequent attempts to write histories, Hayden White says that the status of their works "as models of historical narration and conceptualization depends, ultimately, on the preconceptual and specifically poetic nature of their perspectives."[15] Given the profound resistance to this view, I think it necessary once again to examine historiography as poetry, both in White's capacious yet precisely formulated sense of the poetic as an aesthetic infrastructure of the historical text and also in the apparently more literal sense of historiography written or spoken in poetic form like that of Don Tomás. With this in mind, however, can one really say his verses are equivalent to writing a history?

For the Director of the archive, Tomás Zapata's poetry was not aesthetic embellishment so much as another way of archiving the past. In fact, the Director was adamantly opposed to the idea that one could separate aesthetics from anything. Even though, after years of Soviet and Communist Party propaganda, he was hardly one to take Marxist slang seriously, he insisted that this separation of reality from aesthetics was a bourgeois idea through and through. He was particularly struck by the way Don Tomás would spontaneously respond *in verse* to questions about the past meant to elicit *facts,* for instance, questions about marriage customs, the development of private property in land, the *violencia,* and so forth. It is of added interest that this spontaneously erupting versifying response to questions intended to elicit historical facts was a response to an outsider, a stranger—an *investigator,* as he was at one point called—and that this encounter was seen by Tomás Zapata as demanding truth saying in a mighty, almost cosmic, transition of the status of historical knowledge from a private to the public world—akin to Columbus's "discovery" of America, as discussed above. Can one assert that repetition—of the verses as much as the history they put into words— acquired a qualitatively new status, from the private to the public world, thanks to the encounter of the two different types of historian, the investigator and the versifier, the one who searched for an informant, the other for an audience?

This puts Walter Benjamin's storyteller in a different and, I feel, more comprehensive light than Benjamin's own essay, which isolates the encounter between two individuals sharing more or less the same class and culture position to the extent any difference in experience nevertheless presupposes both the ability to exchange experience and the existence of a wide range of common cultural reference. Such would be the case, for instance, of the encounter between the peasant who rarely left the region with the artisan or servant returning to the peasant's village after years in the cities.

But equally important to modern world history, if not as frequent, is the encounter between strikingly different narrators—like the Poet and the Recorder—different on just about any criterion you care to select. When the Grimm brothers published their stories, for instance, they created in effect a mediation between bourgeois and peasant, a mediation that effectively purified the peasant as a type on whose back all sorts of lofty universals could be packed. Likewise, when Benjamin writes on the art of the storyteller, he in fact writes of a premodern peasant and artisan transformed into the published work not of a peasant or an artisan but of Nikolai Leskov, a writer and commercial traveler—in other words, a salesman. The art of the storyteller then transpires as Leskov's voice partly mediating the world of the Russian artisan and peasant. What is more, Benjamin occupied this very same sort of role in the stories he himself wrote about his sea travel to the island of Ibiza and about the life of the peasants and castaways there.

This mediation between bourgeois and peasant has of course been crucial to the stories that anthropologists have built all their work on since E. B. Tyler published the pathbreaking *Primitive Culture* in 1872, if only because in the field (that sonorous term) it is always by means of stories (occasionally termed "cases") that "information," whether on "kinship" or on "mythology" or "economics" or whatever is in fact transmitted to the Investigator such as the Recorder . . . whose job it is to further mediate to the bourgeois reader. Anthropology is blind to how much its practice relies on the art of telling other people's stories—badly. What happens is that those stories are elaborated as scientific observations gleaned not from storytellers but from "informants."

More could be said about this mediating function crucial to modernity because it has been precisely the role of the peasant and the primitive to endorse modernity's sense of literality—the experiential quality that makes metaphor effective. Modernity's peasant, like modernity's primitive, functions to bring the ancients into the realm of the living no less than the body into the realm of the mind. Language itself rests on this otherwise transparent yet necessary fiction of a bodily link between sign and referent, a link established by the history of class forms in the world historical movement from country to city.

Living Through. Looking Back

The Director and I kept coming back to one feature, which at first seemed merely technical and rather unimportant but which later assumed dense complexity and relevance. This was the fact that Don Tomás was expressing lived experience of the present, which to the Recorder is history.

Constructing America

But as time goes by, as the chronicler ages or dies, this record of the lived present ages too. It slips over the weir of the present into the stream of time to become history. It passes into history as datum and at the same time becomes a history. This is more than a confusion of words—history as the past and history as the record of the past—because it is precisely as confusion that it exercises a special quality of force speaking from within as well as outside events, speaking as expression as well as commentary.

This quality of the present passing into history bestows upon the chronicle and its associated form of the epic the potential to achieve what Freud singled out as the key feature of memory in psychoanalysis. Commenting upon the implications of repetition among people suffering from traumatic neuroses and shock, Freud wrote in 1921, much as he had written about hysteria with Josef Breuer at the beginning of his career in 1893, that the analyst must get the patient to "re-experience some portion of his forgotten life, but must see to it, on the other hand, that the patient retains some degree of aloofness, which will enable him, in spite of everything, to recognize that what happens to be reality is in fact only a reflection of a forgotten past."[16] What I wish here to emphasize is the double action of being part of something yet distant from it, too, of being immersed in an experiential reality and being outside that experience. I think it fair to say that the quality of pastness in the past has to be registered in the very repetition, no less than in the sense that this is, after all, not the past but a memory, in the same way a photograph is both of the past and about the past as well.

Indeed, in his later writing repetition became for Freud more than a sign of repression. It was an end in itself, a compulsion so profound it exceeded even the search for pleasure and amounted to a predisposition to death along with the suffusion of mind and soul in the extrahuman, the inorganic realms of earthly life where there is no history, at least not human history. In people suffering from shock after a terrible fright, repetition took the form of recurring nightmares perhaps, suggested Freud, to create the anxiety that was lacking at the time of the fright—it being his argument that anxiety acted as a stimulus shield preventing fright from creating shock, that is, from imploding the psyche and causing a collapse of mental and physical structure. The curious thing for our discussion of the meaning of history is that this stimulus shield—the mark of modernity— is made up of a consciousness so prone to rapid processing of stimuli that it undermines both memory itself and the ability to experience (*Erfahrung*, which includes the ability to be changed by experience).

This makes you wonder about the function of repetition in poetry—understanding poetry in the plain and popular sense of rhyming verse where words and the rhythms of grammar and image move from speech to song. Truly here is where a modern high culture and popular culture clash and where suspicion towards Don Tomás's verses is most easily aroused. Listen to the disdain for rhyming poetry as opposed to "free verse" in this confident 1911 futurist manifesto of the musician Francesco Balilla Pratella. "Free verse is the only one," he declaims, for "not being bound by the limitations of rhythm and of accents monotonously repeated in restricted and insufficient formulas." And in my opinion he correctly emphasizes the rhythm of rhyming poetry as a *dance rhythm*—that is, where words become incarnate. Listen to his contemptuous dismissal of dancing words.

"The rhythm of dance: monotonous, limited, decrepit, and barbarous, will have to yield its rule of polyphony to a free polyrhythmic process."[17]

This was close to Baudelaire's attitude too. "Which one of us," he asked in the foreword to *Paris Spleen,* "has not dreamed of the miracle of a poetic prose, musical, *without rhythm and without rhyme,* supple enough and rugged enough to adapt itself to the lyrical impulses of the soul, the undulations of reverie, the jibes of conscience?"[18]

Clearly, Don Tomás's verse shares little with this version of modernism—yet is his poetry not as much a poetry of shock as Futurism and Baudelaire, whose poetry was defined by Benjamin as the site where aura disintegrated because of the shock experience of the modern?[19]

Is it not one of the functions of steady, relentless rhythm, no less than of simple rhyme to extol repetition for repetition's sake? When we specify the poetry as epic poetry then we add another type of repetition, that of repeating the past—in verse. The even tone, a certain emotional flatness, at times, the jocularity, wit, and ironies do not so much oppose the repetition of the nightmare as scoop it up and reorient its forces, channeling the anxiety of the stimulus shield into an understanding of the past that comes from being both within and outside it.

When I identify Tomás Zapata's poetry as epic verse and wonder as to its status as historiography, I recall that section in Benjamin's essay on the storyteller where he states that Mnemosyne, the rememberer, was the muse of the epic art among the Greeks and that the epic forms a creative matrix from which a range of very different forms have emerged—the story, the novel, and what we today call histories. This observation provokes one into thinking about similarities no less than differences among such disparate forms of putting the past in words. In this regard I would like to recall Hayden White's contribution to the analysis of

Constructing America

forms of writing history, where he distinguishes between annal, chronicle, and modern forms of historiography. What is intriguing about the epic form, a form intimately related to the annal and the chronicle and thus a form we are likely to think of as antiquated, is that it is nevertheless in some respects extraordinarily modernist as well. Indeed it can be seen not only as an expression of the art of memory but as memory applied in modern times to the aesthetics of shock. And nobody made this clearer for the twentieth century than Brecht, whose poetry and dramatic direction of what he chose to call "epic theater" in this regard has still to be given its due—in good part because it was "accepted" before it was understood. Here was where the poet "in dark times" strapped himself to the ultimate double bind, repeating well-known histories in the theater, the dark house of illusion, to display illusion making. The oft-cited "alienation effect" could be striven for in many ways, but essentially it meant showing showing through a curious succession of effects occasioned by a shock sufficient to jar, but not overwhelm, the intellect such that one moved in and out of a lived experience.

Violence

The stimulus for writing this essay, however, came from surprise over Don Tomás Zapata's response to the *violencia*. Here was the "voice of the people," of the oppressed, the voice of the victim. Here was the voice "from within." What aching void of silence, of pain beyond words, it would fill!

But instead of a private voice what I find is an eminently public one. Instead of emotional involvement I find distancing. Instead of tension and a subsequent catharsis, I find a more or less endless story with a grand mocking flourish of a conclusion, the poet-storyteller making sure to reintroduce himself as the "untragic hero."

Seguro me matarán porqué digo la verdad
porque mi pluma se impone mientras yo pueda pensar
ya no me puedo aguantar y por eso ya aquí escribo
por el peso de mi pluma muchos serían enemigos

Me siento capacitado no solamente para esto
y de paso les aviso que nunca tuve maestro
si al tigre se le conoce por sus pintas que no es una
al hombre se le conoce por el peso de su pluma

Aquí termina mis versos escritos ya por mi mano
en esta forma fue el gobierno de Marco Polo Zambrano.

[For sure I will be killed because I speak the truth
my pen keeps on writing even while I'm trying to think
I can't take it anymore and that's why the writing flows
such that from the power of my pen, the world will come to blows.

That's not the only reason why I feel empowered
and as an aside I should tell you I never had a teacher
if you recognize the tiger on accounts of its stripes, which are more than one
you recognize a man by the power of his pen
here is the end of the verses I have written
thus was the rule of Marco Polo Zambrano.]

Here one is far from the school of magical realism of Latin American and Caribbean writers, climbing to the stars on the backs of what they take to be peasant fantasy. One is far from the attempts at clinical exactitude to be found in reports by groups like Amnesty International, no less than from the emotionally overwhelming first-person accounts of the *violencia* in the north of the Cauca Valley to be found in Alfredo Molano's powerful and powerfully edited transcripts in *Los años del tropel*.[20] To the contrary, in Don Tomás's hands, the epic as spontaneous response to the demands for memory purges the sensational—both from the real horror of the *violencia* as well as from the attempts thereafter through the decades to talk and write about it in Colombia and elsewhere.

He puts on a show, thereby showing showing. Unlike the histories composed by professional historians, he works simultaneously both within and without the reality, therewith indicating its modes of realization. He exposes not merely his personal "values" but achieves the even more important task of exposing as exoskeleton the physicality and soulfullness of the medium of thought—language itself—thereby manifesting the imaginative infrastructure of all our works, of any and every rendering of the past. His is eminently an art form drawing attention to itself as art, as rite, together with self-mockery, never letting us forget for a moment that just as historiography is contrived, so shock can to some extent be outshocked—by being repeated in predictable rhyme, steady rhythm, and turned over by humor so its belly can be scratched while its claws gyrate in mindless, albeit menacing, meanderings. In today's world in which the Colombian *violencia* is no longer restricted to the rural poor of Colombia but is, instead, in so many ways a worldwide phenomenon, we take this to be a singularly important contribution to the "construction of America," no less than it is a construction "by America" driven by the quincentenniality of history's obsessions.

This epic art form, however, presupposes no less than it deserves an audience. And who is that audience? There is no record of Tomás reciting his poems to his neighbors in Puerto Tejada. Even if we presume that happened, we are nevertheless haunted by the image of him sitting alone with his verses rattling inside his skull. What we do know is that twenty years later in another part of the world it is we who form for whatsoever brief a time an audience—thanks to the blunderings of the mysterious Recorder and the good counsel of the fictitious Director of the fictitious Prague archive that I have constructed to provide necessary distance from myself. Through the archive, an encapsulated site of remembrance has been created, a site enacted in the mis-en-scene of this writing based on fragments resurrected by the Director—bits of tapes and scattered notes, chips of time brought glowing from dark files. This site is one of transference (in Freud's sense of psychoanalytic technique) between past and present. Here repetition is allowed to play "in almost complete freedom" such that the obsessions driving history "are at every point accessible to our intervention,"[21] so long as one recognizes, in the words of the angel of history, that "history is the subject of a structure whose site is not homogenous, empty time, but time filled by the presence of the now."[22] It was the angel's fervent hope that against all odds the leap into the past would be into "the open air of history" and not in the arena where the ruling class gives its commands. In attempting this I have found it necessary to construct a closed archival space layered with the debris of the past from which such a leap may occur, and it is this space—every bit as much as the space of marginal peasant existence alongside agribusiness—that has to be recognized and drawn into the equation of how it is that we construct the past while being constructed by it.

The Sun Gives without Receiving[1]

Even though as a child in the 1940s I used to watch my mother sewing up, with the skill of a jeweller, gifts of food parcels to send from sunny Australia to her mother, who had stayed behind in war-torn Vienna, parcels that always contained, as I remember, several pounds of butter, and even though I marveled at how thickly she spread her toast, let alone at her cheerfully acknowledging such unhealthy excess, it was not until I settled down in a hot sugar plantation town in western Colombia in 1970, a town without drinking water or adequate sewage, that I realized that butter could be a sign of privilege, golden and creamy, suspended between solid and liquid, dependent on refrigeration no less than on good dairy cows, a dairy industry, and a nice temperate climate.

Then I heard of the devil contract.

And having made his contract with the devil, he earns much more money but can only spend it on luxuries; on butter, sunglasses, a fancy shirt, liquor . . . If you buy or rent a farm, the trees stop bearing. If you buy a pig to fatten up, it gets thin and dies. Secar *was the word they used. To dry, to dry up like a green tree drying out through lack of water, drying to a crisp in the relentless sun.*

An earlier version of this chapter was originally published in *Comparative Studies in Society and History* 37, no. 2 (April 1995).

And the same word applied to livestock, the pig getting thinner and thinner, wasting away to skin and bone. Secar. *To dry up. Too much sun.*

Why can only luxuries be bought and consumed with the devil's pact? Butter, sunglasses, a fancy shirt, liquor . . . a strange list, I thought, being thrown by the butter, a new sign precariously signalling to me both the difference of my new, third world existence, and the way in which that existence connected with another movement through time and memory, a history of flight from Europe about which my parents never said anything. It was as if it had never happened and that Europe had never existed. "And so it is with our own past," writes Proust. "It is a labour in vain to attempt to recapture it: all the efforts of our intellect must prove futile. The past is hidden somewhere outside the realm, beyond the reach of the intellect, in some material object (in the sensation which that material object will give us) which we do not suspect. As for that object, it depends on chance whether we come upon it or not before we ourselves must die."

But is it just chance as to whether one encounters the right object at the right time? Walter Benjamin says no. That is the wrong way to put it. The times are against it ever happening. History itself has taken the turn whereby people are increasingly unable to assimilate the data of the world by way of experience. The capacity to remember is under siege because, in a shell-shocked world, the capacity to experience has had to atrophy. The enormity of Proust's eight-volume work was testimony, Benjamin argued, to the effort it took to restore experience, in the figure of the storyteller, to modernity; and even so, it was a unique triumph. As for the claims of what Proust called "involuntary memory," triggered by an object, perhaps by preference for an object of gastronomic delight, if not excess, then that object's triggering capacity was, too, a product of history's effect on the human capacity to experience and, hence, to remember. Could it have been different, very different, once upon a time? Benjamin certainly thought so:

> Where there is experience in the strict sense of the word, certain contents of the individual past combine with material of the collective past. The rituals with their ceremonies, their festivals (quite probably nowhere recalled in Proust's work), kept producing the amalgamation of these two elements of memory over and over again. They triggered recollection at certain times and remained handles of memory for a lifetime. In this way, voluntary and involuntary recollection lose their mutual exclusiveness.[2]

The festival is a time of licensed transgression involving excess consumption and excess giving, of squandering and letting go. If, therefore, we are to grant this

Dionysian element of ritual, with its repetitions and renewals, its make believe, divinity, sacrifice, exchanges, bestowal, violence, and pleasures, and if this transgression of the festival has a decisive role in amalgamating the two elements of memory, the involuntary no less than the voluntary, then what are we to make of the ritual with the devil? Is it the transgressive pact that in equal measure creates largesse, demands luxury consumption, and issues forth death and barrenness— a pact we can locate as at the threshold of modernity where Benjamin wants to draw a line distinguishing the capacity of objects to provoke memory? Is the pact with the devil above all the rite that obliterates what Benjamin calls "experience in the strict sense of the word"? And if that is the case, then may it not also be the case that the story itself of the pact with the devil has a striking mnemonic function, the mnemonic of the evisceration of memory, or at least of memory geared to "experience in the strict sense of the word"? The worldwide ubiquity of the story of the devil's pact, let alone the intensity of its drama, would therefore speak incessantly, in repetition heaped on repetition, to the sense of losing, just as it speaks to the lust for gaining. Not losing something. Just losing.

This would take us also into the heart of George Bataille's strange contribution to twentieth-century thought, entwining excess with transgression to create a radically different history and science of political economy, capitalism, and communism, focused not on production but on spending, on what he called "unproductive expenditures: luxury, war, cults, the construction of sumptuary monuments, games, spectacles, arts, perverse sexual activity . . . ends in themselves." But first, in this our age wherein the economy has achieved the status of the natural, underpinning the science and metaphysics of scarcity, and before I tell you some more about the devil, the Great Imitator, and his mighty contract, I need to tell you about his torrid zone of operations.[3]

Sun

Solar energy is the source of life's exuberant development. The origin and essence of our wealth are given in the radiation of the sun, which dispenses energy—wealth—without return. The sun gives without receiving.

—GEORGES BATAILLE[4]

It was from a group of women friends of mine, cooks in the sugar plantations at the southern end of the Cauca Valley of western Colombia, in 1970, to be exact, that I first heard of this devil's pact. With money from the University of London, I was studying the abolition of slavery in the area and was living in a small and predominantly black town of about 11,000 people, a town without sewage or drinking water located at the very southern end of a 125-mile-long valley pressed between two chains of the Andes. At that time three large plantations of many thousands of hectares were being rapidly developed by single owners, three white families—one from the days of the Spanish colony, one descended from the German consul who came to Colombia in the late nineteenth century and made a fortune, and the third, recent immigrants of Russian-Jewish extraction. These three families exerted a mighty impact, consuming many of the plots of the surrounding peasant farmers, descendants of African slaves freed in 1851 who held, usually without title, maybe as much as a quarter of the flat valley land in that area. Consequently, through necessity or choice, peasant farmers were finding work as wage workers on the plantations. A huge influx of black women and men from the forests of the isolated and far-off Pacific coast, hungry for money and adventure, also found work as wage workers in the cane fields. All this was new. Very new. The area was, to coin a favored phrase, yet one sounding a little too like some sort of skin disease, becoming rapidly proletarianized, albeit in an uneven and unplanned manner, creating a multitude of heterogeneous class forms and overlapping occupational niches in the cash economy. This is one timescale of history, one way of talking history.[5]

Situated almost on the equator, this valley was stupendously fertile and flat, with many feet of black topsoil subsequent to lacustrine sediment and volcanic ash raining down for millennia from the mountains onto what had been in prehistoric times a vast lake, which in that era had drained into what is today the Cauca River, running the length of this narrow valley. This is another timescale of history, embodied in the thickness of the good soil itself upon which agribusiness today draws its account.

And what a history it must have been, this prehistory of the warring elements. The hot earth expended itself, erupting onto the plains below, the cool water wearing its way through rock, drop by millennial drop: "That yielding water in motion, gets the better in the end of granite and porphyry" (Brecht's image of revolutionary change, drawn from the Taoist Lao Tzu)—two very different rhythms, two histories in concert. "The *correspondances*," writes Benjamin, "are the data of remembrance—not historical data, but data of prehistory. What makes festive days great and significant is the encounter with an earlier life."[6] And elsewhere Benjamin peruses a note by his friend, T. W. Adorno, concerning the former's elusive notion of the *dialectical image:* "For nature doesn't prevail as eternally alive and present in the dialectic. The dialectic inhabits the image and at the end of his-

The Sun Gives without Receiving

tory cites myth as long gone: nature as pre-history. That is why images . . . really are 'ante-diluvian fossils.'"[7] We might want to ask to what rhythm does Benjamin see this festival corresponding—to the horrific splendor of the earth's eruptive self-evisceration or to the steady wearing down by the yielding water?

The answer is bewildering and quite marvellous, a twofold rhythm of expenditure and cessation of happening, such as Benjamin's prophecy, expressed in his "Theses on the Philosophy of History," that modern memory and social revolutionary tension would act in concert to explode the continuum of history. Yet it is by no means guaranteed that the necessary *correspondances* articulating the past through a dialectical image will coalesce.[8] Such is the character of modern culture. "The past can be seized only as an image which flashes up at the instant when it can be recognized and is never seen again."[9]

And this is also a rhythm of an awesome standstill, "the sign of a Messianic cessation of happening, or, put differently, a revolutionary chance in the fight for the oppressed past."[10] Therefore, if the accent is on the side of the volcanic rupture, what Benjamin elsewhere called the *Jetzteit*, the presence-filled now-time—not homogenous, empty, evolutionary time—it must be appreciated that this rhythm is in the midst of its violence also a time of enormous stillness, as perhaps befits the shifting and rejuxtaposition of the earth's plates, no less than the plates of modern memory in search of *correspondance* in a world without festivals. This is the stillness of shock, suspended out of time. This is the work of the negative, as in Bataille's notion of sovereignty, in which the limit is transgressed.

And high above, the sun, without which nothing can grow, is too hot to stand under, too strong to look at. Soaring clouds clinging to the mountain tops surmount the blues and greens of the valley floor, shimmering with heat at midday, sleepwalking into the long hot afternoons. You quickly learn to seek shade. There are two summers and two rainy seasons of unequal duration. Plants grow in wild abundance. "I will begin with a basic fact," writes Bataille in the opening pages of *The Accursed Share*. "The living organism, in a situation determined by the play of energy on the surface of the globe, ordinarily receives more energy than is necessary for maintaining life."[11] When a peasant planted corn in the 1970s, which was not all that common because tree crops were preferred, she or he would walk in a straight line over the soil with a sharp stick and an apron full of corn seed. Jabbing the stick into the earth, a couple of seeds would be tossed in, and the hole covered with a movement of the foot, often shoeless. No plow. No chemicals. No "improved seed" à la Rockefeller. No watering. And if you wanted, you could get two crops a year: *choclo* or soft sweetish corn after four months or dry corn after six. Few places in the world could match this for fertility or for the contrast between that fertility and the poverty of the mass of the people.

In the 1970s you could see groves of trees in clumps and straggling ribbons, the sign of peasant farms, cocoa trees, coffee trees, large-leafed, almost luminous green plantain trees, all sheltered by the giant red flowering Cachimbo trees ensuring shade. And all around lay the endless stands of plantation sugar cane, shadeless under the fierce sun.

At least a third of the peasant farms were owned and run by women. Capital input was negligible, and little work was required to maintain and harvest the tree crops, which bore fruit on a pretty steady basis throughout the length of the year, ensuring a constant trickle of income. Denied the full force of the sun, weeds barely grew. When the rains poured, the trees soaked up the water. When the sun bore down, the trees slowly released moisture. The forest floor was inches deep in leaf mould that would slowly enter the soil to fertilize it. This peasant ecology replicated the rain forest and as such was, point for point, opposed to the principles of farming imported first from Spain and, in our time of John Deere and American foreign aid, from the Great Plains of the United States, where once Indian and bison had roamed. On the plantations and on those peasant plots succumbing to the axe and bulldozer to make way for the new commercial crops, with their Euro-American style of open-field agriculture, sun and rain made weed growth a primary problem requiring much labor and, from the mid-1970s, chemicals of dubious safety.

If you look at the accompanying photograph I took of a traditional peasant farm in back of an open field, you can see the broad-leafed plantain trees down at the bottom, interspersed by some coffee and cocoa trees. Above them are fruit trees, and dwarfing the grove stands a Cachimbo tree.

The irony is that the destruction incurred by the new mode of production, in which trees are felled for the open-field system, allows this traditional farm to be seen in its glory and grandeur no less than its intricacy. The old ways become exposed at the moment of their demise, reaching for the sky. This photograph captures not only a cross-section through the peasant farm. It also holds still a cross-section through time, a history of domination.

Increasingly, as the spread of the new agriculture leveled peasant farms, one saw a new feature: neatly stacked trunks of trees and piles of firewood. As the trees were cut down, their roots were not present to absorb the water of the heavy rains twice a year, so the land flooded. And where the shade of the green leaves of the

groves of trees allowed the peasant farms to remain cool, now the summer sun burnt the denuded land to crisp tawny hues.

The young peasant men (gamblers) pleaded with their mothers (stoic conservatives) to borrow from the banks and cut down the farms and plant new "green revolution" crops that would make a lot of money fast, crops like soya and other sorts of beans that would require fertilizer and pesticides and money to hire tractors and harvesters. The trees on many plots were felled, but the plans for quick profits nearly always seemed to go wrong, except for the richest peasants. Debts mounted. The old women tried not to give way to their sons' demands. "It gives me little, but it gives," they would say about their ailing plots.

As the plantations sprayed chemicals to kill bugs and weeds, the peasants' trees started to die. The area had been miraculously free of the severest plague that affected cocoa trees, the disease known as witches' broom, but by the 1980s there was scarcely a peasant farm not devastated by this. When ripe, cocoa pods are lustrous and purple and weigh several pounds. When afflicted with witches' broom, however, something amazing would happen. Far more pods would develop, only they would grow into tiny, shriveled, wispy husks, frayed and almost frantic-looking; galloping growth, twisted shapes of dying. So . . . more trees were cut down.

What happened to the trees? Some were taken to the sawmill while still green to be cut into thin strips to make boxes for tomatoes grown by peasants on their newly cleared fields. Others were sold as firewood for the ovens that were miraculously springing up everywhere as peasant farmers turned into brick- and tile-makers. Each of these two very material options for dealing with acute land scarcity, tomatoes and bricks, takes us further down the nightmare of history. The first option is the way of toxic chemicals, the second is that of amputation, a term that will become clear later.

Tomatoes were the first crops that smallholders sprayed with pesticide around 1970, and now in most, if not all, of the country all crops are subject to massive application of such chemicals in a revolution encompassing rich and poor farmer alike. The innocent (and soon tasteless) tomato was the vehicle through which Ralston Purina spearheaded the peasants' use of chemicals in this area, along with the impact of that use on soil and the water.

Now when I walk my old haunts, I see the whiteness of the chemical burnt into the soil, and my throat catches on the smell. An agronomist specializing in toxins came through town in 1992 and declared in a public meeting that the soil has become so contaminated that food grown in it should not even be fed to animals!

Just as startling is the revolution that herbicides have so calmly effected in the 1980s. One day we woke up, and from the centers of agribusiness to the furthest-flung corners of the republic, the peasantry had given up on manual weeding with pala, or machete, and instead were casting powders across the land, saying it was far cheaper that way. Even on the frontier in the Putumayo, for instance, the shamans, immersed in natural remedies and herbs, spray Paraquat to kill "weeds."[12]

In the photographs you can see young men at the sawmill cutting the trees to make tomato boxes. The man operating the saw lost his right forearm awhile back. But he still does the job. With a shiny black leather sheath over his stump, studded with sawdust, he guides the trees into the singing blade, smiling self-consciously. For the moment the violence of the image stills the movement.

As for the second option, that of amputation: the average farm has shrunk to such an extent, to a quarter-acre or less, that now only a desperate act is possible, a delirious last grasp at money by selling the good earth itself to make bricks. Some sell it to men who come in trucks from the massively expanding cocaine-funded city nearby. The going price at the moment is six U.S. dollars a truckload. Compare that with the daily wage of around three dollars. "Se vendío para hueco" (Sold for a hole) they say more laconically than my translation conveys.

Others erect their own brick-making ovens on the farm and then excavate next

to it. This, of course, requires large amounts of firewood, adding to the demand for cutting down traditional agriculture. A quarter-acre farm worked this way with a seven-meter-deep hole dug by a rented backhoe will last about four years until *there is nothing left*. The farm will have gone, and in its place there will be just the hole. The earth here is famous for the bricks it makes. It does not require straw. Just the mud the volcanoes spewed as ash to settle on the lake squelched into a creamy consistency like potter's clay.

In not so many years there may be no land at all other than the cane fields of the plantations amid serpentine waterways of chemically polluted mini-lakes in which kids joyfully swim, stirring the water lilies no less than the earth's memories of the prehistoric lake that once was. Unless of course the latest mode of production takes hold—for now the peasants are being approached by men from the city carting toxic garbage with which to fill their holes—a truly diabolical, unimaginable, turn of events.

Devil's Pact

The cooks in the cane fields in 1972 first told me about the devil's pact, years before the startling turn of events I have just described. They were matter-of-fact about it, words flying in the bustle of pots and starting fires, their good humor dished out in measure equal to the food. Something—I cannot remember

"Se vendío para hueco."

what—caught my ear, and I asked for clarification. Yes, there were these men, usually cane cutters, who had a pact with the devil that allowed them without added effort to cut much more cane than normal and therefore make much more money than normal. (Plantation workers were paid according to their production, not by hours worked.) Most everyone I questioned in the months thereafter was familiar with this. It was uncommon, but not singular. Only once did I come across a person who actually knew, and in this case knew well, a person who had attempted to make a pact with the devil in the cane fields and, in this case, had panicked. He was a young man born and raised in the Chocó on the Pacific Coast on the other side of the mountains—a region notorious, from the point of view of the sugar cane area, for its magic. Relying on a book of magic printed in Mexico bought in the marketplace from the wandering Indian herbalists and healers from the Putumayo, he had secreted himself in a field of mature cane, well above head height, and eviscerated the heart of a black cat. As he tried to recite the prayers indicated in his book, a gale-force wind whipped up out of nowhere and the sky went dark. He lost his nerve, dropped everything, and fled, crashing through the cane as the sky erupted.

But the usual story was of a person distant and anonymous, a shadow on the horizon of human possibility, a profiled caricature of a man engaged by destiny—the man like a zombie uttering strange, repetitive cries as he cut his swathe through the forest of cane, the man with the figurine prepared by a sorcerer, the man instantly fired by the plantation overseer because he was cutting so much more than everyone else, the man teased by his coworkers, "My! What a long way you've come today with your figurine!" Most everyone had some such story to tell.

Years later when I brought up the subject with my old friend, Rejina Carabali, a sister of one of the cooks who had taken me to the cane fields, she told me, "Well, they don't use the devil anymore. They use marijuana." This was a valuable lesson that by necessity I keep unlearning, that things change all the time at the drop of a hat and that an awful lot depends on your perspective at any given time. But I can also discern continuity, a Baudelarian *correspondance* between the devil and hashish—and here Benjamin's definition leaps to mind, that what Baudelaire meant by *correspondance* is something like sympathetic magic between things and "may be described as an experience which seeks to establish itself in crisis-proof form."[13]

It was also said that the field of cane worked by a man under the influence of a devil's pact would be rendered barren. No more cane would sprout after cutting. Sugar cane is like giant grass. You cut it, and within a few weeks it comes up again,

and in a year or slightly longer, depending on sun and rain, is ready for the next harvest. This continues for some five to seven harvests, until the sugar content falls below an economical level. Each lot or field of cane planted at the same time is called a *suerte*, and if some of the cane in a *suerte* has been cut under contract to the devil, then no more cane will come forth from the roots for the entire *suerte*. The whole lot has to be plowed in and replanted. I remember once walking past an open field in which nothing was growing and being told by my companion, who for years had been a ditchdigger on the plantations, that, according to people living in the vicinity, it had been worked by someone with a devil's pact. It was in clear sight of the smokestack of the sugar mill itself. After some months it was put to the plow and planted anew.

There were still other curious features about this when I enquired further. The details of the pact were obscure. Who had the expertise to make them and how they were made was open to conjecture, although the frequent mention of figurines suggested the influence of Indian magic from the Pacific coast, the origin of many black labor migrants.

Two classes of people seemed exempt from making these contracts, namely, women and peasant farmers, the latter being those who owned small farms or worked on them for wages. At that time, in the early 1970s, there were large numbers of women working in the plantations, usually as weeders with the long sharp spade, the *pala*, used by eighteenth- and nineteenth-century slaves. When chemicals were introduced in the 1970s, these women and their children got jobs applying pesticides by hand. Certainly these women were as needy as any man, if not a good deal more so, and thus, on the face of it, should have been enticed by the apparent benefits of a devil's pact. But when questioned, some of my friends would point out that because women had the primary responsibility, either in fact or in principle, for raising children and sustaining the household, it was unlikely that wages from a devil's pact would be useful. In fact they would probably be downright murderous, in just the same way as such wages were described as having to be spent only on luxury goods.

In other words this was inherently barren money. The cane field would yield no more harvests; land bought or rented would become barren; and livestock bought with such money would waste away. Hardly enough money to raise children! This was money that could not turn a profit. It could not serve as investment. Its *negative* quality went further still. It was money that seemed *actively* negative—not just unable to function this way or that but willfully sterilizing nature's proclivity to reproduce.

By the same token, so it was said, you would not expect such a pact from a *peasant* farmer, female or male, because no matter how much that person might desire to increase their income, it would kill the crops. Not even wage workers on peasant plots were ever alleged to have made a devil's pact. Such pacts were exclusively restricted to men selling their commodity—labor power, as Karl Marx called it—for wages in the sphere of the plantation.

Here one would do well to ponder the nature of evil in these (d)evil pacts—the *dangerous* feeling generated by these tales of weirdness, of thresholds transgressed, of depths unexplored and maybe unexplorable. Even to talk of such things seems to run the risk, no matter how slight, of becoming polluted by the powers in question; and it is thus to the coalescence of danger and immorality that I want to draw attention—to a specific focus of practical religion, namely, the poorly understood commonplace of taboo and, hence, transgression. It might be helpful, therefore, to extend the range to consider other places where the devil, to my recollection, has been active in recent economic history.

GOLD

Not so long ago on the Timbiquí River on the hot and humid Pacific coast of Colombia, the *boga* at the front of the canoe, pirouetting between rocks on our downward glide, pointed his paddle to where a man had recently drowned. His canoe had capsized in the flooding river. Although he could swim, he was encumbered by rubber boots. But, added the *boga* nonchalantly, his mind more on the rocks before us, the man died from choking on his false teeth. Here and there the forest's luminous green flashed through the rain in this, the rainiest area in the world.

The chain of mountains runs parallel and close to the coast. The rivers run fast and straight. When they flood, they can create a tidal wave called *la bomba*—a wall of water hurtling through dark walls of rock.

But the drowned man must have been confident. People there grow up in canoes. Just a short hop, I can imagine him saying. Then, his boots begin filling with muddy water, getting harder and harder to kick. His teeth stick back in his throat. How many people there would have a set of false teeth anyway? You need money for that. The jumble of ramshackle buildings and the gaping mouth of the gold mine in the rock face speed past, rusty iron rails extruding from the mine. The buildings had been left behind in the Great Depression by the French mining company. There must have been quite a scramble to get a hold of them, let alone access to the mine. May the best man win.

And I guess he did. For the drowned man was the owner of the mine and, so it was said, in league with the devil. That was how he found gold. That is how anyone finds gold. It was all so momentous, yet ordinary. My thoughts went back to my previous visit, in 1975, when another man had died, clubbed to death one night with brandy bottles, his body tossed into the river. He had come back for Easter week from the plantations in the interior where he worked as a cane cutter or loader. He had made good money, was bedecked in fancy gear—sunglasses, fancy shirts (and butter? I do not know). If you leave the river for the interior, you have to come back a visible success. But if you come back a success, you generate envy. And if you generate envy . . . There is a regionally self-conscious saying on the coast that puts the notion of reciprocity well: "Here on the coast, one hand washes the other."[14]

SPIRIT QUEEN

It was now pretty dark, and behind the shrine of the *Indio Macho* we could see the twinkling lights of the sugar mill with its immense chimney and ascending smoke. Years later it dawned on me that this looming complex of the sugar mill in central Venezuela was no less of a magic mountain than the mountain in whose shadow it nestled and to which pilgrims came in thousands from all over the country. There was a type of kinship between them. Both were shrouded in a mythic reality, although apparently poles apart. The mountain was all fable; the mill was harshly real, albeit with twinkling lights and incessant activity twenty-four hours a day. The workers worked even on Christmas day. They were burning cane fields on Good Friday! They never let up. Perhaps we could see one as fortuitously allegorical of the other, the interesting and perhaps important thing being that while the mountain leapt forth as the obvious work of the imagination, a spectacle and a work of art, the sugar mill at its base did not appear that way at all. Instead, it appeared as something natural, something to be taken for granted. While nature was celebrated on the mountain as part of an enchanted domain of the spirit queen, herself the icon of the nation, the sugar mill was more truly natural in that it was routine and everyday. But when this contrast and kinship dawned on you, then the mill, too, started to appear as enchanted or at least malevolent and haunted and no longer so natural.[15]

Colombian cane cutters in Aguas Negras (about twenty-five miles from the mountain) and all the way from the Pacific coast of Colombia, one of the most remote regions of the world, told me that they would never work for this mill because the owner, a Cuban, by origin, had a contract with the spirit queen so he could maintain his business. The contract required the death of a worker every so often so the devil could acquire his soul. Luís Manuel Castillo, a seventy-four-year-old Venezuelan man, born in Coro, living alone as caretaker on a small farm in the hills about twenty miles from the mountain, told me that when he first heard about the spirit queen he was twenty-two years old and working for the town of Chivacoa's public works department. People said the spirit queen's contract with the Cuban required a dead worker per week! That was in 1940. He remembered that the sugar mill paid a great amount of money to a man to paint its smokestack. Day after day in the heat of the sun, the painter worked, inching his way upwards. When he reached the top, he swayed and toppled in, to be burnt alive in the furnace below. About ten years ago, however, went on Luís Carlos, a different story started to circulate. The spirit queen, it was said, did not want the souls of *the poor*, who were, after all, merely defending their families. Now she wants the owner himself.

LIFE

From the mid-1970s until 1990 I lived frequently with an old Indian healer by the name of Santiago Mutumbajoy.[16] I was intrigued by colonists' attribution of magical power to Indian healers in that area where the foothills of the Andes meet the clouds and rain forests of the upper Amazon. It was there that I learnt one of the most important things that my own upbringing had virtually concealed from me—namely, the singular and overwhelming force of envy. It was envy that the curer had to extract with song and medicine, envy as a substance and power impacted by sorcery into the body of the envied, because just about all serious misfortune was attributed to being magically attacked by an envious other—even the poorest of the poor when they fell sick said it was because someone was envious of them—and envy could be aroused by anything.

And what was it that provoked envy? Well, the fact that the envied other was seen as having more. More what? More cattle? Good looks? Helpful children? More health? More money? No common denominator held the list together, certainly not money, unless it was something to do with the exuberance of life itself. Here the envy of the living by the dead is salutary.

One day an old Ingano- and Spanish-speaking woman brought some children to be cured. They settled down to stay a few days. The children's father had died some months back. Then the mother died. The father had called her, it was explained to me, "from the other side." The dead do this. Now the children might be called too. The healer would find a moment during the day to sit with one of

The Sun Gives without Receiving

the children, sing softly and sweep over the child with his curing fan, blowing medicine and cigarette smoke.

Months later at night, drinking the strong medicine which makes your head swim, singing the while in ebbs and flows of pictures, the topic of these kids came up. I strongly doubt that the healer and I would have talked about them had we not been taking this medicine. The father, an Indian, had died because he had gotten involved with *Satanás,* the devil. He had recklessly bought a book of magic that traveling herbalists sell in the marketplaces and was studying its spells. One day, going out to fish at dawn, he met a stranger sitting in the mist by the river. When he came home, he fell sick with fever and bloody diarrhea. In a few days he died. Then the wife. Now he was calling his children. And the healer? He is calling too. This side. Two sides.

COCAINE

Up in the mountains in another curer's house at about this same time, I met a weather-beaten old colonist, a black man from the coast, who had migrated many years before to the Putumayo, where he now had a small farm. He smiled a lot. He and his son were illegally growing coca, the plant from which cocaine is derived, and were making money for the first time in their lives. He was on top of the world, and his eyes gleamed when he asked me, as though playing a game or rehearsing a lesson, if I knew how to smuggle cocaine past the police and army roadblocks? I shook my head. "Well, you get a dead baby and open up the abdomen, remove the intestines, pack cocaine paste in, sew up the abdomen and, with the baby at the breast the good mother cuddles her precious cargo through the roadblocks and, who knows, perhaps to Miami and New York as well."

OIL

In the states of Morelos and Guerrero in Mexico in the mid-1970s, I heard stories of children's corpses found decapitated, sometimes under bridges. Entire villages were keeping their children at home and away from school. The mutilation of the corpse was described in roundabout ways, ways that clung to and illuminated details as fragments of the holy. An uncle or a friend of one's uncle had attended a funeral for a child and surreptitiously viewed the corpse. Good God! Headless! And nobody saying anything! But we all know, now. In Guerrero a woman told me how a gang of men were digging a hole, looking for oil in southeastern Mexico. A voice spoke out of the hole. "If you want oil you must give me the heads of so many children!" The workers told the foreman. The foreman told the manager. The manager told the president of the republic, and the president told the federal police. "If that's what's required, we'll oblige." This was when Mexico was buzzing with expectation at the bonanza of great oil discoveries.

MHUTI

In Soweto, South Africa,[17] one finds in the newspapers and in almost everyday discussion concern with sorcery known as *mhuti* and its alleged increase. A week ago, so I am told, the mutilated corpse of a Sowetan man was found in a field close to one of the migrant workers' hostels. The heart, the genitals, and the tongue had been removed for *mhuti*. There are accounts of large numbers of students in rural areas (such as Bushbuck Ridge) attacking supposedly successful businessmen whose success is allegedly due to their using such *mhuti*—for example, burying the tongue under the doorway to attract customers; the genitals to promote growth of the business. Babies are said to be often used. "And women? Are their bodies used?" "No!" says my new acquaintance, a woman. "They just get raped."

THE ACCURSED SHARE: *Theories of Consumption Say Nothing (Can You Believe It?) about the Meaning of Consumption*

What might these stories teach us about the theme of this essay: placing consumption in historical perspective?[18] Let me orient my discussion through Georges Bataille's lifelong philosophical project aimed at understanding transgression and expenditure—*dépense*, spending, especially excessiveness of spending, which, of course, is strangely identical with consumption. The excessiveness to which I refer crosses boundaries and connects opposites in bewildering and fascinating ways.

"I am the only one who thinks of himself," Bataille wrote, "not as a commentator of Nietzsche, but as being the same as he." To this we might add an idea from Nietzsche's *Twilight of the Idols (or How to Philosophise with a Hammer)*, in which, in his dispute with Darwinist ideology of "the struggle for life," Nietzsche asserts that prodigality, not "the struggle for life," is the motor of life and human history and that where there is a struggle, the dissimulators, the great mimics, always win over the strong, a point we will have to return to when considering the power of the devil, the Great Imitator, and the problem of the gift.[19] Similarly, where Nietzsche first introduces his notion of "the eternal return," an overflowing sense of limitless expenditure abounds. Addressing the sun in gratitude for receiving its surplus, Nietzsche wants to give away—not give away something but simply "give away"—an act that must take him *under,* like the sun descending at night into the underworld. "Bless the cup that wants to overflow in order that the water may flow from it golden and carry the reflection of your rapture everywhere. Behold, this cup wants to become empty again."[20]

In his first formal statement of the problem at the age of thirty-six, in 1933, Bataille argued that human activity is not reducible to processes of production and conservation, and that consumption must be divided into two parts: one part "represented by the use of the minimum necessary for the conservation of life and the continuation of an individual's productive activity in a given society," but the other part (the accursed share, "accursed" also meaning sacred as in the Latin *sacer*) is consumption as *unproductive expenditure.* Here followed the examples ranging through luxury, festival, war, cults, spectacles, games, art, revolution, death, and sex. Bataille insisted that expenditure, when defined as unproductive and nonutilitarian, clearly accents *loss* "that must be as great as possible for that activity to take on its true meaning."[21] On the whole, he asserted, "a society always produces more than is necessary for its survival; it has a surplus at its disposal. It is precisely the use it makes of this surplus that determines it." The surplus, he goes on to say, in a supremely important comment, "is the cause of the agitation, of the structural changes and of the entire history of society."[22]

"I did not consider the facts the way qualified economists do," wrote Bataille in the preface to the first volume of *The Accursed Share,* subtitled *Consumption.* "I had a point of view from which a human sacrifice, the construction of a church or the gift of a jewel were no less interesting than the sale of wheat. In short I had to try in vain to make clear the notion of a 'general economy' in which 'expenditure' (the 'consumption') of wealth, rather than production, was the primary object."[23] The epigraph to this first volume came from William Blake: "Exuberance is beauty," and the subsequent chapters were so many case studies displaying the manner in which different schemes of life in world history had dealt with excess, the problem of surplus: the sacrifices and wars of the Aztecs; the gifts of rivalry of the Potlatch of the Kwakiutal and their neighbors (just north of Vancouver, Canada); militant Islam; the religious (as opposed to the political) economy of the Tibetan state (in 1917 one out of every three adult males was a monk and the ecclesiastical budget was twice as large as the state and eight times that of the army); the use of exuberant asceticism by Calvinism so as to erase exuberance and thereby fortify capitalism and the bourgeois world; the suspension of luxury consumption for the sake of industrialization in the Soviet Union; and, finally, the Marshall Plan. These case studies were preceded by a remarkable theoretical introduction wherein both the sun and the great world wars of the twentieth century (very much including the Cold War) were dwelt upon as massive spending, meaning *dépense,* wasting, or unproductive exuberant expenditure. By such shock tactics, and many others, Bataille hoped to accomplish what he so often saw as impossible (*The Impossible* being the title of one of his works of what he called fiction)—the understanding and the pinning down of the useless and its entailments in human pleasure, cruelty, and subsistence. This concern with excessiveness led him, as I have stated, to a wonderfully diverse economic science conflating death, sex, laughter, violence, and the sacred (in the modern, no less than in the nonmodern, world). What brings these things together is the mobile and passionate mix of attraction and repulsion entailed by the way in which expenditure mobilizes prohibitions and transgressions in a ceaseless, twofold, instantaneous movement.[24]

This, then, is quintessentially a theory of consumption if ever there was one. Indeed, theory here seems a somewhat limited term in that what Bataille came to call *general economy* cannot avoid applying its precepts to itself, as befits a concern with excess and transgression when "the very heavens open," such that Bataille speaks of "the apex of a thought whose end jumps the rails on which it is travelling."[25]

The Gift

What then of my stories? What then of criticism? The important thing is to stay within the compass of their force and imagination. We must not commit stories to the servile operation of getting them to say something that could be said otherwise—for example, to see them instrumentally, as devices to achieve some other thing, such as equality, limits to individualism, morality tales against greed, prodigality, and capitalist logic. I have myself previously suggested how the devil's pact, as I heard about it in the sugar plantations of western Colombia, *constellated*—I use the word advisedly—with amazing precision the argument set forth by Karl Marx in the first section of *Capital* concerning the complex movement of use-value and exchange-value in the constitution not only of the commodity-form but of what Marx called "the fetishism of commodities" as well.[26] A good deal of the power, not to mention the mysteries for further interpretation, created by this suggestion lay additionally in the tension I perceived between the gift-economy features (as laid out by Marcel Mauss) of peasant farming in that region, on one side, and the commodity-form of the recently created plantation sphere destroying peasant agriculture, on the other.[27]

What saves such an analysis from the all-too-common servility of functionalist method as cultural critique is the exoticism of its reference and, hence, its power to estrange familiar ways of relating to market exchange, production, and consumption. But estrangement is not necessarily guaranteed by the exotic, and here I want to return to Marcel Mauss's influential essay on the gift, which, thanks to Bataille, becomes open to new interpretations that, if observed, would have radically altered the history of anthropology in this century. For Mauss's gift has by and large been understood as emblematic of balanced exchange, constituting therewith "the total social fact" that is, in Claude Lévi-Strauss's paraphrase, "an event which has a significance that is at once social and religious, magic and economic, utilitarian and sentimental, juridical and moral" and entails the famous casting of the economic in precapitalist societies as the obligation to give, the obligation to receive, and the obligation to pay back.[28]

The very word, *obligation,* as in the obligation to give, sets up the question that assails Bataille (and, for that matter, Mauss) because of the singular and supreme contradiction within the gift as something spontaneous and generous, on one side, and calculated and self-interested on the other.[29] Mauss establishes this on the first page of his text, where he writes, "We intend in this book to isolate one important set of phenomena: namely prestations which are in theory voluntary, disinterested and spontaneous, but are in fact obligatory and interested."[30]

Bataille's decisive move is to intervene at the point of "the obligation to give." He bends every rhetorical trick he knows, and then some, to get the reader to break out of customary thinking to be able to acknowledge the excruciating quality of the fathomless contradiction implicated in the obligation to give, with its "mixture" of generosity and self-interest; and he tries even harder still to get the reader to appreciate what he would call the "quality of sovereignty" implicated in the gift as profitless expenditure ("The sun gives without receiving").

Contrary to this, Mauss puts the stress on the obligatory nature of giving in a way that makes it seem more like obeying a rule than giving per se. But of course the whole problem raised is what is giving per se? Bataille admits to the mixture of generosity and self-interest in giving, as in Potlatch, but argues on logical and sociological grounds that "we cannot give precedence to the principle of rivalry over the sovereign generosity that is at the origin of gift-giving; to do so would be to reverse the terms of the discussion."

Calculation would be on the side of the giver . . . The game would end if this were the case. Even if the giver feigns it, at bottom it is still generosity that overwhelms. And doubtless it was a rule, in these archaic forms, that the giver should feign, but his generosity would still not have taken effect without excessiveness. Ultimately it was the one who overdid it who prevailed and whose sovereign character compelled respect.[31]

This is not to contradict the existence of exchange or even balanced exchange. Rather, it is a matter of where the focus of analysis lies and what the implications are of that angle of vision. A utilitarian reading focuses on the gift as a mutually beneficial exchange, in which I get some thing out of this, and so do you—Adam Smith's truck, barter, and exchange, writ into the deceptive ideology of the gift no less than a universal law. Against this vision of society as a clockwork of calculated mutual advantageousness, a Bataillian reading posits an additional and ineradicably subversive feature—namely, the trauma given to the coherence and equilibrium of the social world by giving and spending for the hell of it—and asserts this, together with taboos against expenditure, as indispensable to what makes up human culture and what makes human beings human. In the mysterious space between this sort of spending and the taboos prohibiting it lies a whole world, an amazing world, one we seem to know a great deal about but cannot quite get our tongues around, partly for metaphysical reasons, partly because of the fierce pressure of organized religions or the moral systems they have left in their wakes, and partly because of political forces of cultural and psychic repression.[32] Bataille's work is dedicated to the impossible task of delineating this world: Humanity is faced with a double perspective: in one direction, violent pleasure, horror, death—precisely the perspective of poetry—and in the opposite direction, that of science or the real world of utility. Only the useful and the real have a serious character. We are never within our rights in preferring seduction: truth has rights over us. Indeed, it has every right. And yet we can, and indeed we must, respond to something that, not being God, is stronger than every right, that *impossible* to which we *accede only by forgetting the truth of all these rights, only by accepting disappearance.*[33]

Now the Marxist interpretation I made years ago of the devil's pact in the cane fields was that it was an exquisitely precise expression in the realm of popular culture of the commodity-form from a "gift point of view." And while the devil contract can be seen as a striking, if morbid, confirmation of the gift principle as balanced exchange, the gift of largesse being paid for by the dissemination of barrenness and death, what I now see as special to it and deserving emphasis is its sheer excessiveness—the plethora of its interpretive possibilities such that its analysis is interminable, the overflowing "too-muchness" of its key terms, the violent movement between those terms, and the dreadful proximity here of the gift to death, of creation to destruction.[34] An old and ubiquitous tale, the devil's pact seems to be trying to tell us something important about the gift, about the ways it articulates investment versus spending as life-and-death issues around the pivot of transgression.

At this point Bataille's rendering of the gift makes a lot of sense. First, he allows, indeed forces, me to dwell on the existence of the devil and ask bigger and better questions about the face of evil in history. Second, he makes me ask why do all my stories entail such gross transgression of prohibitions, beginning with the illicit magical pacts themselves, and then the dissemination of sterility in the cane fields, murder of children or illicit use of their cadavers, as with the oil and cocaine, and the body parts in the *mhuti* used by successful businessmen? Third, what is one to make of the restriction of the wages of the devil to the purchase of luxury goods by men, of the actively negative, deathly effect of such wages as investment? *Secar* was the word used. The land and the animals of the man making the pact dry up and die. Women do not make the pact because that would prevent growth of children. The money is quintessentially infertile. It is blatantly not capital. It cannot reproduce.

These stories are wounds, signs of rupture accessing the marvellous in the fullness of what Bataille called sovereignty, meaning the mastery of nonmastery.

These extremes of wealth and death, of disfigured corpses, of the use of the cadavers of babies and children, of luxury and barrenness, speak to the unspeakable mystique of the excessive, the abrogation of the useful, and the sensuous no less than logical intimacy binding overabundance to transgression in a forwards and backwards movement of attraction and repulsion that is difficult to put in words—of "thrust and counterthrust, ebb and flow of a twofold movement, the unity in the violent agitation of prohibition and transgression."[35]

In the diversity of his metamorphosing forms, his secrecy, incongruities, and fiery splendor, the devil is the epitome of such a twofold movement of attraction and repulsion. As the figure of the impure sacred, he irradiates the wild energy of this vortex. As the Great Imitator he opposes not only God but the possibility of ontological anchoring of steadfast meaning that He constantly dangles before us. As the paramount sign of evil, he was always a little too interesting and a little too seductive to be trapped by Christian *ressentiment* into a simple dialectic of otherness. There was always this overflowing surplus of resolute irresolution, for he is the salutary figure of transgression—so now we might better follow Hegel's moving statement of the negative in which, in the famous preface to *Phenomenology of Mind,* he says (and Bataille, influenced by Kojève, uses this quote):

> But the life of mind is not one that shuns death, and keeps clear of destruction; it endures death and in death maintains its being. It only wins to its truth when it finds itself utterly torn asunder. It is this mighty power, not by being a positive which turns away from the negative, as when we say of anything it is nothing or it is false, and, being then done with it, pass off to something else: on the contrary, mind is this power only by looking the negative in the face, and dwelling with it. This dwelling beside it is the magic power that converts the negative into being.[36]

The Negation of the Negation

Arguing that what expenditure gives rise to, as with the festival, is not a return to animality but access to the divine, Bataille draws our attention to what he sees as the curious dynamic of transgression, to the prohibition of prohibition, to what he called "the negation of the negation"—a movement in which repression increases "tenfold," projecting life into a richer world. As an exemplary account of the negation of the negation, the filiation with the enemy of God, the devil, gives expression to this richer world, raising the specter of Bataille's "sovereignty"—that "void in the face of which our being is a plenum, threatened with losing its plenitude, both desiring and fearing to lose it . . . demanding uncertainty, suspension."[37]

"Is there still any up or down? Are we not straying as through an infinite nothing?"[38] What happens when the sun overflowing in its diurnal passage goes down into the underworld where the devil is, taking Nietzsche along for the ride? For Nietzsche so wants to give without receiving, like the sun itself. Or rather he receives from the sun and then wants to give away, following the sun, without any expectation of return.[39] He simply wants to give away—a phrasing that in its cliff-hanging suspension should remind us of that disturbing statement of Bataille's comrade-in-arms, Roger Caillois, in his 1935 essay on mimicry, in which he writes of wanting to be similar, not similar to some thing, "just similar."[40] Might we then want to reformulate this "giving without receiving"?

For Nietzsche argued that "giving without receiving" (and here we make the

truly radical, the truly marvellous leap that the gift can entail) implied a particular theory of representation encompassing both the joy of becoming and the joy
of destruction, namely, the discharge of "all powers of representation, imitation,
transfiguration, transmutation, every kind of mimicry and playacting, conjointly. The essential thing remains the facility of the metamorphosis, the incapacity *not* to react." Such a person "enters into every skin."[41] That is the Dionysian
impulse. But the devil, the Great Imitator, most emphatically does not "give
without receiving." He strikes a deal and exacts a price. The devil must be that
principle of unbridled cleverness, the victor throughout history, who appropriates the Dionysian gift of giving without receiving *and* the power of mimicry
therein.[42] That is quite another impulse, equally extreme—its ultimate and satanic deception being, of course, the illusion that real transgression has been
achieved. But that "tremendous event is still on its way, still wandering; it has not
yet reached the ears of men."[43]

Aftereffect

If my stories have the function of making us consider *consumption* as something
a good deal more than the effect of need—basic or culturally promoted, if indeed
there is any difference—and indicate that consumption skirts and at times partakes of a mysterious, even sacred, power, it behooves us to return to what is my
consumption of these stories.

The stories' relation to the events they depict is reminiscent of Bataille's pointedly antiutilitarian interpretation of the paintings of animals and hunting in the
Lascaux caves not as images the magical power of which shall ensure the success
of the hunt and the satisfaction of need but as images demanded by the opening
to the sacred consequent to the violence of violating the prohibition against
killing. This leaves the status of the image, no less than the devil stories, in a
strange vacuum of testimony, sanctity, and obligation—not unlike the gift itself,
reminiscent of Benjamin's evocation of the way experience ("in the true sense of
the word") was facilitated by collective ritual and festival, amalgamating the voluntary with the involuntary elements of memory. Thus, the stories speak to God,
to the world, we might say, not so much to have a social function, satisfy a need,
or even betray a cause. They come *after* the event. As gifts about the gift, they
come through me along a long chain of anonymous storytellers to you and function in a sovereign, not a useful, way—to be consumed, in other words, inside
themselves as ritual art expended in a storm of negation. And this is, after all, the

lot of our disciplines of History and Anthropology, their fundamental power lying in their stockpiling the excess without which meaning and representation could not exist, namely, the belief in the literal basis to metaphor—that once upon a time, or in distant places, human sacrifice and spirit possession and miracles did occur, and ghosts and spirits, sorcerers and witches, gods and people making devil's pacts did walk the face of the earth. History and anthropology become, together with the folk tale and a certain type of popular wisdom, the depositories and proof of those unbelievable acts required now by language to carry off its tricks of reference, its tropes and figures, and if the play of expenditure, of *depénse,* has moved from the sacred nature of the person to the fetishistic power of things in a universe bound to the appearance of the useful, we stand all the more in debt to the wild exuberance of these devil stories, like the sun, instances of giving without receiving, endorsement of sheer expenditure—as when, before the "efficiencies of scale" in the factory system of the sugar plantation and the poverty no less than the destruction it has wrought, the earth emptied itself out and ash floated onto the still lake.

Under the paving stones—THE BEACH!
—Graffiti, Paris, May '68

"Who needs the beach? I've got McDonald's!"
—Television commercial, USA, 2005

The Beach (a Fantasy) 4

Prologue

The ultimate fantasy would be to write about a fantasy because as soon as you realize it's fantasy, it changes. But where does it go? What happens to it? Freud suggested fantasy was a montage of sight and sound drawn from prior experience
that disguises that experience and represses memory of it. But if the fantasy increased in intensity beyond a certain point, it too would be repressed, and a physical symptom would take its place.[1] Might writing be just such a symptom, particularly in the form of the cut up that meets Freud's montage head-on? "Cut ups?
but of course. I have been a cut up for years. . . . I think of words as being alive like
animals. They don't like to be kept in pages. Cut the pages and let the words out."[2]

The History of the World

The history of the world, says the American poet Charles Olson in his little book
on *Moby-Dick* entitled *Call Me Ishmael* (1947), could be summed up by three

This essay was written for the conference "Fantasy Spaces: The Power of Images in a Globalizing World,"
organized by the Research Center for Religion and Society of the University of Amsterdam, 1998. It was
first published in *Critical Inquiry* 26 (winter 2000), ©2000. My epigraph comes from Chris Lamping's
e-mail signature.

oceans, the Mediterranean, the Atlantic, and now the Pacific (Homer, Dante, and now Melville).[3]

The Disappearance of the Sea and Its Fantasmatic Recovery

Yet how unthinkable Olson's proposition has become. Not because of the ordering but because of its substance. For now so few of us have any direct experience of ships or the sea even though we are mightily dependent on the ocean and its histories through the commodities brought in the hulls of ships. Joseph Conrad's writing is not a reflection of the sea and a worldwide experience of it so much as an anxious premonition of its disappearance as a key element of nature from human experience. Conrad retired from the sea shortly after receiving his master's certificate, just when sail gave way to steam, which is when radical experiments in modernism were born. This displacement of everyday experience by commodities caught Karl Marx's eye, too, in his notion of fetishism. The point of this concept is not the occlusion of reality but its phantasmatic displacement propelling strange flights of imagination and even stranger ways of juxtaposing time and place.

Today the ports of wood and stone are either no longer used or have been demolished. Concrete container terminals have replaced them in moonscaped industrial sites far from the people who go as tourists to the gentrified old ports where sailing ships are resurrected as museums. Yet we are told that the whole world is unified as never before into the One Big Market, which must mean immense amount of shipping and human dependence on seaborne freight. The conduct of life today is utterly dependent on the sea and the ships it bears, yet nothing is more invisible.[4] How different it must have been until well into the twentieth century when ships and sailors filled the horizon of Western experience from Ulysses onward! Is this what Joyce sensed would happen when he backtracked on Melville and demythologized Ulysses, forgot the great white male and instead had his Ulysses be a fumbling everyman, a Dublin Jew named Bloom, barely making it through life, masturbating on the beach? "'She is our great sweet mother,'" declares "stately, plump Buck Mulligan," "'the snotgreen sea. The scrotumtightening sea.'" And he turns abruptly to Stephen Dedalus. "'The aunt thinks you killed your mother.'" "'Someone killed her,' Stephen said gloomily."[5]

Sea provides the medium of travel for Homer concerning the adventures of Ulysses, while for Joyce it establishes the setting for inner travel as inner speech.

Has nobody reading Joyce's *Ulysses* seen the significance of this inner speech as travel, that the sea has disappeared into our heads and that this is why he begins on the utterly strategic location of the beach between sea and land? The book is a seascape of mind flowing in and out of Western history in which the movement of the sea onto the shore, immense, restless, and mesmerizing, is the movement of the unconscious mind sifting images, just as the author sifts styles in the mad inheritance we call a language, a language on the edge of empire. We overhear young Stephen Dedalus talking to himself as he walks the beach. It could just as well be language talking to itself, "shellcococoacolored."

Forgive my playing with his playing with its playing as we are all swept up for the "flood is following me. . . . These heavy sands are language tide and wind have silted here. And there, the stoneheaps of dead builders . . . A school of turlehide whales stranded in hot noon, spouting, hobbling in the shallows. Then from the starving cagework city a horde of jerkined dwarfs, my people, with flayer's knives, running, scaling, hacking in green blubbery whalemeat . . . Do you see the tide flowing quickly in on all sides, sheeting the lows of sands quickly, shellcocoacoloured?"[6]

Young Dedalus's eye wanders to a dog playing at the water's edge. (Such a site for play, this edge.) Now we see the dog. Through Stephen. We no longer listen to Stephen talking to himself via the sea but to the dog via Stephen. The animal's consciousness has displaced the historical consciousness, just as the historical was displaced by the primeval, which is to say by a dying sea and a mother's green bile torn from a rotting liver. The dog is "looking for something lost in a past life."[7] Sniffing at the sand. "His snout lifted barked at the wavenoise, herds of seamorse. They serpented towards his feet, curling, unfurling many crests, every ninth breaking, plashing, from far, from farther out, waves and waves."[8] This is language moving into the sea as our very bodies might, ending up newly buoyant and happy somewhere between its watery moving energy and the human facility with mimesis. "Listen: a fourworded wavespeech: seesoo, hrss, rsseeis, ooos. . . . In cups of rocks it slops: flop, slop, slap: bounded in barrels."[9] Beyond representation. Bounded in barrels. And at the very end of this first section of Joyce's *Ulysses*, the end before we meet Bloom bustling in his kitchen frying kidneys for his lady love upstairs, young Dedalus sees Joseph Conrad's ship disappearing into the slipstream of time behind our very backs. "He turned his face over a shoulder, rere regardant. Moving through the air high spars of a threemaster, her sails brailed up on the crosstrees, homing, upstream, silently moving, a silent ship[10]" Joyce has suddenly changed tack here at the end "rere regardant" with this fulsomely self-conscious lyrical moment coming out of nowhere, going home, this all-too-silent ship.

As the ships sailed home into oblivion across the "snotgreen sea" sometime after World War Two, so the beach became increasingly popular in the affluent West, and the sea underwent a phantasmatic recovery by virtue of a new structure of feeling: Billy Butlin's camps by the sea; topless Swedes and Germans basking by the water's edge, leaving the Spaniards on the Costa del Sol aghast, tightening their kerchiefs; Greek peasants in the Peloponnesus selling off their coastal plots to the floods of Germans because the peasants never built on the exposed seaside of the slopes on account of pirates. But all this has changed. That sort of piracy belongs to the past, and the beach is where just about everyone wants to be.

Vietnamese Fishermen

In Sydney, where I was born in 1940, the coastal beaches and harbor waterfront were with few exceptions where the working class lived or where they would go on Sundays to surf or, in the case of the harbor, drink Toohey's lager and gamble on the sixteen- and eighteen-footers—wide-beamed racing dinghies with huge amounts of sail and crew. The ferries hired to follow the race would heel over almost as much as the racing dinghies as the inebriated followers would anxiously cram the rail. There were corrugated iron shacks in the deep bays like Mosman and Castlecrag in which poor people lived close to the oysters clinging to the orange-faced sandstone that like a curtain hung at the water's edge. Soft she-oaks whispered sad tunes to the receding tide, and their delicate needles felt soft underfoot. Today they are not called she-oaks but casuarinas. The name change says it all, a certain, critical distancing has occurred, a more precise, even scientific nomenclature contains the nature we love. Suburbs, like the previously working-class waterside area of Balmain, for example, are now among the wealthiest in Australia. Famous city beaches such as Bondi and Coogee, with their hideous brick homes and squat apartment buildings, which were lower-middle-class and working-class areas, are now battlegrounds for people with money fighting for their place in the sun. They will do anything just short of murder to get their "harbor view" or be by the beach. Twenty years ago they wouldn't have given a shit.

Today it's the strangest thing to watch the ferries from the city disgorge their well-heeled passengers off the wharf at Long Nose Point at Balmain, for instance, as they come home from a tiring day in the law firm or stockbroker's office. A real

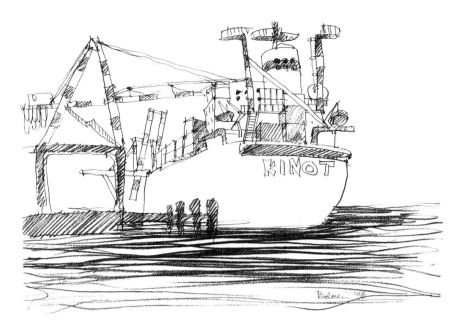

Line drawing by Clive Buhrich, Balmain '98.

oceangoing ship at anchor in the harbor around there is now a rarity, a museum piece, perhaps, that the locals have placed to create authenticity as illustrated here by the drawing in 1998 of the ship *Kinot* by my architect friend, Clive Buhrich.

Each passenger hopping off the ferry forms a quiet monument to the self, set into a noble tranquility by the gentle harbor crossing, God's newfound gift to the mentally spent. As they spring invigorated onto the shore of their new, if not quite yet natural, habitat, a waterside working-class suburb converted into luxury housing, there is a curious anachronism, a slight shuffling of the cards of world history as impoverished Vietnamese families, taking advantage of the public space offered by the wharf, pull in their fishing lines to make way for the ferry. Nobody speaks. The Vietnamese seem not to be aware they really shouldn't be there even though it's perfectly legal. Indeed they seem far more naturally part of the scene than the tired white professionals stepping ashore. The Vietnamese are an unknown entity. They come in the early evening from remote slums in battered cars for which it is difficult to find parking around the renovated waterfront. Now and again it is reported in the media they eat dogs. They are quintessentially foreign and out of place. Yet they blend intimately with it and fish just about all night long, it seems, with their flashlights and thermoses, and they fish with the same mix of pleasure and boredom as did the white Australian working-class men before them who have, it seems, around this harbor at least, become quite extinct, other than in their reincarnation in these refugees from Southeast Asia.

To me the oddest thing is the stillness of the encounter between those coming off the ferry and these people fishing. It is as if the latter didn't really exist, that they are invisible and are seen straight through. Yet they're the ones actually using the water as something other than real estate. Perhaps with time they will pass into the spectacle as part of the flora and fauna, the flora having been carefully selected and planted as Australian Wild.

Benjamin cites Adorno's letter to him, dated 5 August 1935, ruminating on the mysteries of the "dialectical image" so dear to Benjamin's practice as a writer enamored of Proust and Marx. At one point Adorno speculates that as the world becomes increasingly subject to market forces and "things lose their use value, they are hollowed out in their alienation and, as ciphers, draw meanings in." Benjamin agrees that such "'hollowed out' things" are increasing at a rate previously unknown in world history and that in their very hollowed-outness, torn between death and meaning, they naturalize subjective intention, one's hopes and one's anxieties.[11] In this regard I wonder if these strange silhouettes of "hollowed out" businesspeople stepping off the ferry, no less than the quiet people fishing on the wharf, more nature than culture, have absorbed into themselves the dead past of these waterfront suburbs, their dead boat-building industriousness and once-busy social life? In which case, that moment when the boat hits the wharf to unload its passengers, that moment in the dusk after work, that is the dialectical image. You feel the shudder radiating along the creaking wooden wharf. It goes way down the piles into the ocean floor. Softly.

Mates of the Kurlalong

With his love of children's literature, Benjamin would surely be among the first to acknowledge the role of the adult's imagination of the child's imagination in the constitution of the dialectical image and its claims on prehistory. And it is with the confidence born of this self-nourishing circuit that I can claim that the renaturalization of the harbor as archaic second nature was foreseen by a book I read as a ten-year-old in 1950. It was called *Mates of the Kurlalong,* in which a group of animals escape from the Sydney zoo, located on a steep, rocky hillside plunging into the harbor, and take over a ferry, the giraffe being the engineer and having to find room for its neck down in the cramped engine room.

Are there rights to remembrance granted expatriates, such as myself, for whom the childhood past across the seas lies preserved under glass, awaiting a hand to shake it into life? "He is driven not merely to awaken congealed life in petrified objects," mused Adorno in his portrait of Benjamin, "but also to scrutinize living things so that they present themselves as being ancient, 'ur-historical' and abruptly release their significance."[12]

Down in the bay from where I lived as a kid, there was a wharf with slips and a large boatshed. Its owner, who lived on this beautiful site at the head of the bay (Sailor's Bay was its name), repaired boats and before that had been a champion cyclist, which in those preyuppie days was a very working-class sport. Fishing off the wharf for leatherjackets, my eye would idle over the yachts at anchor. There were about ten. That's all. But today you can hardly see the water there are so many. What's more, when I was a kid many of those yachts had been built by their owners. Years it would take. Hard to imagine today. Later, aged fourteen or so, I joined a sailing club on the other side of the bay at Seaforth, racing eleven-foot-long boats called Moths with one enormous sail and a nineteen-foot mast. The club consisted of men, all of whom who worked at a trade, like carpentering or plumbing.

It was an unusual place where I grew up, a sandstone peninsula jutting into the Middle Harbour. I am told that in the 1920s or 1930s the easiest way to get there was to row a dinghy from the Spit, a narrow tract of land to where trams ran from the inner city. Mainly oddballs lived there, communists, refugees from central Europe like my parents, and artists. By and large, respectable people shied away even though it was in a sense middle-class and professional, culturally, if not economically. It was covered with she-oaks and soaring white-skinned eucalyptus trees. In summer cicadas would sing. Now that I'm older I feel the song as much as hear it. They were singing so loudly and so many it seemed like the summer air as a whole was vibrating despite the stillness that hung over the land in the drowsiness of those far-off summer, days that seemed to never end. The entire peninsula would be vibrating. We knew the different types of cicadas by their names handed down immemorially as in a secret society from child to child, names such as Black Prince, Greengrocer, Chocolate Soldier, and Flowery (for some reason I now see this spelled as *Floury*) Baker. Black Prince was all black, speedy and elegant, while Flowery Baker was rounded and cumbersome in its whirring flight, light green with a yellow fluffed abdomen. They would sing to their heart's delight, but no sooner were we close by their tree than a terrible silence would descend.

Perhaps it is from these hunting expeditions I learned whatever skill I have as a reader and researcher, let alone my sense of the environment, the important

Drawing by Clive Buhrich, The Spit '98.

point being to keep one's find alive. And although we assiduously traded the fruits of the chase with each other and learnt some of the painful lessons of scarcity and value, some cicadas being harder to catch than others and therefore worth more, I can't say that I learned much about business, perhaps because we were first and foremost collectors, not budding capitalists.

All around was water, saltwater from the Pacific. But very few people had boats or were in any sense, I think, oriented to the sea. The only person that comes to mind was Ern Claridge who had worked his way up in a small company selling hot water systems. He was a kind, portly man with a great laugh who lived with his wife and daughter in a stone house fifteen minutes' walk from the water's edge. It had been built for an actor and had a star-shaped living room that could serve as a theater, and just about every afternoon he would go down to the harbor and row out in a clinker-built wooden boat and fish until nightfall. He smoked huge Havana cigars and loved white wine, both of these habits being distinctly unusual for a real Australian, but his credentials were assured by his sitting in the bath for hours of a morning and going carefully through the racing guide, then calling his bookie, before departing for work. I seem to remember he caught a lot of fish. What is my point? Of all the people I knew in my "middle-class" peninsula suburb laid out in the beautiful bay of the beautiful harbor, he was one of the

The Beach (a Fantasy)

very few adults I can remember who made use of the sea, only minutes by foot from our homes. I find this remarkable.

Down from where I lived on the steep hillside and maybe half a mile from the roadway, there were four or five houses built of wood and corrugated iron, illegal building materials dating from another era, probably the Great Depression. Who lived there? I never knew. Whoever they were, they were a foreign element. They must have come and gone in boats or surreptitiously up and down the zigzag paths only they and we children knew about. I do remember however that the doctor who looked after me, as I was often sick, told me he once had to run all the way down there to attend to what was called a New Australian, a Yugoslav, I think, who being "new" had failed to heed warnings about sharks and was in the habit of swimming back and forth across the bay in the morning. An unthinkable practice. He had been bitten in half, so it was said, by a shark, no doubt inspired by the same attitudes towards migrants as held by Old Australians, and when my dear doctor, Walter Keller, who was once a Rugby Union football star and still pretty fleet of foot, got there it was too late. Now yuppies and latter-day hippies have pushed the previous dwellers out and elbowed their way into that hidden colony on the water's edge by the mangroves, the sharks, and the ghosts of their victims. And doctors no longer sprint down craggy hillsides or consider house calls part of their job.

Nothing captures the world change in the orientation to the sea more dramatically than the fate of the shark. When I was a kid you couldn't put your toe in the water for fear of sharks. When the tiny sailing boats three of us had heeled under the impact of a squall, we were exquisitely careful to retract our toes, and you never ever waded or heaven forbid! went swimming outside of a sharkproof area, of which there were pitifully few. Apart from the New Australian bit in two, there was the schoolteacher we all heard about who, merely wading, had been yanked into the water and lost her leg. When we were older and started surfing in the ocean, we sometimes saw a trawler inching its way between the beaches, hauling in nets. It was Nick Gorshenin, as I remember the name and spelling, attending to the shark nets laid in front of all Sydney beaches. I never actually saw a shark, but I could easily imagine their torpedo-long bodies writhing in his cruel nets as they were joyfully hoisted aboard and given the treatment they deserved. You can imagine my surprise, therefore, when upon my return in 1995 I found kids gleefully jumping into the harbor (did they do it to spite me?) and people swimming outside the net at Nielsen Park where as teenagers we use to carouse, drink beer, sing, make love till the early hours but never, ever swim outside the net. Yet now it's as if the shark no longer exists. A new era has dawned. The sea has come to mean something else, and its demons have been laid to rest. Or instead the demonic has been displaced onto the panic of skin cancer and fear of raw sewage and mercury in the water.

Across the bay from where I grew up, there was of all things a liver red–brick working-class suburban bungalow. Absolutely stereotypically typical suburbia. But also, totally incongruous because it was so isolated in the bush. Nothing else for miles around. It belonged, as I remember, to one H. C. Press, and from its heights descended elaborate wooden steps and bush paths zagzagging down to a jetty and a sharkproof swimming pool made of wooden palings where, as a twelve-year-old I used to sneak in with friends on hot weekday afternoons, rowing across the bay. Press had been an eighteen-foot dinghy sailing champion and on retirement from his real job had built this little park by the harbor to rent out for weekend excursions from the city. Hence the butchers, the bakers, and the candlestick makers' unions would hire ferries and spend the day picnicking, while the middle class and the wealthy were nowhere to be seen. The latter chose to live and raise children on the leafy "north shore," which, despite its name, was inland with no trace of the ocean. As I said before, they were indifferent to the harbor and the sea.

A mile or so through the bush along from H. C. Press was an extraordinary thing, a castle, adding to the wonderful working-class fantasy that the Press picnic grounds brought to life. A castle! In Australia! We kids called it Dr. Willis's castle, for some reason, but I myself later suspected it really belonged to one John Mystery, who wrote scary but not well-known books and whose face I seem to remember seeing as a drawing the size of a postage stamp in the frontispiece of one of those books, where details of the publisher are printed, together with what for me was compelling evidence, a profile of that same little castle. Once or twice we nerved ourselves to row across the bay, haul the boat up under the overhanging trees, and creep up a wide, smooth path in the forest to peer at the garden rendered all the more beautiful by the surrounding bush. Hidden further up the slope, we discovered a dam, maybe fifty feet across, its waters dark and tranquil. Nothing could seem more mysterious than this cement artifice so perfectly blended with nature.

We never dared get closer to the castle, and we never once saw a person. That entire stretch of headland was deserted, except for these two idiosyncratic phenomena, H. C. Press's liver red–brick working-class bungalow, at one end, and John Mystery's stone castle, at the other. The bay lay still and empty, shimmering in the beauty of its translucent green water irradiated by shafts of blue and gold sunlight. I can still touch them as I write. Today the land has been developed by one L. J. Hooker and is covered by huge and ugly houses, while on weekends the bay is littered with yachts and motorboats, often tied one to the other so as to make more of a party or perhaps squeeze as many vessels into what has become, in reality, not a natural waterway but a parking lot.

This reconfiguration of money and the sea began and has been completed in my lifetime, this total reversal of value and forced exodus of the economically weaker from the seaside. It is by no means as dramatic or as consequential as the appropriation of the land from the Aboriginals that was begun in the late eighteenth century, the land having been legally defined by the British government as without owners, much the same as was done to the Palestinians by the Israelis this century but was achieved freely by the anonymous force of the market instead, the market of fantasy.

The Archaic

I spent Christmas of 2004 in a lighthouse on a deserted island, home to wild pigs and horses off the westernmost extremity of Europe a few hours from Santiago de Compostela. The lighthouse keeper, who had two brothers working in the same profession, told me there remained but eighty lighthouse keepers in Spain and that she was the only woman. More and more the lighthouses are automated. In the United States I believe they all are; automated lights blinking their greetings of welcome and warning to what are basically automated vessels far out to sea. As we walked back to the lighthouse in the late afternoon, the sea alight with flickering color, she raised the fingers of her right hand between her eye and the sun setting on the sea. Between the sinking sun and the horizon there was room for two fingers only. At fifteen minutes a finger, she said, that means we have only half an hour to get the light of the lighthouse lit. These fingers are among the last sign of the human being as seafarer, fingers interposed between sea and sun as night blankets the ocean.

During the many years of the Franco dictatorship—a dictatorship essential to the United States as source of military bases—this island had been refuge to peasants fleeing the mainland. They had terraced the land and carved out a livelihood growing crops and raising livestock. It is said they lived better than people on the mainland. After the dictator died, the island was taken over by a relative of one of Franco's generals who expelled the peasants to make the island into a resort. Where the peasants had built their tiny village, he built a crenellated wall a few meters high, suggesting a castle battlement. By the jetty he got workmen to construct a statue of a mermaid. But other than the lighthouse keeper, there were no human beings on the island anymore. Once I saw the new owner out at sea in a powerful cabin cruiser. It was a choppy day, and his boat was pitching like a crazy thing as he circumnavigated his island.

There was life on the island, to be sure. There were wild animals, witnesses to a previous age of peasant occupation. And there was the lighthouse keeper with her light sweeping in wide circles across the night, carrying its message of danger and comfort to the mariner. Yet this was all the more reason why the island seemed more dead than alive, a ghostly place inhabited by memories I, for one, would be unlikely to access.

Nature does not so much disappear as exist in layers of such histories, with each layer written across the one before so that the earlier layers continue to be visible in a smudged-out and sometimes surprising way. How curious that the wildness of the animals was itself probably due to this very same history whereby docile farm animals were now unapproachable, galloping in headlong flight or stock still at a distance like cardboard cutouts, a newborn foal nuzzling its mother's stomach. Through the dense undergrowth, the spiraling, burrowlike paths of wild pigs went deeper into nowhere, the beginnings of time itself, while overhead the white lighthouse kept time at a standstill. Surrounded by sea, history surfaced as prehistory. I think of this revaluation of the sea as testimony to the force of the archaic in modernity, a coming into fullness of a "second nature" in which objects and landscapes, along with indigenous people, acquire radically intensified meaning as the physical melts into virtual reality.

"The beginning of man was salt sea, and the perpetual reverberation of that great ancient fact, constantly renewed in the unfolding of life in every human individual, is the important single fact about Melville." So says Olson in his *Call Me Ishmael.*[13]

But the current turn to the sea I am describing would seem to be quite different, not something to be *inhabited* but something to be *contemplated* as an expensive backdrop or as a yachting playground for Republican millionaires like William F. Buckley, Jr., testing their manhood against the elements on weekends and in continuous radio and radar contact with the Coast Guard. Down market there is the one-week getaway to the Caribbean with black waiters in tuxedos standing in the blue sea with martinis on a tray, or the two-week cruise on a tarted-up ocean liner that once plowed the seven seas on a regular passenger route. It is hard to imagine the sailors Melville describes in the mid-nineteenth century, for example, or Conrad's, at the end of the century, having the advantage

The Beach (a Fantasy)

of the "second nature" that such alienation from the sea and physical nature provides. For it is by virtue of separation and loss that the sea acquires a new magnificence, as when Benjamin, sensing the demise of storytelling in European cultures, notes that at that point it is "possible to see a new beauty in what is vanishing." It is not commonly recognized that it was on his journeys from Germany to Spain and from Barcelona to Ibiza, in 1932 and 1933, respectively, that Benjamin was seized with enthusiasm for the art of storytelling and even wrote stories—about the sea—himself. Ibiza represented for him an archaic reality, an anachronism, on the margins of Europe, and in one sense ships were for him, I suggest, capsules of the archaic. Ships are nomadic wanderers through time. And this is one reason why they so powerfully concentrate the art of storytelling and do so in ways that touch on the epic dimensions of world history and the exploitation of labor as much as on the retaliation by nature. Certainly this is so for *Moby-Dick* and B. Traven's *Death Ship* as well as Conrad's *Heart of Darkness*.[14]

This rupture into modernity of the archaic as "second nature" gives quite a different sense of historical progression to that of Olson's chronological sequence through the three oceans, Mediterranean, Atlantic, and Pacific. For with the surfacing of the archaic, we become aware that different orders of time may *coexist* with a past precisely because that past is both real and fictional, nature and "second nature," reminiscent of Freud's depiction of fantasy as a play with memories involving montage and overlays. As a site of such fantasy production, the beach's job is not to conceal but reveal and revel in revealing just such play, announcing itself as playground and transgressive space par excellence, displacing by far all previous rituals of reversal and pleasure. The beach, then, is the ultimate fantasy space where nature and carnival blend as prehistory in the dialectical image of modernity.

Dialectical Image

As a presence surfacing in montages and overlays in modernity, the archaic provides both the power and the texture for what Benjamin called the dialectical image. The vital nerve here lay with what was seen as the dynamic architecture of the commodity, a surreal object of such cultural influence and such self-transformative, shape-changing magnificence that, far from demanding oppositional practice, it invoked mimetic strategies to take advantage of its futuristic powers. What encouraged play and trickery was what Georg Lukács called the commodity's "phantom objectivity," defining culture across the board as too, too

spookily real, making much of history as a tragedy that has passed into nature and where everything is on hold, as if awaiting something from us, the survivors, to break the silence. Breton called it the "fixed-explosive."[15]

"In the dialectical image, the past of a particular epoch is also 'the past from time immemorial'" wrote Benjamin.[16] The dialectical image contains time within itself, the cinema compressed into a still-shot, and this is the messianic moment of stillness in the flow of time, arresting thought and allowing reality to collide and roll over it in search of another and until then unacknowledged history in a struggle to redefine the past and its meanings.

The sea must be a paramount instance in the West of "'the past from time immemorial,'" and I can think of no better example of a dialectical image than the postcard that serves as frontispiece, here reproduced, to the English edition of Klaus Theweleit's *Male Fantasies*. He found this card in his mother's photo album, as she lay "unconscious from a stroke and on a journey that is no journey. When people die," he adds, "we look at their photo albums and hear the voices that belonged to the images."[17]

Pacific

It is this I yearn for and fantasize, the "southern sea," as it was first called by Europeans, writing here in a dark room in New York City. It is winter, perfect time and situation for fantasies about the beach. But my history reverses Olson's history of the three oceans. I trace the movement of my life in reverse order to world history, back through history, as is the way of fantasy, back through oceans of time from the Australian Pacific to England, then across the Atlantic to Colombia, and now I live on a coast, the East Coast as they call it, of the Atlantic, a coast I find ugly and cannot, will not, understand because every time I approach it I am reminded of something infinitely more splendid, bobbing in a line beyond the breaking waves waiting for the big one. We sung to strange gods like Huey, to send us one of these Big Ones, and he would oblige. Above the sound of the waves I could hear cicadas in the eucalyptus trees in the midday heat on the headland. It was magical escape, beyond words, the fate well known to the surfer trying to convey the sensation of waves. This bears a direct relation to the fragile freedom, always already lost, of what Hakim Bey calls the "temporary autonomous zone," such as pirate utopias.[18] Truly nothing remains but green twilight and green lightning in this sea of sadness at the unrecuperable loss that memory registers. All or nothing, I say. The real beach or the urban sublime with its rat poison and iron rails rusting into oblivion, home to the homeless. "I have blown a hole in time with a firecracker," says William Burroughs, the Survivor, at the end of *Cities of the Red Night*, a book dedicated to pirate utopias in the Caribbean and Madagascar. "A few may get through the gate in time. Like Spain, I am bound to the past."[19]

Atlantic

Years later I read of the same despair with that depressing English coast by Sylvia Plath, author of an exquisite memoir, "Ocean-1212W," written for the BBC in 1962 towards the end of her short life, which a sailor from Baltimore, named Alicia Rabins, also a poet, brought me. The title refers to the telephone number of Plath's Austrian grandparents whom, living on the seaside, she would as a little girl call via the operator from her own house, on the bayside of a Boston headland of the Massachusetts coast, until the age of nine when her father died and her mother took the children to live away from the sea. It was gone. Utterly and forever. Along with the loss of childhood and the loss of the father.[20]

Much has been made of the death of Plath's father, not least by her late poet-laureate husband, Ted Hughes, anxious to find in that death her death, killing herself at the age of thirty-one in 1963, a few months after their marriage broke up.

As if you descended in each night's sleep
Into your father's grave
You seemed afraid to look, or to remember next morning

What you had seen. When you did remember
Your dreams were of a sea clogged with corpses,
Death-camp atrocities, mass amputations.[21]

Ted Hughes had in mind poems like "Daddy," the most infamous of her Ariel poems written at fever pitch, sometimes two to three a day, in the months before she took her own life. The second and third stanzas:

Daddy, I have had to kill you.
You died before I had time
Marble-heavy, a bag full of God,
Ghastly statue with one grey toe
Big as a Frisco seal
And a head in the freakish Atlantic
Where it pours bean green over blue
In the waters off beautiful Nauset.
I used to pray to recover you.
Ach, du.[22]

"Ach, du" ties the sea to language as much as paternal power is tied to memory, the next stanza implanting the German tongue in Polish towns scraped flat by incessant war. His is a phantom presence ("I could never tell where you / Put your foot, your root") such that she could never talk to him, "the tongue stuck in my jaw."):

It stuck in a barb in a wire snare.
Ich, ich, ich, ich,
I could hardly speak.
I thought every German was you.
And the language obscene
An engine, an engine.
Chuffing me off like a Jew.
A Jew to Dachau, Auschwitz, Belsen.
I began to talk like a Jew.
I think I may well be a Jew.[23]

"In the waters off beautiful Nauset." A place for a prayer. "A head in the freakish Atlantic." His head? A headland? The same thing? "I began to talk like a Jew."

Off to Auschwitz. "Where it pours bean green over blue." In any case, language going, going, gone, this Atlantic that, in Peter Linnebaugh's recovery of William Blake's recovery of mythical Atlantis, in an article entitled "'All the Atlantic Mountains Shook,'" is seen in its African, European, and New World immensity as a criss-crossed multicultured history alive in the present.[24] More than a passageway to the New World, so the argument runs, this busy busy ocean provoked a new way of thinking about the world, most especially about idiosyncrasy replacing the norm, what Paul Gilroy, following Linnebaugh's extraordinarily suggestive essay, called "the black Atlantic," an anarchic mix of sailors and slaves and riffraff plying the waves, planting the plantations, loading the ships on both sides, all sides, of that ocean, humming with creolized languages and music and preindustrial visions of the Rights of Man that were, given the ways of ships and the sea, by no means rigidly bound to the categories of the nation-state. It was a new deal, a volatile and heterogeneous mass drawn from wherever the Atlantic washed ashore.[25] More a subaqueous influence and a utopic vision, a piratical antiauthoritarian potential *something,* waiting to be sprung, this reemergent Atlantis cannot displace the dystopia of African slavery or the fact that the life of the sailor was nasty, brutish, and short. Instead the two realities, slavery *and* the Rights of Man, have to be recognized as two sides of the one coin, and this is why the Atlantic mountains shook. It could have been different. It still could!

Mediterranean

Now, at last, I have seen the sea with my own eyes and walked upon the beautiful threshing floor of the sand which it leaves behind when it ebbs. How I wished the children could have been with me! They would so have loved the shells. Like a child, I picked up a good many because I have a special use for them.
—GOETHE, *Italian Journey, 1786–1788*

A black Atlantic directs us to the unwritten history that would alter the terms of historical reckoning as presently constituted, beginning with the search for an alternative to the father's signifying authority, which I take from Plath's. The transformation of language into play and into body ("And a head in the freakish Atlantic") is Nietzschean in the Dionysian sense of pleasure accompanied by equally great pain in a trancelike state of altered consciousness as one enters into the image and no longer contemplates it from a safe distance.

A black Atlantic asks us to examine how a freakish Atlantic underlies and coexists with a northern European love affair with its exotic south, given that southern Italy and Greece, Provence and Spain, provide vivid and life-enhancing primitivist fantasies concerning the sea and the beach, implicating sensuousness and the body naked to the elements. Witness Goethe in Italy, discovering his childhood by the beach, as I do writing this essay.

Freud had in him, relates his biographer, friend, and colleague, Ernest Jones, "the dichotomy, not rare, between the call of the North and that of the South. The high ideals of duty spoke for the North. There was Berlin, for instance, with its restless activity and unceasing impulse for achievement. But for pleasure, happiness, and pure interest the South was preeminent." He showed Freud some poems from Browning expressing his love for Italy, at which, Jones recalls, Freud smiled, saying, "'I have no need for that; we have our own enthusiasts.'"

> O Woman country
> Woo'd, not won,
> Loved all the more by earth's male lands
> Laid to their hearts instead.[26]

Recall Nietzsche's attachment, appropriately expressed in his use of Italian (*La gaya scienza*) for the title of his most suggestive work, *The Gay Science* (1882), and a century before that, Goethe's *Italian Journey, 1786–1788*. Far from being something restricted to past centuries, the South remains a sexualized site, as we witness in the work of W. H. Auden and Elizabeth Mayer, translators of Goethe's *Italian Journey* and who, in 1962, assert Italy to be Goethe's sexual awakening based on the evidence of portraits painted of him before and after his return to Germany. The latter show a "masculine, self-assured face," they claim, "that of man who has known sexual satisfaction."[27]

Such brazen use of physiognomy says more about attitudes to Italy than it does about Goethe's alleged sexual experience. But that is not the point. What is evoked here is the way the idea of physiognomy is nourished. As a pervasive instrument for navigating social space, the art of reading the secrets of the soul from the exteriority of the face bears an intimate relationship to what the North holds to be the dissimulating face of the sensuous South. For in this scheme of things, sensuousness is tantamount to superficiality, and superficiality means both a person without depth, a human-animal, so to speak, as well as a person with too much depth, so to speak, meaning a liar and a cheat. Nietzsche's philosophy is built on this, as is Karl Marx's economics.

In his justly famous section on the "primitive accumulation" necessary for modern capitalism, Karl Marx evokes this issue of secrecy and "decadence" in the South, where he writes that the "villainies of the Venetian thieving system formed one of the secret bases of the capital-wealth of Holland to whom Venice in her decadence lent large sums of money."[28] This early modern history of capital's dependence on the (secret of the) South is, moreover, a relation among trading ports, the Venetian empire, in decline, and the burgeoning port city of Amsterdam. Not only are these maritime cities but both are built on canals along whose turbid waters came the spices and silks from the East. Indeed the canals not only *are* the city but remind us that these cities are in essence continuously operating salvage operations squatting on swamps and mud in precarious co-existence with the sea. The huge defenses of Venice were described by Goethe in 1786 as built of "uncemented stone blocks" protecting the city from storms and high tides, a city built on protuberances poking out of the muddy swamp that had been formed by "the interaction of tides and earth" as the "primeval ocean" gradually fell.[29]

These prehistoric places of entry and exit where the coast breaks into neither one thing nor the other, anastomoses of islets, lagoons, and peninsulas—natural canals, we could say—seem to have been selected out by a historically informed nature as the generically fertile zones for generating money and trade, just as the prehistoric space-substance that is neither water nor land is where life began and to which it will return. It took a seafaring nation operating out of an island with the largest navy in the world, namely, England, to complete this process by adding the factory system to the African American plantation system.

What specific secret Marx had in mind in this financial relationship between Amsterdam and Venice, I cannot say. Certainly Venice had long been associated with sexual license. Its reputation for "decadence" brings to mind Richard Sennett's observation that "sensuality was a crucial element in the image of Venice in Europe, and in the Venetians sense of themselves." Around the sixteenth century, this included high- and low-class prostitution, "a flourishing homosexual subculture devoted to cross-dressing, young men lounging in gondolas on the canals wearing nothing but women's jewels," and also, the sensuous body of the ghettoized Jew as the incarnation of attraction and repulsion.[30] The first ghetto in history was in Venice. Both Jews (from 1397) and prostitutes (from 1416) were forced by the city to wear yellow as their distinguishing color, the prostitute displaying a yellow scarf, the Jew a yellow Star of David (or a hat). The public executioner was always a Jew. Likely to be thought of by Christians as the quintessential depository of leprosy, syphilis (at first said not to be brought by Columbus but by

Jews), other venereal diseases, and mysterious powers of pollution, these same Jews were the moneylenders, without whom the long-distance trade in spices underlying Venetian naval power would be brought to a halt. Hence Shakespeare's *Merchant of Venice* and, of course, his pound of flesh.[31]

At the crossroads of Western trade with the Orient for silks and spice and all things nice, Venice conflates sensuousness and transgression with the market and the jangle of gold coin, not to mention the specter of the yellow executioner in the background. This interplay came to be called capitalism, which in essence is not only a matter of "primitive accumulation," looting gold and silver from the New World, as it is a question of finding the right mix of transgression and taboo—precisely where the Orient and the West interpenetrated to their utmost.

Venice can be thought of as the ur-scene of capital—and it is a heightened expression of this scene that settles into the collective dream life of Northern Europe in later centuries as "the beach," our paradise, our Eden, from which we have been banished and to which we eternally return.

Here the margin between land and sea where life began is where the repression sustaining civilization takes a transgressive dive and where, moreover, it is to be seen doing so where children play building sandcastles and adults play at being children on their way to being sea-creatures. Beyond the beach, the sea, to what in Thomas Mann's *Death in Venice* is the empty eternal, the nothingness into which the gaze of the northern visitor, uptight, middle-aged von Aschenbach escapes from the rigor his life as a writer demands.

Von Aschenbach's own body, if only he knew it, is to serve as Thomas Mann's beachhead, a playground of passion let loose, like line from an angler's reel, only to be jerked into place by dying forces of artistic creativity dependent upon repression. This is the ultimate and terrible cruelty, this image of creativity as the sublimated product of repression, creativity as something that can only exist at a cost, as a denial of instant gratification. Yet here, on this body as beachhead, do we not glimpse the possibility of the spirit set free from the restricted economy of Freud for whom the north travels south to the beach to stoke the primitive fires of the flesh and then returns to the north to advance the spirit?

"'You see,'" said a friend in Munich, "'Aschenbach has always only lived like *this*,'" and he closed his fist tightly. "'Never like *this*'—and he let his open hand hang."[32]

But miraculously in Venice the hand opens. He is on the beach, where life forms began. He is watching the boy with whom he has fallen in love playing in the sand before leaving Venice. This boy is locked in Aschenbach's gaze. The boy is walking now into the water, wading to the sandbar. He is slowly pacing back and forth on this narrow strip of unsubmerged land divided from the shore by a width of water, an apparition walking as if on water with his floating hair "out there in the sea, in the wind, in front of a nebulous vastness."[33] On impulse he turns towards Aschenbach, his eyes seeming to call and beckon to the horizon. He is still. The beach is still. Just them. Everything is frozen. And as Aschenbach struggles to clamber out of his deck chair and project his body into the flight path of his eyes, Mann kills him—and thus disposes of his writerly fantasy of forbidden love wrought from the water's edge. Nietzsche would have it quite otherwise; the beach and its waves and beyond them the sheer eternal emptiness open up history to a "reverse experiment" whereby we humans could return to the life of sea animals whose enjoyment is not bound by the fear of pleasure.

When Marx collapses "the villainies" and "decadence" of the Venetian "thieving system" into one of the secrets of capital and specifically does so in relation to moneylending from south to north, it is hard to escape the feeling that this "secret" is already secured by many centuries of intricate cultural practice fusing money, sex, magical pollution, ethnic division, and transgression. Mann is simply turning the wheel, crucial to which are the many centuries of Venetian power built on trade with the Orient for silks, spices, dyestuffs, medicines and perfumes—luxury goods soaked in the aura of the Middle East, Ceylon, India, the Malay Archipelago, China, and Japan.

After all, what is a luxury? It is a ravishing commodity aimed at titillating if not entrancing the human body, its taste buds, its arousal by color such as lapus lazuli and indigo, its love of mosaics, and the smooth cool touch of silk. It is the immersion of the body in the commodity. It is the enclosure of the body by the commodity. It is also—and this is what separates it from nonluxuries—a consciousness as to these unconscious pleasures, as when one buys a prostitute.

The "secret" of capital turns out to be its dependence on the hothouse mix of sensuality and transgression at the crossroads of Europe and the Orient. Fetishism is not a consequence but the magical precondition for the commodity and, hence, for mature capitalism, to function. That is why we witness the spectacular "return" of the archaic within modernity as much as within our very bodies, tied as they are to the history of the world as the economic history of three oceans.

Will and Wave

"Will and Wave" is the title Nietzsche gives to a passage in *The Gay Science* surging with the ordered disorder inherent to what I call the Nervous System, that sense of reality as always one step ahead of one's grasp.[34] This of course is writing, dissembling itself face-to-face with a dissembling world.

So? You mistrust me? You are angry with me, you beautiful monsters? Are you afraid that I might give away your whole secret? Well, be angry with me, arch your dangerous green bodies as high as you can, raise a wall between me and the sun—as you are doing now! Truly, even now nothing remains of the world but green twilight and green lightning. Carry on as you like, roaring with overweening pleasure and malice—or dive again, pouring your emeralds down into the deepest depths, and throw you infinite white mane of foam and spray over them.[35]

Walter Kaufmann sees "Will and Wave" as a deliberately purposeless piece of writing, a Dionysian moment in which childish play is allowed a space, as on the beach, just prior to Nietzsche's first formulation of the eternal return as the sign of meaninglessness and lack of purpose in the apparent design that is world history.[36] Yet surely the point of such Dionysian "moments" is that they transgress time as well as custom, so as to seem anything but "moments" fixed to a cordoned-off site licensing disconformity?

For the beach is precisely the scene where prehistory became human history, as when Nietzsche, citing the enormity of the break with what went before the invention of guilt and instinctual repression, "turning man against himself," compares it with the fate of sea animals forced to become land animals or perish. "I do not think there has ever been such a feeling of misery on earth, such a leaden discomfort."

Here the Dionysian play of will and wave acquires premeditated political force. For the whole point of Nietzsche's work was to try for "the reverse experiment," undoing the repression that turned man against himself. It should be possible, *"in principle*—but who has sufficient strength?"[37] No accident, then, that the reverse experiment has to be down there at the water's edge, edge of history, edge of repression, "turning man against himself," the most fateful mimetic act of all, and this is why I have chosen to dwell on the beach along with Stephen Dedalus sifting images in the mad inheritance we call language.

The Beach (a Fantasy)

In Nietzsche's fable, the disaster struck when the animals crawled onto the beach out of the sea to become humans turned against themselves. They did this by using the instincts to subdue the instincts. The pre-Socratic sense of interconnectedness and flow was displaced by decontextualizing logic and state-friendly models of cause and perspective. The Judaeo-Christian world came to condemn the body as sinful, and Dionysus was not effaced but appropriated as the devil.

In today's world, in the West, and much of the developing world as well, the sea has been rediscovered not as part of everyday life but as a commodity in itself—"the sea"—like the latest-style SUV or, better still, as real estate investment with a view. Even the middle class can get a piece of the action, like visiting a bordello, with a time-share condominium, a two-week cruise, or a week at an expensive resort in a poverty-stricken third world country such as Thailand or Jamaica. Could anything be further from "the reverse experiment" that Nietzsche thought should be possible? Has not the reverse experiment itself been subject to commercial appropriation?

Returning to Winthrop on the Massachusetts coast in the winter of 1958, Sylvia Plath found it "shrunk, dulled, wrinkled its dense hide: all those rainbow extensions of dreams lost luster, shells out of water, color blanching out."[38] Goethe rediscovered the imagination of the child when, at Venice, for the first time in his life he saw the sea and strode along the beach at low tide and found shells. The surf was breaking on the beach in high waves. He loved what he called "the beautiful threshing floor of the sand" left when the waves went out to sea again. "Like a child, I picked up a good many," these same shells that a mere century and a half later make Plath despair and ask whether "our minds colored the streets and children then and do so no longer." She could have been echoing Nietzsche as to the fate of sea animals forced to become land animals or perish. "I do not think there has ever been such a feeling of misery on earth, such a leaden discomfort."

"We must fight," she went on in her journal, "we must fight to return to that early mind . . . We must recreate it, even while we measure baking powder for a hurry-up cake and calculate next month's expenses. A god inbreathes himself in everything. Practice. *Be* a chair, a toothbrush, a jar of coffee from the inside out: *know* by feeling in."[39]

The beach. Something we enjoy, an eternal childhood we continuously lose to green twilight and green lightning, afterimage of waves arching themselves between myself and my sun.

Practice!

Underlying all our mystic states are corporeal techniques,
biological methods of entering into communication with God.
—M A R C E L M A U S S , "Les techniques du corps," 1960

The sorcerer generally learns his time-honored profession in good faith,
and retains his belief in it more or less from first to last; at once dupe and
cheat, he combines the energy of a believer with the cunning of a hypocrite.
—E D W A R D B U R N E T T T Y L O R , *Primitive Culture*, 1871

Viscerality, Faith, and Skepticism
A N O T H E R T H E O R Y O F M A G I C

Habituated as we are these post–9/11 days to the dramaturgy of Homeland Security—who can still remember the color-coded warnings of terror whenever the president's ratings were falling or the advice to place plastic sheeting on the windows?—there is one act of theater that still seems fresh and daring: the revealing glimpse of stately being provided by U.S. Attorney General John Ashcroft when he ordered Justice have her fulsome breast covered by suitable drapes. It was as if he had taken to heart what, according to students' notes, the learned anthropologist Marcel Mauss had said in Paris sometime in the 1920s, that "underlying all our mystic states are corporeal techniques, biological methods of entering into communication with God."[1] Later on with untold millions watching the 2004 Super Bowl on television, the singer Janet Jackson had a wardrobe malfunction in which her dress slipped to reveal for an instant the breast that the attorney general had had to cover up. Laws were instantly drafted against indecency in the media. A year later the noted evangelist Pat Robertson told viewers on his television show that the United States should kill Venezuelan president Hugo Chávez, described in the *New York Times* as "a leftist whose country has the largest oil reserves outside of the Middle East." Claiming that "this is even more threatening to hemispheric stability than the flash of a breast on television during a ballgame,"

An earlier version of this chapter was originally published in Nicholas B. Dirks, ed., *In Near Ruins: Cultural Theory at the End of the Century* (Minneapolis: University of Minnesota, 1998).

the Reverend Jesse Jackson called for the Federal Communications Commission to investigate, just as it did when Janet Jackson's breast was exposed.[2]

Mauss hardly needed to add that clothing—that second skin—goes hand in hand with "corporeal techniques" for reaching the holy. One has only to think of the passions aroused by the veil in Islam, nuns' and priests' habits in Christianity, the scarlet robes of cardinals, the pope's miter, the orange robes and haircuts of Buddhist monks, and the layers of black and white cloth, white string, and large black hats of Jewish men's orthodoxy, let alone the postures and body movements for praying, to get the point, strange as it may seem. Even nudism is a kind of religion. It is strange, is it not, that something so intensely spirited and spiritual as communicating with God should be so tied to the flesh and, at the very same time, be so tied to covering it, uncovering it, and even mutilating it?

Intense it certainly is. Those of us fortunate enough to live in the United States have become acutely aware these days of such "corporeal techniques" that in media form allow the populace to enter into communication with God, techniques so downright earthy and body-saturated that they leave the Christian and Muslim penitents lashing themselves to bloody frenzy far behind, no less than the nuns of early modern Europe glorying in their infected wounds. In Flemish painting of the fifteenth and sixteenth centuries it is common to see Christ the Crucified with a neatly made, vagina-shaped, incision on his right chest, level with the nipple. In one painting I know of, the wound emits golden rays of fine droplets that take up a good third of the painting. Leo Steinberg has dedicated much of his formidable scholarship to the ubiquity in Renaissance painting, north and south of the Alps, of what looks like a large, sometimes very large, erection on Christ's part while on the cross.[3] What is just as noteworthy is the cover-up. For not only is Christ naked except for an awkwardly bulging sheet, but centuries have passed without mentioning this unmentionable, as likewise with the equally large number of paintings of the Virgin adoring the baby Christ's dick. If it wasn't for the fact that people choose, perhaps unconsciously, not to see this, one can only imagine what a busy time people like the attorney general could be having in the War against This Terror.

But fortunately for us those barbarous displays of spiritual devotion devoted to covering and uncovering the body are long past. Today in the West, church and temple have long been sanitized, and the evidence lies safely ensconced in the no-less-sanitary and no-less-hallowed rooms of art museums. Instead, religion has found other and better "corporeal techniques for entering into communication with God," absolutely life-and-death issues including fanatical opposition to abortion, gay marriage, embryonic stem-cell research, euthanasia, condoms, and the sale of "morning-after" pill. (But not Viagra.) That this opposition wins national elections and hence shapes the fate of the world is now painfully obvious, and thus these corporeal techniques merit closer examination.

In the sorts of societies traditionally studied by anthropologists, in which religion was in the hands of so-called shamans, witch-doctors, and sorcerers, such corporeal techniques can be viewed as forms of conjuring based on sleight of hand, which is what assures them their ability to enter into communication with God. This is conjuring, but with a twist. And what is this twist? It is quite marvelous and amounts to *the skilled revelation of skilled concealment*—witness Janet Jackson's briefest of brief revelations and the attorney general's cover-up. Witness the crucified Christ's erection that nobody sees. What we have here is an art form dedicated to cheating, or should I say contrived misperception, a corporeal technique that not only evokes something sacred but that involves deceiving oneself as well. Religion is certainly strange. In the mid-nineteenth century in Oxford, England, the celebrated founder of anthropology, Sir Edward Burnett Tylor, put it like this:

> The sorcerer generally learns his time-honored profession in good faith, and retains his belief in it more or less from first to last; at once dupe and cheat, he combines the energy of a believer with the cunning of a hypocrite.[4]

By "sorcerer," Tylor was not necessarily thinking of attorneys general, but it is established in the ethnographic record that law in so-called primitive societies is very much a matter of sorcery, if by that term we include, as is generally the case, medicine and religion. What is more, Tylor puts his finger on something timeless here, fascinating and timeless, which is that faith seems to require that one be taken in by what one professes while at the same time suspecting it is a lot of hooey.

At once dupe and cheat, Tylor said—truly an amazing state of affairs, mixing recognition with denial, blindness with insight. Here faith seems to not only happily coexist with skepticism but *demands* it, hence the interminable, mysterious, and complex movement back and forth between revelation and concealment. Could it follow, therefore, that magic is efficacious not despite the trick but on account of its exposure? Let me flesh this out, beginning with what for me stands as the primal scene of conjuring on the part of the sorcerer.

In his wonderfully evocative and informative autobiography, Lucas Bridges, son of a missionary turned sheep farmer, tells us how he grew up playing with Indian children around 1900 on Isla Grande, one of many islands, peninsulas, and waterways that make up Tierra del Fuego. He learnt at least one of the native languages, and by the time he was an adult he was tempted to learn the ways of the sorcerer, ways which were, in essence, very puzzling because the fear of magic coexisted with disbelief in the magicians. Note that magic, in the form of killing by means of sorcery, was common. The first among the Ona Indian superstitions, according to Bridges, was "fear of magic and of the power of magicians, even on the part of those who, professing that art, must have known that they themselves were humbugs. They had great fear of the power of others."[5] He went to say that "some of these humbugs were excellent actors," and it will be useful for us to follow him in his description of what he calls "acting" and observe the focus, if not obsession, with the "object," an object withdrawn from the interstices of the living, human, body.

> Standing or kneeling beside the patient, gazing intently at the spot where the pain was situated, the doctor would allow a look of horror to come over his face. Evidently he could see something invisible to the rest of us. . . . With his hands he would try to gather the malign presence into one part of the patient's body—generally the chest—where he would then apply his mouth and suck violently. Sometimes this struggle went on for an hour, to be repeated later. At other times the *joon* would draw away from his patient with the pretense of holding something in his mouth with his hands. Then always facing away from the encampment, he would take his hands from his mouth gripping them tightly together, and, with a guttural shout difficult to describe and impossible to spell, fling this invisible object to the ground and stamp fiercely upon it. Occasionally a little mud, some flint or even a tiny, very young mouse might be produced as the cause of the patient's indisposition.[6]

As an aside let us take note of the eyes of the great medicine man, Houshken, perforce an expert in physiognomy. He was over six feet tall and his eyes were exceedingly dark, almost blue black. "I had never seen eyes of such color," muses Bridges, and he wondered whether Houshken was nearsighted. Far from it. For not only was the man a mighty hunter, but it was said that he could look through mountains.

Viscerality, Faith, and Skepticism

These are also the sort of eyes that can look through the human body, as was brought out when Bridges allowed another famous medicine man, Tininisk (who twenty years later became one of Father Martin Gusinde's most important informants), to induct him into the ways of the medicine man. Half-reclining naked on guanaco skins by the fire sheltered by a windbreak, Bridges's chest was gone over by the medicine man's hands and mouth as intently, said Bridges, as any doctor with a stethoscope, "moving in the prescribed manner from place to place, pausing to listen here and there."[7] Then come those eyes again, those eyes that can see through mountains, the mountain of the body. "He also gazed intently at my body, as though he saw through it like an X-ray manipulator."

Having eyes like these eyes is helpful for seeing through the world, but perhaps the implication this carries is misleading. For penetrating as these eye are, it could be the nature of the material looked through that is special. For it seems that solids, like the body, are, under certain conditions at least, unstable and transparent.

The medicine man and his helper stripped naked. The medicine man's wife, one of the rare women healers, took off her outer garment, and the three of them huddled and produced something Bridges thought was of the lightest gray down, shaped like a puppy and about four inches long with pointed ears. It had the semblance of life, perhaps due to the handlers' breathing and the trembling of their hands. There was a peculiar scent as the "puppy" was placed by the three pairs of hands to his chest, where, without any sudden movement, it disappeared. Three times this was repeated, and then after a solemn pause Tininisk asked whether Bridges felt anything moving in his heart or if he could see something strange in his mind, like in a dream?

But Bridges felt nothing, and eventually decided to abandon what he had found to be a fascinating course of studies because for one thing, he would have to frequently lie, "at which I was not very clever," and for another, it would separate him from his Ona friends. "They feared the sorcerers; I did not wish them to fear me, too."[8] Yet, although his desire to learn magic waned, it never completely left him.

Some twenty years later Father Martin Gusinde was informed by the Indians that the "puppy" was made of the white feathers of newborn birds and a shaman's entire body, other than the skin, was made of this stuff. It was this substance that gave the shaman his special powers—his penetrating sight, his ability to divine, to reach out and kill, and sing as well.[9]

When he later met up with the famous Houshken, about whom he had heard so much, Bridges told him he had heard of his great powers and would like to see some of his magic. The moon was full that night. Reflected on the snow on the ground, it cast the scene like daylight. Returning from the river, Houshken began to chant, put his hands to his mouth, and withdrew a strip of guanaco hide three times the thickness of a shoelace and about eighteen inches long. His hands shook and gradually drew apart, the strip stretching to about four feet. His companion took one end and the four feet extended to eight, then suddenly disappeared back into Houshken's hands to become smaller and smaller such that when his hands were almost together he clapped them to his mouth, uttered a prolonged shriek, and then held out his hands, completely empty.

Even an ostrich, comments Bridges, could not have swallowed those eight feet of hide without a visible gulp. But where else could it have gone but back into the man's body? He had no sleeves. He stood butt naked in the snow with his robe on the ground. What's more, there were between twenty and thirty men present, but only a third of them were Houshken's people and the rest were far from being friendly. "Had they detected some simple trick," writes Bridges, "the great medicine man would have lost his influence; they would no longer have believed in any of his magic."[10]

Houshken put on his robe and seemed to go into a trance as he stepped toward Bridges, let his robe fall to the ground, put his hands to his mouth again, withdrew them, and when they were less than two feet from Bridges's face slowly drew them apart to reveal a small, almost opaque, object, about an inch in diameter, tapering into his hands. It could have been semitransparent elastic or dough but whatever it was, it seemed to be alive, revolving at great speed.

The moon was bright enough to read by as he drew his hands apart, and Bridges realized suddenly the object was no longer there. "It did not break or burst like a bubble; it simply disappeared." There was a gasp from the onlookers. Houshken turned his hands over for inspection. They were clean and dry. Bridges looked down at the ground. Stoic as he was, Houshken could not resist a chuckle, for there was nothing to be seen. "Don't let it trouble you. I shall call it back to myself again."

By way of ethnographic explanation, Bridges tells us that this curious object was believed to be "an incredibly malignant spirit belonging to, or possibly part of, the *joon* (medicine man) from whom it emanated." It could take a physical form. Or it could be invisible. It had the power to introduce insects, tiny mice, mud, sharp flints, or even a jellyfish or a baby octopus into the body of one's enemy. "I have seen a strong man shudder involuntarily at the thought of this horror and its evil potentialities."[11] "It was a curious fact," he adds, that "although every magician must have known himself to be a fraud and a trickster, he always believed in and greatly feared the supernatural abilities of other medicine-men"[12]

Viscerality, Faith, and Skepticism

At this juncture I want to draw your attention to several things about the sleight of hand involved here in the manipulation of the human body. First, there is the use of the body as a receptacle, a "holy temple," whose boundary has to be traversed. This is the basic, the essential, staging for the perpetual play of moving inside and outside, implanting and extracting . . . whether it be the shaman's body, the patient's body, the enemy's body, or the body of a novice shaman during training.

Then there is the exceedingly curious object that is said to be a spirit belonging to the body of the medicine man; it appears to be alive yet is an object all the same; it marks the exit from and reentry into the body; it has a remarkably indeterminate quality—note the weird elasticity of the guanaco strip and the semitransparent dough or elastic revolving at high speed—all acting like extensions of the human body and thus capable of connecting with and entering into other bodies, human and nonhuman.

There exists a Central European version of this weird doughlike spinning thing and it is called Odradek, the hero of a one-and-a-half page story, "The Cares of a Family Man."[13] The author, Franz Kafka, tells us that the origin of the name Odradek is perplexing, and from his account it is impossible to know whether Odradek is a person, an animal, or an object. Odradek seems like a person in some ways, can speak and respond to questions, for instance, and can move fairly nimbly, like an animal. Yet it is nothing but an old star-shaped cotton reel with bits of different colored thread and a couple of little sticks poking out either end. It lurks on thresholds and cul-de-sacs, on the stairs and in the hallway. When it laughs it is like the rustling of dead leaves. We are unsure as to whether he can die.

Kafka himself did not employ sleight of hand. His writing was sufficient. Odradek was an extension of Kafka, his body no less than his mind, similar to the "puppy" of white feathers of newborn birds emerging from Tininisk to enter the body of his patients or victims. Kafka's stories are not stories at all. They rely on gesture, the bodily equivalent of words, words that suddenly shoot out of syntax and take on a life of their own, like the Selk'nam revolving dough emergent from the shaman's mouth. Kafka never felt at home in his body. He was bound to empathy and metamorphosis. Remember the man who became a bug? And the facial tic that tics away on its own?

In Kafka's account, Odradek is both exotic and familiar, fantastic and ordinary. Perhaps this is the same for the "puppy" among the Selk'nam described by Lucas Bridges and by Father Gusinde. Such creatures are more than creaturely; they are sudden appearances and equally mysterious disappearances; they are movement, most notably bodily movement, meaning not only the place of the body in space, nor simply rapid extension of limbs in what is almost a form of dance, but also movements of egress and ingress, of insides into outsides and vice versa combined with a movement of sheer becoming in which being and nonbeing are transformed into the beingness of transforming forms.

Such creatures refer us to the metamorphosing capacity of curious unnamable animated objects able to become more clearly recognizable but out-of-place things such as baby octopi or mud or a flint in the body of the enemy rendered sick and dying, a capacity on the part of these creatures not only for change but also for an implosive viscerality that would seem to hurl us beyond the world of the symbol and that penny-in-the-slot resolution called meaning.

Above all at this point, I want to draw attention to the spectacular display of magical feats and tricks and to wonder about their relationship to the utterly serious business of killing and healing people. This combination of trickery, spectacle, and death must fill us with some confusion, even anxiety, about the notion of the trick and its relation to both theater and science, let alone to truth and fraud. We therefore need to dwell upon this corrosive power creeping along the otherwise imperceptible fault lines in the sturdy structure of language and thought, splicing games and deceit to matters of life and death, theater to reality, this world to the spirit world, and trickery to the illusion of a world without trickery—the most problematic trick of all. Here one can sympathize with Friedrich Nietzsche where he writes that "all of life is based on semblance, art, deception, points of view and the necessity of perspectives and error," no less than with the attempt by Horkheimer and Adorno to position not Eve and the tree of knowledge of good and evil but shamanism and its magic as the true fall from grace onto the first faltering steps of Enlightenment and what has come to be called science, imitating nature so as to control nature, including human nature, transforming the trick into techniques of domination over nature and people.[14]

Faced with this world based on semblance, art, and deception, Nietzsche advises us not to labor under the illusion of eliminating trickery on the assumption that there is some other world out there beyond and bereft of trickery. The trick will always win, especially when exposed. What we should do instead is practice our own form of *shamanism*, if that's the word, and come up with a set of tricks, simulations, and deceptions in a continuous movement of counterfeint and feint strangely contiguous with yet set against those weighing on us. It is something like this *nervous system*, I believe, that Nietzsche had in mind with his *Gay*

Viscerality, Faith, and Skepticism

Science, a "mocking, light, fleeting, divinely untroubled, divinely artificial art" built around the idea, if I may put it this way, that exposure of the trick is no less necessary to the magic of magic than is its concealment.[15]

"TO DESCRIBE ANY CONSIDERABLE NUMBER OF TRICKS CARRIED OUT BY THE SHAMANS, BOTH CHUCKCHEE AND ESKIMO, WOULD REQUIRE TOO MUCH SPACE"

When Catherine the Great opened up the wastes of Siberia to European explorers in the eighteenth century they were first not called *shamans* but *jugglers*—jugglers as in *conjurers.* The name *shaman* came later, being the name used by one of the indigenous cultures, that of the Tungus, for one of several classes of their healers. From its inception, the naming and presentation of the figure of the shaman by anthropologists was profoundly linked to trickery by means of startling revelations about ventriloquism, imitations of animal spirit voices, curtained chambers, mysterious disappearances and reappearances, semisecret trapdoors, knife tricks, and so forth, including—if *trick* is the word here, and why not?—sex changes by men and women.

By the last quarter of the twentieth century, so-called shamans came to be thought of by anthropologists and by laymen as existing everywhere throughout the world and throughout history as a universal type of magical and religious being, and the trickery tended to be downplayed as the mystical took center stage. The term itself had become early on diffused throughout Western languages, thanks to the ethnography of Siberia begun in the late nineteenth century, the phenomenon thus joining an illustrious company of colonially derived native terms enriching European languages such as *totemism, taboo, mana,* and even *cannibalism,* words at once familiar yet mysterious as if freighted by their indigenous meanings and contexts.[16]

Hearken to the wonderful tricks presented by Waldemar Bogoras for the Chukchi shaman he met in Siberia, Bogoras's 1904 monograph being one of the high points in the birth of shamanism as a Western object of study.[17] Bogoras was fascinated, for instance, by the shamans' skill in ventriloquy creating soundscapes so complex and multiply layered that it seemed like you had become immersed in a spirit world. Bogoras took pains to capture the trick of voice throwing onto a wax cylinder, phonographic record, and was surprised that he could do so, delighted by his own trickery. The shaman sat over there, throwing his voice, but the voice emerged right here, out of the phonogram! I heard the same thing a century later, two years ago in the oral examination of a doctoral student who had gotten hold of a copy. This was one of those especially fine tricks from everyone's point of view. To the white man it conflated two magics, that of the mimetically capacious shaman with that of the modern mimetic machine. To the native it must have been satisfying to have another happy client.

Another form of trick performed by a shaman was wringing her hands to make a large pebble reproduce a continuous row of small pebbles on top of her drum. Bogoras tried to trick her into revealing her trick, but he was unable to. This is an important moment in the Western investigation of shamanism and we should not let it pass unnoticed no matter how much our attention is focused on the shaman's tricks. It is a touching moment when the anthropologist tries to outsmart the shaman, something you don't generally come across as recommended in standard texts on field methods such as *Notes and Queries.* We shall observe it in detail later with E. E. Evans-Pritchard in Africa in the early 1930s.

Another of this shaman's tricks was to rip open the abdomen of her son to find and remove the cause of illness. "It certainly looked as if the flesh was really cut open," said Bogoras. On both sides, from under the fingers flowed little streams of blood, trickling to the ground. "The boy lay motionless; but once or twice moaned feebly, and complained that the knife had touched his entrails." The shaman placed her mouth to the incision and spoke into it. After some moments she lifted her head, and the boy's body was quite sound. Other shamans made much of stabbing themselves with knives. Tricks are everywhere. As Bogoras concludes, "To describe any considerable number of tricks carried out by the shamans, both Chuckchee and Eskimo, would require too much space."[18] Yet can we resist mentioning a couple more? Upune, for instance, "pretended to draw a cord through her body, passing it from one spot to another. Then suddenly she drew it out, and immediately afterward pretended to cut it in two and with it the bodies of several of her children, who sat in front of her. These and other tricks resemble to a surprising degree the feats of jugglers all over the world. Before each performance, Upune would even open her hands, in the graceful manner of a professor of magic, to show us she had nothing in them." The greatest trick was not that of being able to descend and walk in the underground but to change one's sex, thanks to help from the spirits, a change that could well eventuate, at least in the case of a man, in his taking male lovers or becoming married to a man. Such "soft men," as they were called, were feared for their magic more than unchanged men or women.[19]

A CAN OF WORMS

Every year from 1975 to 1997 I would visit the Putumayo region of Colombia's southwest, a strikingly beautiful landscape of cloud forested steeply sloped ravines saturated in sorcery. I lived with my shaman friend, Santiago Mutumba-joy, a well-known indigenous healer using hallucinogens and music, and at one point, before the guerrilla war became really serious, we were thinking of setting up a dual practice. I would do the Western medicine, he would do the rest. He would laugh a lot and loved jokes, usually in the form of gossip or stories about people and the strange situations in which they found themselves. There was one joke he loved in particular. It summed up centuries of colonial history and the ways by which history played a trick on itself: Europe's conquest of the New World imputed magical powers to the savage such that modern-day colonists of the region, poor whites and blacks, and lately well-to-do urbanites, would seek out forest Indians for their alleged shamanic powers. Santiago Mutumbajoy found this uproariously funny, a trick to beat all tricks, as if keeping in reserve the other sort of magic, the "true" magic we might say, that came from centuries if not millennia of Indian history and culture. But of course was it possible in practice to separate these two sorts of magics?

But the joke was on me in other ways as well. Like when I asked him how he became a shaman. When he was young and recently married, he replied, his wife was constantly ill. He and she consulted shaman after shaman at great expense with no relief until, one day, they heard that a white doctor was being sent by the government to the nearby town to treat Indians. They dressed in their finery, including swathes of necklaces of tiny colored glass beads, and walked to town. "Make way for the Indians! Make way for the Indians!" people said. On the balcony of a two-story house was the doctor. To her consternation he made his wife take off her shirt and began to palpate her chest, drumming one finger on top of another, laid flat, such that hollow booms followed muffled ones. He said she was anemic and gave her parasite medicine. A small boy they met going home explained there was more than one type of anemia.

When she defecated a day or so later she expelled a lot of worms. "Look here!" she exclaimed. Santiago Mutumbajoy went over and looked. A great rage seized him. All those shamans had been fakes. And at that moment he decided to become a shaman.

"A PECULIAR STATE OF MIND . . . IT WOULD BE WONDERFUL IF A MAN COULD TALK WITH ANIMALS AND FISHES."
"It is perfectly well-known by all concerned," wrote the eminent anthropologist Franz Boas toward the end of his career, that "a great part of the shamanistic procedure is based on fraud; still it is believed in by the shaman as well as by his patients and their friends. Exposures do not weaken the belief in the 'true' power of

shamanism. Owing to this peculiar state of mind, the shaman himself is doubt-ful in regard to his powers and is always ready to bolster them up by fraud."[20]

At the risk of being odiously pedantic, allow me to try to catch this slippery fish of Kwakiutl shamanism by itemizing its contradictory components as they come across here in Boas's rendering. I am aware that all I demonstrate is that the more you try to pin this down, the more it wriggles, and this is, I guess, my labored point, to watch the figure of logic emerge as a vengeful force of pins and points bent on restraint.

1. All concerned know that a great part of shamanistic procedure is a fraud.
2. Yet shaman, patient, and friends all believe in shamanism.
3. Moreover, exposure of shamanism's fraudulence does not weaken belief in it.
4. But contrary to points 2 and 3, the presence of fraud does make the shaman doubt his or her worth.
5. Point 4 has the effect that the shaman resorts to (further) fraud.
6. Now start with point 1 again.

A student of Franz Boas, Irving Goldman, emphasizes that "the Kwakiutl shaman relies heavily on elaborate tricks in his public demonstrations. He devises hidden trapdoors and partitions, and uses strings to cleverly manipulate artificial figures. He is in appearance the modern magician."[21]

Well, not quite. After all, magicians who screw up are not usually killed. After all, it's only a trick. But hearken to Stanley Walens. "Anthropologists have often wondered," he says, "why it is that the natives do not complain that the shamans are performing tricks and not real cures. They have found it difficult to explain the seeming paradox that while Kwakiutl shamans are admired for their abilities at legerdemain, if a shaman bungles one of these tricks, he is immediately killed."[22]

At this point, let us pause and cast an eye over the strategies one might pursue to understand fraud as somehow not fraudulent at all but something true and even efficacious, what I keep referring to as the *trick as technique*. One could find relief in Boas's statement that not all but only a (great) part of the shamanistic procedure is based on fraud and hope that the lesser part may turn out to be the more important. One could interrogate the meaning of *belief* as in "still it is *believed* in by the shaman as well as by his patients," thus forcing the issue about the difference between belief as in a personal psychological state, versus belief as in "tradition" as some sort of cultural "script" (the British "intellectualist' approach to magic versus the French à la Emile Durkheim and Lucien Lévy-Bruhl), and so forth. One would also want to ask questions such as to what extent is belief ever an unflawed, confident, and consistent thing anyway? How much does one have to "believe" for shamanism to work? And so on (a well-worn path, actually).

Or one could play the E. B. Tylor maneuver taken up, as we shall see later, by Evans-Pritchard, that because procedures for verification or falsification of the efficacy of magical healing are either not available, not practiced, or by definition inapplicable, *there is always a way of explaining failure away* (e.g., malevolence or ritual error on the part of the healer, a stronger sorcerer or spirit at work in the background). This argument is usually packaged with another: that this infamously "closed system," about which so much has been written as regards Africa, is in some yet to be plausibly connected way associated with the yet to be explained belief that *although any particular shaman may be fraudulent, shamanism is nevertheless valid* (believed in, plausible, worth a shot?). It takes more than a few bad apples . . .

Or one could substitute *simulation* or *mimesis* for *fraud*. This has remarkable fallout poetically as much as philosophically and is uncannily resonant with the ethnographic record itself—as we shall later see. With this, perhaps, our fish would stop wiggling and start to swim, a manner of "resolving" contradiction I find preferable to that of pins and points.

Boas's intimate knowledge concerning this "peculiar state of mind" came from his forty-year relationship with his Kwakiutl informant George Hunt and the ten thousand pages of material they published, plus several thousand more existing in manuscript form. Franz Boas's texts on Kwakiutl society have been described by Stanley Walens as "one of the monuments of American cultural anthropology."[23] Walens also points out that the "degree to which the excellence of Boas' work is the result of the meticulousness and diligence of both men [Hunt as well as Boas] has never been amply discussed."[24] Irving Goldman describes these texts as "probably the greatest single ethnographic treasure [in existence]."[25]

Hunt and Boas's conversations concerning Hunt's shamanic experiences began in 1897 and reached a peak almost thirty years later in the 1925 *auto*biographical text of Hunt's that was published in both Kwakiutl and in English in 1930 as "I Desired to Learn the Ways of the Shaman."[26] This text was miraculously delivered from obscurity two decades later by Claude Lévi-Strauss in a famous essay entitled "The Sorcerer and His Magic,"[27] which was an attempt to provide what must seem now more of an *expression* of faith, as in structuralism, than an *expla-*

nation of faith, as in magic, the point being that Hunt, known at the beginning of the 1930 essay as Giving-Potlatches-in-the-World, becomes by his own admission a famous shaman not so much despite but because of his profoundly skeptical attitude.

In fact, over the twenty-nine years from 1897 to 1925, Hunt *had given Boas no less than four accounts of his experience in becoming a shaman,* and it was for Boas remarkable how the last account—the one that became published as "I Desired to Learn the Ways of the Shaman"—eliminated what Boas called all the supernatural elements in the earlier versions, in which Hunt vividly described his mysterious fainting fits as a child; finding himself naked in the graveyard at night; the visits by powerful spirits such as the killer whale named Tilting-in-Mid-Ocean who told him how to cure the chief's sick boy the following day; how the down indicative of disease just appeared of its own accord in his mouth as he was sucking out the disease; how killer whales accompanied his canoe; how he ate of the corpse of the shaman Life-Maker, and so forth. Most of the time, it seems, in the early versions, he was falling unconscious, passing out into these other realms, while in the last version, that of 1925, Hunt takes the position, as Boas puts it, that "his only object was to discover the frauds perpetrated by Shamans."[28] Small wonder then that confronted with contradictions such as these, and resolute to the facts at hand, Boas—unlike the fledgling field of British social anthropology, in the pioneering hands of Bronislaw Malinowski with his functionalist formula relating part to whole—never came up with a general theory or panoramic picture of Kwakiutl society.

At one point Boas commonsensically noted that the skepticism displayed by Kwakiutl people toward magic should be seen as a political defense because Indians did not want to come across to whites as irrational and so would fake a critical attitude toward shamanism. (How things have changed now that "shamanism" has become a darling of the white man!) Hence at one stroke we could dismiss questions concerning the place of skepticism in faith and simply view such perplexity as mere artifact of another sort of fraud—or is it mimesis?—namely, that of Indian self-representation to whites at that time and place. But then of course another hypothesis intrudes, that if fraud is an essential part of (Kwakiutl) shamanism, or at least of its "greater part," as Boas elsewhere states with much vigor, and if skepticism exists alongside such fraud, then it probably wouldn't require much effort, if any at all, to "adopt" (as Boas puts it) a skeptical attitude toward shamanism when talking to whites, and this would hold true for two connected reasons. The first is that skepticism is part of the greater part and that the

Viscerality, Faith, and Skepticism

Indian is merely being honest and is in fact giving "the native's point of view" in admitting to the fraud, and the second is that insofar as one is being fraudulent vis-à-vis the white interlocutor, presumably one has had much practice with fraud and skepticism in discussing shamanism with fellow Indians anyway.

And what are we to make of the fact that Hunt's scathingly skeptical 1925 autobiographical account of shamanism comes not at the beginning but after forty years of friendship with Boas and that it is the earlier, not the last, versions that are mystical and not skeptical? Does not this timing tend to contradict Boas's attempt to interpret the veracity of his Indian informant when he states that as a general rule the Indian is likely to stress skepticism with whites in order to appear rational? Wouldn't the later version be more likely to be more honest and less concerned with creating a good—that is, rational—impression? What was there to hide about the culture after forty years?[29]

In any event, the colonial relationship through which such sensitive and imaginative activity as shamanism is to be conveyed inevitably becomes no less part of our object of study than the activity itself. To get to the truth about shamanism, we start to realize, means getting to the truth of an intercultural relationship objectified by means of autoethnographic intercultural texts such as the fourth version over three decades of "I Wished to Discover the Ways of the Shaman."[30]

But this is most definitely not to say that the pervasive influence of colonialism accounts for skepticism with regards to the autoethnography of magic. On the contrary. The magic at stake here first and foremost concerns the way in which the colonial presence provides yet another figure to be caught in the legerdemain of revelation and concealment.

Perhaps an outline of Hunt's meteoric shamanic career, as he presents it in his final, 1925, text, will assist us here, although the comforting sense of a career does scant justice to the zigzagging through contradiction that is entailed. First let us dwell on the fact that from the first line of his account, he presents himself as *the arch-doubter, yet wants to learn* the ways of the shamans.

The tension here seems so carefully highlighted that it would surely be reasonable to venture the hypothesis that learning shamanism means sinking ever deeper into ambivalence—an interesting dilemma, perhaps, even a mystical exercise?— doubting it while believing it, doubting practitioners but not the practice, such that continuous oscillation without any resolution is what this learning process is all about.

"I desired to learn about the shaman," he starts off, "whether it is true or whether it is made up and whether they pretend to be shamans." His doubting is all the more striking given that the two shamans with whom he is involved were also, as he states, his "intimate friends."

His first step is to be the target of a shaman's vomited quartz crystal during a public healing ceremony. He himself, we might say, becomes a display object, a ritual within a ritual, a trick not unlike the trick with the concealed down in the mouth that he later learns for healing. Next he appears as a powerful shaman in the dream of a sick boy, the son of a chief, whose dream acts as a detailed script full of technique for the subsequently effective cure he practices on the young dreamer, and with this his fame is ensured, his name is changed, and a succession of shamanic competitions ensue as he travels the land in search of truth and technique in which he exposes other shamans as fakes or at the least puts the healing efficacy of their techniques in grave doubt, such that they are convinced that he possesses a *secret* more powerful than their own.

At this point it should be noted that there is a curious substitution of *secret* for *sacred*. Irving Goldman tells us, for instance, that in many places "the Hunt manuscript is more precise [than Boas's edited and published version] in rendering Kwakiutl meanings. For example, Boas characteristically converts Hunt's 'secret' to 'sacred.'"[31] The implications of this seem devastating. We are immediately alerted to a sort of game, even a conjuring game, in which the sense of something as secret has to be maintained at a pretty high level in the community of believers, but the secret itself must remain secret. What is important is the demand here for the continuous evocation of revelation and concealment.

From the outset Hunt not only privately doubts shamanism but goes out of his way to publicize the fact. It seems culturally important to do this, making it clear that he is "the principal one" who does "not believe in all the ways of the shamans, for I had said so aloud to them."[32]

Yet far from his being the "principal one," he lets you know that one of the first persons he meets after the quartz has been shot into him asks, "Have you not felt the quartz crystals of the liars, the shamans, the one that they referred to that was thrown into your stomach?. . . . You will never feel it, for these are just great lies what the shamans say."[33] And the head chief, Causing-to-be-Well, the next person with whom he speaks, similarly disabuses him: "They are just lies what the shamans say."

Just about everyone, so it seems, revels in declaring shamans to be fakes and rarely lets an opportunity slip to insist on this elemental fact. What's more, each

Viscerality, Faith, and Skepticism

time Hunt, known here as Giving-Potlatches-in-the-World, serves as a target of opportunity for the *revelation of this fakery,* his *desire to learn the ways of the shamans redoubles.* One really has to admire his enthusiasm—no less than that which the accomplished shamans bring to bear to the task of revealing their secrets.

Take the case of the famous Koskimo shaman Aixagidalagilis, he who so proudly sang his sacred song,

Nobody can see through the magic power
Nobody can see through my magic power.

But when Giving-Potlatches-in-the-World (i.e., George Hunt) cured the patient whom Aixagidalagilis was unable to cure, and did this through his *pretense* of trembling and through his *pretense* of sucking out the bloody worm of disease (I am merely emphasizing here what he says in his text), then Aixagidalagilis implores Hunt to reveal his secret:

I pray you to have mercy and tell me what stuck on the palm of your hand last night. Was it the true sickness or was it only made up?[34]

This from the man who used to sing, "Nobody can see through my magic power."

"Your saying to me is not quite good," responds Giving-Potlatches-in-the-World, "for you said 'Is it the true sickness, or is it only made up?'"

Note that this is the very same Giving-Potlatches-in-the-World who has just finished singing his sacred song on completing his successful cure in front of the assembled throng, humiliating Aixagidalagilis:

He tried to prevent me from succeeding, the one who does not succeed. Ah, I shall not try to fail to have no sacred secrets.[35]

Having been bettered, an amazing thing occurs. Aixagidalagilis pours out his secrets: "Let me tell you the way of my head ring of red cedar bark," he says.

Truly, it is made up what is thought by all the men it is done this way. Go on! Feel the thin sharp-pointed nail at the back of the head of this my cedar bark ring, for I tell a lie when I say that the alleged sickness which I pretend

Viscerality, Faith, and Skepticism

to suck out from the sick person. . . . All these fools believe it is truly biting the palm of my hand."[36]

Once they lose out in competition, established shamans beseech Hunt for the secret of his technique. In doing so, however, they seem even more concerned with telling him theirs. In fact their predisposition to confess their secrets is breathtaking. The secret teaching of shamanism has thus built into it this emphatic and deliberate tirade of revelation![37]

Thus the ways by which the deception was achieved is divulged in passionate and loving detail. And what a world is revealed! Nothing seems to have been without pretense, other, of course, than this exposure itself (and the double-headed serpent with the head of a human in its middle, about which more below). "It would be wonderful," Aixagidalagilis says at one point, "if a man could talk with animals and fishes. And so the shamans are liars who say they catch the soul of the sick person, for I know we all own a soul."[38]

It is his daughter, Inviter-Woman, who then recounts what happened to this cynical manipulator that is her shaman-father—of the great unholiness that befell herself and him when, on account of his shame, they fled the haunts of men and in their wandering came across a creature lying crossways on a rock, which they recognized as the double-headed serpent, with a head at each end and a large human head in the middle. Seeing this they died, to be brought back to life by a man who told them he would have brought them good fortune, but because she was menstruating they would have trouble until they died.[39] And from then on they were driven out of their minds. She was laughing as she told this, and then she would cry, pulling out her hair, and her father, the great pretender, died crazed within three winters. And the moral? "Now this is the end of talk about Aixagidalagilis who was believed by all the tribes to be really a great shaman who had gone through (all the secrets). Then I found out that he was just a great liar about everything that he did in his shamanism."[40]

Thus, we might say, shamans might be liars, but menstruation and double-headed serpents are not without a decidedly nasty potential. And surely this is one of those tales that not only belies the satisfaction of a moral or any other system but delights in exploiting the idea of one? This we might with truth call a "nervous system," in which shamanism thrives on a corrosive skepticism and in which skepticism and belief actively cannibalize one another so that continuous injections of recruits, such as Giving-Potlatches-in-the-World, who are full of questioning are required. They are required, so it would seem, to test and there-

Viscerality, Faith, and Skepticism

with brace the mix by serving not as raw material of doubt positioned to termi-
nate as believers, nor yet as cynical manipulators, but as *exposers*—vehicles for
confession for the next revelation of the secret.

Technique is thus revealed as *trick* and it behooves us to inquire further into this
momentous distinction—recalling how fundamental a role the passage from
trick to technique is in Horkheimer and Adorno's beguiling argument regarding
the role of mimesis in the shamanism that in their opinion stands, so to speak,
as doorway to Enlightenment and modern technology. Here I am indebted to
Stanley Walen's reading of shamanic tricks as technique in the Boas-Hunt texts
because of his pointing out the awesome magic of mimesis in which the practitioner sets up a performance, which, through its perfection, spirits will copy. This
follows from the fact that the Kwakiutl believe their world is mimetically doubled
in several ways, that "animals and spirits lead lives exactly equivalent to those of
humans. They live in winter villages, perform dances, wear masks, marry, pray,
and perform all other acts that humans perform." When the shaman sucks disease from the human body, the spirits are there, sucking too. In this way magic
involves what Walens calls "the magnification and intensification of a human action to a greater level of power."[41] Hence he can claim that there is no real paradox involved in shamanism, because the tricks turn out to be models or scenes
for the spirits to follow, and it is the spirits who ultimately supply the cure.

The apparent paradox is a result of the way Enlightenment disenchants the
world such that for most of us spirits are to be explained rather than providing
the explanation. It is devastating, I think, to read Walens when he tells us that the
shaman is at all times dependent on the spirits and that "Kwakiutl pay no attention to the thoughts of the shaman while he is performing the act because the
spirits effect the cure using the shaman as their instrument and the shaman's
thoughts are irrelevant to the efficacy of his cure."[42]

In the Hunt text we read of a shaman talking to his rattle and getting it to swallow the disease of a sick man. Then he says to the spectators: "Did you see my
rattle as it bit the palm of my hand after it had swallowed the great sickness?"

Then he tells the song leaders to sing after him the words of his sacred song.

Do those supernatural ones really see it?
Those supernatural ones see it plainly, those supernatural ones
No one can imitate our great friends the supernatural ones
Wae.[43]

Viscerality, Faith, and Skepticism

Nevertheless, a fundamental objection raises itself here: how does this explanation invoking spirits help us understand the continuous anxiety about pretense and the continuous excavation of fraud through revelation of the secret? In other words, given the creation of these marvelous simulacrums that instigate action on the part of the spirits, why is there continuous concealment and revelation, this other play of viscerality, faith, and skepticism, this play-within-the-play?

I doubt there is a satisfactory answer to this. Yet there is a clue where Walens points out that the "critical part of the cure is the fluidity, skill, and physical perfection with which the shaman performs his tricks, for it is the motions of the tricks (reinforced by their exact duplication by the spirits) that effect the cure."[44]

"Motions of the tricks." Walens calls it fluidity. I call it sheer becoming in which being and nonbeing are transformed into the beingness of transforming forms. In other words, "fluidity" to me suggests mimesis as a sort of streaming metamorphicity rather than replication as with a photograph. In the language set forth by *The Golden Bough,* this is magic of *contagion* and not of *likeness,* what Roman Jakobson, the famous linguist, inspired by the terms set forth in *The Golden Bough,* later called *metonomy,* meaning a sense of physical connection, versus *metaphor,* meaning likeness. Yet neither of these terms do justice to the fluidity that Walens refers to as "the critical part of the cure" because they are both too static and draw attention away from the sheer becoming and instead direct it towards the end result.

What is required of us, I suggest, is that we adopt a particular view of what it is to reciprocate. We have to wrench ourselves away from the idea of reciprocation as a contract between humans and spirits responsible for effecting the cure. Instead it is the fluidity of the mimesis that is at stake and not some form of instrumentally conceived mutual aid. By this I mean that the performer is neither asking for a gift nor entering into a contract with the spirits so much as *gearing into their world* through the perfection of his performance of *beingness.* In later life, Nietzsche saw this as essential to the Dionysian state, in trance or ecstasy, with music and dance, the Dionysian character becomes totally plastic and protean in a rush of becoming other. This is not so much becoming any specific other so much as becoming becoming itself.

Perhaps we could say, therefore, that the crucial thing is the repetition of concealment and revelation, for which moving in and out of the human body is the quintessential staging. "The characteristics of the physical movement made by the ritualist are of the greatest importance," says Walens, "for the particular qualities of the movement he makes during the performance of the ritual will be repeated exactly in form, but with greatly increased power by the spirits."[45]

Viscerality, Faith, and Skepticism

An immensely suggestive feature is left hanging here, along with perfection and skill. "As long as the shaman performs his actions fluidly," insists Walens, "the spirits are conjoined by cosmic forces to use their power to cure."[46] And whatever fluidity is, it is not *bungling*. "The shaman who bungles his tricks," Walens goes on to say, "forces the spirits to perform actions that are as disjointed, undirected, and destructive as his." Not only does this bungling not result in a cure, but far worse, it actually kills people by unleashing what Walens refers to as "uncontrollable chaotic power on the world." For this reason, the bungler must be immediately killed before he or she can do greater damage. To say the least, this puts Giving-Potlatches-in-the-World's desire to learn the ways of the shaman in admirable perspective. If what Walens states is true, then it would seem almost suicidal to be a shaman.

I am reminded of Boas describing the reaction of members of the seal society when they notice a mistake in the dancing or singing of the performer in the Winter Ceremonial; they jump from their seats and bite and scratch the person who made the mistake, who then pretends to faint, meaning that the spirit has taken the performer away. Members of the seal society sit on the platform of the house or stand during the dances to be certain of discovering mistakes. It is said that in former times, if the cannibal dancer fell while dancing, he was killed by the other cannibal dancers, often at the insistence of the dancer's father.[47]

Whatever we might mean here by sacredness, it surely has a great deal to do with the flow in technique in Kwakiutl shamanism, a shamanism that bears heavily on the facility with which soul can be dislocated from the body, implicating not one but several bodies and energies flowing into and out of one another across borders accessed by dream, surrealism, and animal visitations. Take the toad or the wolves come down the beach vomiting foam over the human body while the others lie dying on account of the holocaust brought by white society in the form of smallpox, reducing the Kwakiutl population by an unbelievable 80 to 90 percent from 1862 to 1929. (The precontact population has been estimated as between 15,000 to 20,000 persons.)[48]

As I understand it, the flow is in the song, the body of the song, which takes speech to another plane of being's being. Flow is what is going on between animals and humans—as from the very beginning of Kwakiutl time when the original ancestors took off their animal masks and skins to present their human selves. The flow is also from the clothes, presumably of the white people, the flow of the pox. "After we had stepped from our canoe," recounts Fool, describing how he became a shaman, "we found much clothing and flour. We took them and ten

Viscerality, Faith, and Skepticism

days later became sick with the great smallpox. We lay in bed in our tent. I was laying among them. Now I saw that all our bodies swelled and were dark red. Our skins burst open and I did not know that they were all dead and I was laying among them. Then I thought I also was dead." Wolves came down to the beach, whining and howling, licking his body, he recounted, vomiting foam, which they put into his body. They tried hard, he explains, to put foam all over his body, continuously licking him and turning him all over. When it was all licked off, they vomited over him again, licking off the scabs of smallpox in the process.

All manner of incredible things happen here, beginning with the devastating smallpox left by the white man. Then there is the fact that the wolf speaks as a human and it is the same wolf who said his name was Harpooner-Body that Fool had saved out at sea on a rock earlier choking to death on a bone. The wolf not only vomits foam over the dying Fool but nuzzles his nose into his sternum as if trying hard to enter into him too. Perhaps Fool is making all this up, equivalent to the legerdemain for which shamanism is famous. But then this weaving in and out of other realities, akin to weaving in and out of other bodies, is what living in that Kwakiutal world is all about. "He sat down seaward from me and nudged me with his nose that I should lie down on my back, and he vomited and pushed his nose against the lower end of my sternum. He vomited the magic power into me . . . Now I was a shaman."[49]

Above all, however, what I find outstanding is a certain quality of flow-within-flow provided by materials such as vomit and foam, how they are made to cover the human body while with equal assiduity they are then removed through licking. This amounts to the same action as concealing and revealing, reinforced by the fact that it is clothes, outer coverings, that are left on the beach that attract the Indians, and that the smallpox has one its leading manifestations, the pustules and redness of the swollen skin, blowing out as an envelope from the frame of the body. What is more it is the wolf's insides—its tongue—licking up the exteriorized material from its deeper insides—its own foam-vomit—that clinches this engagement of insides with outsides, endlessly repeated at the point of immense death there on the smallpox scene of the beach. "Now I saw I was lying among my dead past nephews."[50]

"We might say," says Walens, "that the Kwakiutl play games as much with the spirits as with their human opponents."[51] In this regard it is illuminating to read the vicissitudes of Boas's translation of the Kwakiutl name of the stupendously important Winter Ceremonial, when the spirits emerge in their fullness from

Viscerality, Faith, and Skepticism

November well into the following year and take over the life of the villages. This is when humans impersonate the spirits. They enact the myths pertaining to the origins of human acquisition of supernatural powers from some fifty-three human-animal doubles such as Wolf, Killer Whale, Eagle, Thunderbird, and Man Eater ("Cannibal Dancer").[52]

The name of the Winter Ceremonial, *tsetseqa,* is curious. Boas says it means "fraudulent" or "to cheat," as well as being synonymous with *to be good-minded* and *happy.* "For instance, when a person wants to find out whether a shaman has real power or whether his power is based on pretense, he uses the same term meaning 'pretended, fraudulent, made-up' shaman. Even in the most serious presentations of the ceremonial, it is clearly and definitely stated that it is planned as a *fraud.*"[53] In *The Mouth of Heaven,* Irving Goldman tries to mitigate this curiousness by arguing that Boas's translation is crude. It should, claims Goldman, using Boas's posthumous grammar, mean *imitated.*[54]

Here, I think, fortuitous as it may be, we have located the core of the riddle, especially when one notes that Boas had, according to Goldman, "in an earlier stab at translation" suggested that the stem of the word for the winter ceremonial, *tseka,* meant *secrets.*

There is a certain anxiety, even pain and craziness, here, as Goldman heatedly insists that to imitate is not necessarily to secularize. Who ever said it was? What's the problem? All these words start to swim in multiple and multiply conflicting configurations of overlapping associations and streams of reversible meanings:

fraud
simulation
exalted
imitation
secret
happiness
sacred

From here on, the ground becomes steep and slippery and perhaps only fools dare go further, as the impenetrable mysteries of representation and reality, within Western philosophy alone, not to mention Kwakiutl, emerge full force.

Yet if there is a moral, it might be this: that the real novice-shaman in "I Wished to Discover the Ways of the Shaman" was Franz Boas and, beyond him, by im-

plication, the science of man he came to spearhead and the momentous historical moment of modernity that spawned this science. This, of course, very much
implicates us too and yet gives us the choice provided by this insight. For the
point of the text as I read it (and as is amply confirmed by Boas's later commentary) is not that Boas as a neutral observer and recording angel somehow lucked
out and found the one unique Enlightenment individual ready to challenge
hocus-pocus and give the inside story to our man from New York, nor even that
there seems to be a ready supply of such skeptics, but that the text in itself, an artifact of the fledgling science of anthropology, especially one given over to giving
the natives' point of view, is an utterly perfect instance of the confession of the secret, the very acme of the skilled revelation of skilled concealment— in this case
using a scholarly inflected academic anthropological text—another form of
"winter ceremonial," another form of rite, as the vehicle for carrying this out.

In other words, this text is not so much about shamanism as it is shamanic in
its conformity to the cannibalistic logic of having to have ever-fresh recruits
for ceaseless confession, such that in its very skepticism lies its profound magic,
making it difficult to accept Lévi-Strauss's conclusion that at the end Giving-
Potlatches-in-the-World seems to have lost sight of his fallacious technique and,
by implication, has crossed the threshold from skepticism to faith, from science
to magic. For Levi-Strauss's mistake lies in not having taken with enough seriousness the necessity for skepticism in magic as relayed through rituals of exposure and unmasking and, second, in not having seen the text "I Desired to Learn
the Ways of the Shaman" as in itself just this very ritual transposed into textual
form and readied as science by the anthropologist. Leaving this text as Kwakiutal-
speak in the mode of Boas or recruiting it as does Lévi-Strauss for the purpose of
validating structuralism, misses the point but also the invitation that such ritual
offers—that it lives as magic and makes claims even on us non-Indians in its re-
quest for a reciprocal response composed in equal measure of confessional responsibility and judicious and intricately moving medleys of skepticism and
faith, continuously deferred through the opening and closing of the secret.

For we have our tricks to develop too, "the trick of the floating quartz crystal," we
might call this, involving a heightened sensitivity to fluidity, mass, and movement no less than to ecstatic moments of appearance and disappearance of
objects inside and between bodies as when the liberated quartz crystal vomited
out by the shaman Making-Alive enters the body of our friend here, Giving-
Potlatches-in-the-World. "'Now this one will be a great shaman,' said he."[55] This

Viscerality, Faith, and Skepticism

suggests a certain fluidity of performance with human identities, if not with the logic of becoming itself, the song leaders beating fast time as Fool looks upward, watching the quartz float around in the cedar beams, while Making-Alive staggers like a drunk around the fire in the middle of the house in front of a great mass of onlookers.

Might we not say that the reality of shamanism hangs on the reality of this fragment of flickering light in tumbling stone, passing between intestines through streams of vomit, lost for the moment in a graceful float up there in the cedar rafters?

There are many issues here, but keep your eye on the quartz crystal floating free. For who knows how short or long a time it stays up in the air heavy with the tension of bodily interconnection? The quartz is a trick and the trick is a figure and the figure of the trick is one of continuous movement and metamorphosis in, through, and between bodies, carrying power one jump ahead of its interpretation. The language of true or false seems not just peculiarly inept here but deliberately so.

At one point, struggling to understand the place of theater and spirit impersonation in the Winter Ceremonial, Irving Goldman seems to be stating that mimetic simulation is a way of keeping hidden things hidden while at the same time revealing them, of keeping secret things secret while displaying them. "The ceremonies deal with the secret matters that are always hidden and can be experienced, therefore, only in a simulated form."[56]

I can think of no better way of expressing my thesis regarding the skilled revelation of skilled concealment.

DANCING THE QUESTION

Indeed, skepticism is included in the pattern of belief in witchdoctors. Faith and skepticism are alike traditional.[57]

Witchcraft was ubiquitous in Zande life when Evans-Pritchard, fondly remembered in anthropological circles as EP, carried out fieldwork in the watersheds of the Nile and Congo rivers in the early 1930s, and it was witchcraft, oracles, and magic that were the focus of interest of his first publication about these people in a book that through the sheer brilliance of its writing and intellect came to define the field of study of magic, and much else besides. Yet at the outset, it should be emphasized how curiously unclear this transparently transparent book actually is when any particular point is examined, how certainties dissolve into ever more

mystifying contradictions magically dispelled, momentarily, as it were, by the author's self-assured explanations of the multifarious aspects of magical phenomena. I take this to be striking confirmation of how magic begs for and at the same time resists explanation most when appearing to be explained and that therefore in its unmasking, magic is in fact made even more opaque, a point given a special twist here through the technique, or is it a trick? of (what Clifford Geertz has called) EP's "transparencies."[58]

Now, witch-doctors are those persons, generally male, whose task it is to divine the presence and identity of a witch in this witch-infested Zande land and heal the sicknesses arising therefrom. They belong to corporations with group secrets. Initiation into the group is long and arduous. These secrets are the knowledge of medicines together with what EP calls their "tricks of the trade," principal of which is the actual extraction by hand or mouth of objects such as bits of charcoal, splinters, black beetles, or worms from the body of the victim of witchcraft. There are plenty of other tricks too, such as vomiting blood, extracting worms from one's own person, resting heavy weights on one's chest, and shooting black beetles and bits of charcoal from one's leg into the body of somebody else, even

Viscerality, Faith, and Skepticism

over large distances. But no trick is as secretly guarded, in EP's narrative, as that of extracting the witchcraft object from the body of the sick. Whether we are to call these tricks or techniques, I for the moment leave for you to decide. (That is pretty much an EP sort of sentence, in both senses of the word.)

The doctors would not divulge their secrets to EP. He in turn decided that entering into the corporation himself would be counterproductive and so instead paid for his Zande servant, Kamanga, to undergo initiation in order to "to learn all about the techniques of witchdoctors." Kamanga, we are told, was a gullible man with profound faith in witch-doctors.[59]

EP was able to learn even more by using the secrets elicited by Kamanga to play on rivalries between doctors. But he felt sure that certain things, notably the extraction of witchcraft objects, would not be told to Kamanga because he had been "straightforward," as he says, in telling the doctors that he expected Kamanga to pass on all he had learned. "In the long run, however," EP adds, striking a militant note, "an ethnographer is bound to triumph. Armed with preliminary knowledge nothing can prevent him from driving a deeper and deeper wedge if he is interested and persistent."[60]

We seem a long way from Nietzsche's gay science, in which "We no longer believe that truth remains truth when the veils are withdrawn. . . . What is required for that is to stop courageously at the surface, the fold, the skin, to adore appearance."[61] But like most of us, EP just has to get to the bottom with his wedge driving deeper and deeper—his aim is to expose the exposure of the witchcraft object extracted through the surface, the fold, the skin, as if penetrated by surgical incision.

What's more, his obsessive search for truth seems to share a good deal with the doctors whose secrets he is intent on uncovering. Like them he uses artifice and like them he extracts worms, or their equivalent: "It would," he declares, "have been possible by using *every artifice* to have eventually *wormed out* all their secrets, but this would have meant bringing undue pressure on people to divulge what they wished to hide."[62] And while the anthropologist digs deep, be it noted, the witch-doctor brings the secret to the surface, counterposed movements destined to meet in the pages of the monograph, a triumphant conjunction of movements through which the anthropologist is drawn into a ritual scheme, neither of his own choosing nor understanding—that in telling the witch-doctors his servant is to reveal to him the secrets they tell to him, he is thereby fulfilling to the letter the need for unmasking that the secrets of their magic actually demand. In other words, there is this oblique ritual of exposure of the secret within the witch-doctors' ritual, which the presence of the anthropologist has here drawn from its otherwise obscure existence.

Such rituals of exposure seemed common enough. Young nobles loved to expose witch-doctors by tricking them—an activity EP refers to as "testing" and as "playing a joke." He tells us how a commoner friend of his, Mbira, once placed a knife in a covered pot and asked doctors to divine what lay within. The three doctors danced in the fierce sun the better part of the day, trying unsuccessfully to ascertain the contents, and, grabbing the opportunity, one sought out Mbira in his hut and pleaded he be secretly told the answer and thus avoid humiliation. Mbira refused, calling him a knave.[63] Only a people imbued with a measure of skepticism could indulge in such activities, EP points out (neglecting to wonder at the witch-doctors' motivation in agreeing to participate in such tests), and yet Mbira believed firmly in every kind of magic, was himself a magician of standing, and consulted witch-doctors when he had a problem. But I want to go further and ask why a sincere or even just your middling sort of skeptic would want to indulge in such sport given such skepticism? And the answer, I submit, has a good deal to do with the need for rites of exposure built into rites of magic in order to strengthen magic itself.

There is in EP's book a dramatic moment of great poignancy concerning rites of exposure, and as an aside, I would like to note how wonderfully postmodern this 1930s straight-from-the-hip text is, how it has sneaked into the canon for other than what it is, you might say, with its anecdotal form of analysis; its studious, almost manic aversion to theory in place of storytelling; its constant swerving away from what is supposed to be the point; and, above all, the way its contradictions not merely pass for a seamless argument regarding the explanation of witchcraft, for instance, but are indispensable to it. The "closed system" of witchcraft consisting of a web of mutually reinforcing propositions impervious to contradiction, made famous by this book, is exemplified by the book itself. The book is the best example of the witchcraft it purports to explain.

Far be it for me to expose such exposure. Instead I want to recall that memorable day EP out-tricked the trickster when his servant, Kamanga, under the tutelage of his instructor, Bogwozu, was about to wipe the body of a sick man (another servant of EP's) with the poultice of grass prepared by Bogwozu. This, we are told, is standard medical practice. It is wiped over the abdomen of the patient with the aim of extracting an object of witchcraft, which, if extracted, is shown to the patient, who is then likely to recover. But it was this technique that, to EP's chagrin, the witch-doctors stubbornly refused to impart to Kamanga because

Viscerality, Faith, and Skepticism

"they were naturally anxious that" EP "should not know their trade secret.[64] It was a complicated state of affairs, made even more so by the fact that Kamanga himself stubbornly held to the belief that there was no trickery involved in this technique. Now I want you to concentrate on the complexity of this situation in its various shadings of gullibility and trickery, faith and skepticism.

First, the anthropologist tricks the witch-doctor:

> When the teacher handed over the poultice to his pupil I took it from him to pass it to Kamanga, but in doing so I felt for the object which it contained and removed it between my finger and thumb while pretending to make a casual examination of the kind of stuff the poultice consisted of and commenting on the material.
>
> It was a disagreeable surprise for Kamanga when, after massaging his patient's abdomen through the poultice, in the usual manner of witch-doctors, and after then removing the poultice, he could not find any object of witchcraft in it.[65]

Then, the exposure:

> I considered the time had now come to stop proceedings and I asked Kamanga and his teacher to come to my hut a few yards away, where I told them that I had removed the charcoal from the poultice, and asked Bogwozu to explain how it had got there. For a few minutes he pretended incredulity and asked to see the object, since he said that such a thing was impossible, but he was clever enough to see that further pretence would be useless, and, as we were in private, he made no further difficulty about admitting the imposture.[66]

We can read this as yet another crass instance of colonial power flexing Enlightenment muscle against primitive magic, staging its own rites of scientific method right there in the heartland of magic. We could also read this a quite different way, that the anthropologist was doing little more than the culturally appropriate thing. For just as Mbira took delight in ridiculing witch-doctors as described above, so the anthropologist was following a well-worn path, although there are no instances described of Zande's being as sneaky or as daring as EP in actually removing the key to the trick midway through the healing of a sick person. After all, it is one thing to test a doctor's powers. It is another thing to trick him and, who knows? thereby contribute to the death of the sick person.

In any case, the point to consider here is whether the anthropologist was himself part of a larger and more complex staging in which exposure of tricks is the name of the game and that what we are witness to via the text is an imaginative, albeit unintended and serendipitous, rendition of the skilled revelation of the skilled concealment necessary to the mix of faith and skepticism necessary to magic.

Finally, we have to consider the effect that the teacher's confession and the revelation of trickery had on the young pupil: It seems like unmasking actually adds to, rather than eliminates, the *mysterium tremendum* of magic's magic.

> The effects of these disclosures on Kamanga was devastating. When he had recovered from his astonishment he was in serious doubt whether he ought to continue his initiation. He could not at first believe his eyes and ears, but in a day or two he had completely recovered his poise and *developed a marked degree of self-assurance which if I am not mistaken he had not shown before this incident.*[67]

We see this paradoxical impact of unmasking again when the anthropologist, constantly on the lookout for "tricks," fails to see that he is instead party to the skilled revelation of skilled concealment. For example, Kisanga, "a man of unusual brilliance," told EP how a witch-doctor begins his treatment:

> When a man becomes sick they send for a witch-doctor. Before the witch-doctor comes to the sick man he scrapes down an animal's bone and hammers it till it is quite small and then drops it into the medicines in his horn. He later arrives at the homestead of the sick man and takes a mouthful of water and swills his mouth round with it and opens his mouth so that people can look into it. He also spreads out his hands to them so that every one can see them, and speaks thus to them: "Observe me well, I am not a cheat, since I have no desire to take anything from any one fraudulently."[68]

"Some training in trickery is essential," writes the anthropologist in that confidence-restoring tone that talking about other people's trickery seems to always instill.

In the first place, the Zande has a broad streak of skepticism towards his leeches who have therefore to be careful that their sleight-of-hand is not observed. . . . If the treatment is carried out in a certain manner, as when the *bingba* grass is used as a poultice, he will be frankly suspicious. But if the witch-doctor sits down on a stool and calls upon a third person to cut *kpoyo* bast and make a poultice of it, rinses his mouth with water, and holds his hands for inspection, suspicions will be allayed.[69]

It is hard not to feel these ostentatiously demonstrative acts of denial are saying the very opposite and that everyone knows (and probably enjoys) that. It is also hard to believe that the anthropologist is alone in detecting skilled concealment of trickery as when he writes, "If you accompany a witch-doctor on one of his visits you will be convinced, if not of the validity of his cures, at least of his skill. As far as you can observe, everything which he does appears to be aboveboard, and you will notice nothing which might help you to detect fraud."[70]

EP is so busy looking for concealed trickery he doesn't realize that he might be a privileged witness of its skilled revelation and that the secret of the secret is that there is none or, rather, that the secret is a public secret, something generally known but that cannot generally be articulated. This is not a question of seeing more or seeing less or seeing behind the skin of appearance. Instead it turns on seeing how one is seeing. Whatever magic is, it must also involve this turn within the known unknown and on what this turn turns on, namely, a new attitude to skin. As Nietzsche would have it, the biggest secret of all is that there is no "underneath" or "behind." God is dead and metaphysics is magic.

DEFERRAL, PERFORMED

The way I read him there are by EP's reckoning two ways by which faith manages to live with and overcome skepticism concerning witch-doctors. One is what was noted by E. B. Tylor by way of *probabilities* wherein one says that even though most doctors are fake, there are some who are not, and it is often the case, says EP, that a Zande never knows whether any particular doctor is a cheat or not and hence faith in any particular practitioner is tempered by skepticism. There is, in other words, a rock-steady ideal of the truly endowed witch-doctor who can divine and cure the evil effects of witches, and now and again the ideal appears actualized. Let it be noted that the probability of the ideal being actualized increases the farther you go from home; the magic of the other is more truly magical, and faith lies in distance and hence difference.

The second way by which faith coexists with and even triumphs over skepticism lies in the use of *substances*, of which there are two: herbal medicines; and the human body, as with the body of the witch, inheritor of witchcraft substance, *mangu,* and as with the witch-doctor's medicine-laden body in motion, dancing the questions.[71] If the first mode, that of probabilities, rests on the logic of the general and the particular, the ideal and the actual; the second rests on the heterogeneity of matter as force.

It is *deferment* that these two apparently dissimilar explanations for the coexistence of faith with skepticism have in common, a continuous and relentless deferral —a positing and flow of intellection that stands in marked contrast to the driving of the wedge, the wedge itself being driven by the quest for the catharsis of the triumphant revelation of the secret. The explanation through probabilities refers us back to where we started in the middle of the problem of magic's truth, which is a truth continuously questioning its own veracity of being. Circular reasoning and doublings back are the movements of intellection here, not the wedge. Deferral also lies here in the power of the "stranger effect," meaning that truth lies in a never-attainable beyond and that cheating is merely the continuous and expected prelude to the mere possibility of authenticity, for behind this cheat stands the shadow of the real in all its perfection, but even this real is strange and never homely or destined for homeliness for all of that. Authenticity is that beyond that is permanently beyond the horizon of being.

As for medicines, in many ways the bedrock of the entire system of witch-doctoring, subject of careful instruction over years of training and of much secrecy as well, deferral could not be more obvious on account of the massive, world-consuming tautology on which the medicines rest; namely, that not only do they serve as the basis for faith in witch-doctoring, as EP's text tirelessly informs us, but the medicines are themselves the quintessence of magical power, and so we end up with no end in sight but that of tracing an endless circle in which magic explains magic. It is medicine that ensures magical power, as in accuracy of divination. "Thus my old friend Ongosi used to tell me," the anthropologist informs us, that "most of what the witch-doctors told their audiences was just *bera,* just 'supposition': they think out what is the most likely cause of any trouble, and put it forward, in the guise of an inspired oracle, as a likely guess, but it is not *sangba ngua,* the words of medicine, i.e., it is not derived from the medicines they have eaten."[72]

To become a witch-doctor, one must learn the medicines and partake in the communal meal of these medicines with other doctors as well as be taken to their legendary source, a stream in the watershed of the Nile and Congo rivers, where, in caves, some of the more powerful plants are to be found. There are many mag-

Viscerality, Faith, and Skepticism

ical things about medicine, beginning with the fact that medicine connects the interiority of one's body with other bodies and with substances exterior to one's body. Indeed it is with medicine that the very force of being—as opposed to meaning— is best established, medicines being the fluid flow by which the exterior penetrates the interior to fundamentally empower the soul of the doctor-in-training.

The novice must hold his face in the steam of the cooking pot but with his eyes open so that the medicines will eventually allow him to see witches and witchcraft. The medicines are served in a highly ritualistic way, with the server offering the spoonful of medicine from the cooking pot to the mouth of one man, only to quickly remove it as he goes to swallow it by offering it to another. Incisions are made on the chest, above the shoulder blades, and on the wrists and face, and medicine is rubbed in.[73] The medicines are spoken to as they are being cooked and as they are being rubbed into the novice's body. As soon as a novice has eaten medicine, he begins to dance.

Medicine must be paid for, that is, it must be reciprocated by another gift otherwise the medicine may not work, and payment must be made in sight of the medicine. "Purchase is part of the ritual conditioning of the magic which gives it potency," we are told, and this seems to imply some humanlike mentation and capacity for retribution on the part of the medicine itself, as much as of a dissatisfied vendor. EP tells us of a witch-doctor placing money—an Egyptian piaster—of his own on the ground when treating a patient, explaining "that it would be a bad thing if the medicine did not observe a fee, for it might lose its potency."[74] At one point, EP refers to this exchange as a gift.

If angered, a witch-doctor can use magic to remove the magic of the medicine he has "sold" to a novice by taking a forest creeper and attaching it to the top of a flexible stick stuck in the ground to form a sort of bowstring, to which he brings a few drops of the magic of thunder such that the medicine will roar and break the creeper, the top half flying on high, the lower staying in the earth. As the top half flies, so the medicine flies out of the novice.[75] This is one of the very few instances where magic depends on metaphor—as opposed to substances in contact with one another. By far the bulk of the instances supplied in this long text referring to witch-doctors are visceral and concern flows of physical force and interruptions to such flows in chains of metamorphic connectedness.

In any event, it certainly seems like that what we have here are powerful instances of magic explaining magic in a circular, albeit staggered, manner, and that this is the movement of deferral par excellence in which the very idea of a secret behind a facade to be unearthed by the zealous ethnographer driving his wedge is extraordinarily naïve.

Nowhere does the existence of deferral intrinsic to the mix required of faith and skepticism find more dramatic expression than in the witch-doctors' séance of divination. "A witch-doctor does not only divine with his lips, but with his whole body. He dances the questions which are put to him," states the anthropologist in what must be the most exquisite description of dance in anthropological writing, comparable to that of Maya Deren.[76]

He dances the questions. His body moves back and forth in the semicircle bounded by the witch-doctors' upturned horns filled with medicines. He kicks up his leg if annoyed by the slackness of the chorus of young boys and may shoot black beetles into them. The spectators throw their questions concerning the witchcraft bothering them. Back and forth, question and answer, another circle is being traced as the doctor leaps and swirls through the heat of the day for hours on end as the answer is ever more re- fined through clever elimination of alternatives and leaps of intuition. Gongs and drums resound. Back and forth go the questions and the answers as the public secrets of envy and resentment are aired in this flurry and fury of intellect and bodies in motion.

The dancing is ecstatic and violent. The dancer slashes his body, and blood flows. Saliva froths around the lips. The medicines in the body are activated by the dance, just as the medicines in their turn activate dancing. When a question is put to a particular doctor, he responds by going up to the drummers to give a solo performance, and when he can dance no more, as if intoxicated, he shakes his hand bells to tell the drummers to cease and, his body doubled over, looks into the medicines obtained in his upturned horns on the ground and he voices his oracular reply. He dances the question, and the dancing is spectacular. "The dance of the Zande witch-doctors," writes the anthropologist, "is one of the few performances I have witnessed in Africa which really comes up to the standards of sensational journalism. It is weird and intoxicating."[77] Here trickery is deferred, transmuted into theater where theater meets the magic—the weirdness and intoxication—of a ritual. The various dichotomies of trick and technique, intellect and intuition, secrecy and public secrecy, are deferred by a series of other types of knowledge given in a body dancing the question under an open sky. This is neither a question of replacing mind by body nor of sense by the senses but of giving to the skilled revelation of skilled concealment a density and fluidity almost sufficient to dispel the craving for certainty that secrecy inspires. It is this

Viscerality, Faith, and Skepticism

revelation of the already known, the public secret, that the witch-doctor dances in his dance of faith and skepticism.

TURNING TRICKS

All along I have been asking myself, What, then, is a trick? I keep thinking of the way a trick is a subterfuge but also something that highlights nature's mysteries as well as those inherent to social institutions and personal relationships. I think of the tricks performed by an acrobat or by a diver performing twists and somersaults or a cardsharp pulling aces. All these tricks require inordinate skill, inordinate technique, inordinate empathy with reality. Wouldn't this make the trick equivalent to technology, that inner knowing, the art and magic, which has to be added to technology so it fully functions? By the same token, is magic cheating on technique, or is it instead the supreme level of technique, so rarified, so skilled, that it passes from mere technique to something we might dignify as magical or sacred—as with a musician, a brain surgeon, or a short-order cook?

Like a gambler or a shaman, the practitioners of such skills take on the laws—the natural laws—of chance and scorning distance they use mimesis to merge with the object imitated. This is a sexual act as that devout gambler, Walter Benjamin, noted in describing gambling as an erotic passion whose thrill lay in cheating on fate.[78] This brings us back to the beginning, to those "corporeal techniques" that Marcel Mauss said underlie all our mystic states for entering into communication with God. As I have tried to show, such techniques of the body notably employ sleight of hand involving revelation and concealment, that is to say, skilled revelation of skilled concealment. Whether God really listens is another matter, but between the bosom of Justice and that of Janet Jackson, we can surely plot the curve of our epoch and its hopes.

Viscerality, Faith, and Skepticism

Transgression

At first sight it seems strange if not absurd and confusing to claim that transgression is a key component of religion: strange because mainstream religions in our time seem more concerned with controlling and eliminating transgression, and confusing because transgression turns out to be the quintessence of intellectual and emotional uncertainty, and this must be of great significance for what is referred to as sacred. Doubtless these issues would be best explored and enunciated through historical study of a particular religion in a particular location in order to eschew the universalizing pseudotruths that plague the study of religions. But because historical and concrete exploration itself presupposes a dialectical dependence on principles of analysis, it is my aim, in the limited space here, to provide an elaboration of transgression in terms of negation and its connection with taboo.

Much has been made of the implications in Latin-derived languages, and hence in Christianity, of the negation built into the word "sacred" in its meaning of accursed as well as holy, impure as well as pure, and thus its suggestion, at least poetically, of a deep wound and the necessity thereof in holiness per se. This sense of negation as within and constitutive of the sacred has been most widely explored in modern Western discussions of the concept of taboo at the turn of the

An earlier version of this chapter was published in Mark C. Taylor, ed., *Critical Terms for Religious Studies* (Chicago: University of Chicago Press, 1998).

century: for example, Freud's elegant summary of its connotations *combining* sacredness, purity, danger, the unclean, the uncanny, and the forbidden.[1] The salient property of danger present in this fascinating complex of negation, with its mutually nourishing oppositions, is its considerable if undefinable power to attract and repulse (compared by numerous authors with electricity!).

Another striking instance of the dominant role of negation is Emile Durkheim's obsessive discussion of the sacred as that which (1) is not profane and exists separated and set apart and (2) is hedged in by prohibitions, as if the sacred is first and foremost the worshipful negative. Whether one agrees or not, one can only be struck full of wonder at the perverse and unexpected nature of this carefully worked-out framework for analysis and stand perplexed at the dizzying logic unleashed as the negative negatively defines something ineffable (we recall the "electricity").[2]

The power of the negative, however, cannot be construed as a simple barrier, because in being separated, something is connected as much as it is dislocated from that which it is set apart, and it is on the curious tension of negations embodied in this relationship that we need to focus attention. Nor can such tension be assimilated to the telos of order characteristic of both the semiotic paradigm of French structuralism (as in the work of Claude Lévi-Strauss) and the scaled-down version of this semiotics emerging from the British structural functionalism apparent in Mary Douglas's elaboration of the idea that impurity is disorder, and that "ideas about separating, purifying, demarcating and punishing transgressions have as their main function to impose system on an inherently untidy experience."[3] What emerges from this is what a tough time transgression is going to have of it intellectually, in that its very being transgresses deeply embedded norms of intellection, of making sense through making order.

But would we have gotten into the issue of transgression if we hadn't expected a rough ride? As a first approximation we have to consider that the barrier crossed by transgression does not so much exist in its own right as erupt into being on account of its being transgressed. Second, we have to try to understand that this barrier is one of repulsion and attraction, open and closed at the same time. On this basis, then, in which we can see the encounter of Nietzsche with Hegel, negation should be understood as an endlessly discharging circuit of taboo and transgression, as if fearsome barriers were erected precisely in order to be crossed. Moreover, it is in the charged space thus opened up by transgression that we encounter empowering and sacred ritual caused by and causative of this "space."

Take for example the initiation rites for young men and boys described for the turn-of-the-century Thonga (in present-day Mozambique) by the Swiss missionary Henri Junod in his *Life of a South African Tribe*. Junod relates how the boys are placed in a self-contained, separated, and heavily tabooed fenced-in compound for three months, during which time serious transgressions of other taboos, including sexual transgressions, have to occur to bring about the mystical transformation of the boys into men. Important too are the secret formulae transmitted by the older men to the initiates, which include what are considered obscene images and ideas. Girls are subject to similar rites on a reduced scale, and we see the same curious logic of transgression involved in funerals, war, and the moving of a village.[4]

In post–World War II anthropology, Victor Turner built on Junod's work and the latter's use of Arnold Van Gennep's idea of rites of passage to accentuate the importance of a so-called liminal period outside normality, a period involving an enclosed, set-apart, theatrical-like space of make-believe for the representation and visceral realization of sacred force.[5] It is striking how in Turner's hands this liminal period has been V-chipped or censored such that the force of negation and hence of transgression, is virtually erased. Indeed, with the passage of time and the further development of the idea, his depictions became increasingly balmy and innocent, with erotic, obscene, sadistic, cruel, and licentious features bleached out—much like the trajectory described by Nietzsche and Bataille for the evolution of Christianity itself. Even more important is that Turner was by no means alone among anthropologists in consciously or unconsciously avoiding transgressive features and their importance in religion, even though the material that came to light around this time from serious ethnographic work in highland New Guinea (let alone what existed in the earlier ethnographic record in general) could hardly be accommodated to such a genteel view.

It is useful philosophically to speculate as to why there has been such aversion to meeting the transgressive material head-on and analyzing its religious significance. The sort of detail brought to light by Junod or the questions posed decades later in 1929 by E. E. Evans-Pritchard in his brief paper "Some Collective Expressions of Obscenity in Africa," were rapidly forgotten (but not by that oddball nonanthropologist and one-time member of the recently resurrected College of Sociology Roger Caillois, in his *Man and the Sacred*).[6] Likewise pushed aside for serious consideration were the presence and crucial importance of transgression in the Christian church of the Middle Ages with regard to liturgy as well as to feasts such as carnival, no less than in the Dionysian elements in the religion of ancient Greece and Rome and the tantric and "left-handed" currents of Hinduism, Buddhism, and Islam.

A telling symptom of the evasion was the virtual torrent of enthusiastic publications such as Max Gluckman's "Licence in Ritual," which concerns "rituals of reversal" in which, for a brief time of licensed transgression, rulers become servants, kings or queens are humiliated, men dress as women or vice versa, and things serious are exposed to ridicule and monstrous reflection.[7] In the writings of modern scholars, it is impossible to escape the utilitarian explanation that such excitements were merely part of a social narrative whose function was to enforce the status quo, yet such analyses in themselves, so to speak, were generally enlivened by a surreptitious countermove as these same scholars, searching for an escape from such a tedious conclusion, identified with the temporary madness and ecstasy of what they were writing about. In other words, the claims to stability and function were not completely containable. There was always this excess creeping out from under the scholarly depictions with their inevitable functionalist stamp of approval. Could the reversal and the transgression expressed beckon to another world altogether different and no less wonderful than terrifying?

This dilemma was especially marked in reactions to the celebrated work of Mikhail Bakhtin on Rabelais and carnival.[8] Here the "licensed transgression" of another era, early modern Europe, becomes nostalgically wrought by Bakhtin's reading into carnival and the poetics of the laughing belly the heroically lost cause of humor and dream in the struggle against Stalinism that was taking place as he was writing his study in semiexile in the far reaches of the Soviet Union in the 1930s. The pathos of the Cold War ensured that Bakhtin's "message," once translated decades later into English, would be purified in scholarly reflection on laughter, while the horror of the gulag would remain unexamined as no less a mark of transgression than carnival. For all his references to the belly and genitals, Bakhtin's sense of the transgressive was interpreted as allied with the angels and eminently respectable, while writers in the tradition of de Sade or Bataille, for instance, can never be assimilated in this or any other way, and their laughter remains mired in death, the corpse, and eroticism. Indeed, here we are forcefully made aware that transgression necessarily finds terrible application in the study of the sacred dimensions of violence in our time, as with the Holocaust and the ever-increasing ethnic conflicts of the late twentieth century.

In most instances it would seem that the aversion to trying to think through the nature of transgression in religion was not directly due to the analytic predilections of any particular theoretical school but could be attributed to the influence of taste and morality in modern times simply closing down massive areas of human experience as consolidated by the combined action of Christianity and Enlightenment in harness with the utilitarian postulates of capitalist common sense. It is this blocking of feeling and the capability of expression that Georges Bataille identifies as his subject and the source of his anxiety in his preface to his *History of Eroticism,* where he describes how we "manage in any case to substitute empty thinking for those moments when it seem[s] to us, however, that the very heavens [are] opening." As against this he wanted to "lay out a way of thinking that would measure up to those moments." This representational pathos will forever remain the challenge that is transgression.

Surrealism and Profane Illumination

We can gain some insight into this representational pathos by invoking surrealism (with which Bataille was closely associated), as with André Breton's concepts (in *Mad Love*) of "convulsive beauty" and the "fixed-explosive."[9] For not only do these concepts convey the dilemma in representing transgression, but in their artistic practice surrealists resurrected the stimulating impact of the unsayable through cunningly crafted contradiction in visual image, poetry, and unusual forms of narrative. At its best this amounted to what Walter Benjamin, in his essay on surrealism, termed "profane illumination," playing off against the mystical sense of *illumination* (rather than *Enlightenment*) to give it a sense at once secularized and materialist while maintaining something mystical as well.[10]

Moreover, such an illumination was in Benjamin's eyes dependent upon a nondiscursive reality emphasizing image and viscerality and amounting to a specific challenge to the meaning of meaning. For surrealism, life "only seemed worth living," he wrote, "where the threshold between waking and sleeping was worn away in everyone as by steps of multitudinous images flooding back and forth, language only seemed itself where sound and image, image and sound interpenetrated with automatic precision and such felicity that no chink was left for the penny-in-the-slot called meaning."[11] It is only from an epistemological enthusiasm such as this that we can begin to follow Bataille's astonishing essays of the 1930s (*Visions of Excess*), exemplary as much of transgression as of the problem of its representation, let alone do justice to those aspects of religion and ritual energized precisely on account of the representational dilemmas thus made manifest.

Let us therefore take up body and image not as symbols or as symptoms but as vehicles for the transgressive in religion. Pride of place should be given first to the cadaver and then to menstrual blood, compared with which polluting and hence sacred power, other components and features of the body, female or male, are usually quite inferior in terms of sacred, transgressive potential. Yet so as to grasp something of the scope with which human cultures have endowed what we might call the religious or religiously worked upon body as the sacred art form, let us not overlook the removal of the clitoris; male and female circumcision; cutting into the underside of the penis; masking; body painting; covering the face with tattoos; cranial "deformation"; flattening the forehead; letting of blood; knocking out teeth; filing the teeth; carving the teeth; scarifying the body, arms, and legs; human sacrifice; eating the body of the other; and hacking off a finger joint while praying to the sun (an automutilation figured by William Burroughs[12] and of consummate interest for Bataille[13] as shown in his study of relating Vincent van Gogh's amputation of his ear and suicide to the sun and to the evacuation of mythic meaning from such acts by modern life).

During the years 1907–1916 when he visited the Crow Indians, the esteemed anthropologist Robert Lowie says he saw few old men with their left hands intact.[14] In the early 1830s after visiting the Crow, George Catlin saw young Mandan braves of the upper Missouri River place their left hands on buffalo skulls and chop off the little finger. Some then also amputated the forefinger, leaving the two middle fingers and thumb since they were essential for handling a bow. Several of the chiefs and dignitaries had in years past also cut off the little finger of the right hand as an even greater sacrifice. But this was as nothing to what immediately went before when the young braves had the musculature of their upper torsos skewered with stakes to which ropes were attached, allowing them to swing suspended from the rafters of the medicine lodge while their companions on the ground twirled their bodies around until they fainted with pain. This was accompanied by four old men "incessantly beating upon the sacks of water and singing the whole time, with their voices strained to the highest key."[15] Then followed something between a race and a dance in which heavy buffalo skulls were attached to the stakes through the ligaments of the leg and arm muscles—not through the muscles themselves—which the young men had to drag while running until the flesh was torn out with the splint.

Then there is human blood, not just the fearsome blood of menstruation, which becomes its own sacred theater and the epicenter of pollution in general, but men's attempts at equivalence to such bleeding as in the scene well portrayed in Kenneth Read's *High Valley*, which recounts his experiences in 1950 among the Gahuku people in the Asaro River valley in the eastern highlands of New Guinea. Read saw initiated men standing in the brightly lit shallows of the river ostentatiously displaying their genitals and masturbating in front of hordes of other brilliantly painted and feathered men, the sacred flutes crying. Then one by one, each man stepped forward with rolls of razor sharp leaves, "flourishing them like a conjurer in a spotlight," and plunged this vicious instrument up his nose so as to tear at the mucous membrane and force blood to flow. The watching men ululated while the wounded man himself was so distraught with pain that, strong as he was, his knees were trembling and it seemed as though his legs would buckle under him.[16] It was this act, understood by Read as in part motivated by a need to exorcise the polluting effects of women, to which the male initiates had then to succumb for the first time in their lives, following which they were forced to swallow large canes doubled over into a long narrow U-shape. Read experienced it this way:

> Leaning forward from the waist, he placed the rounded section in his mouth, straightened, tilted his head, extended the line of his neck, and fed it into his stomach. My throat contracted and my stomach heaved, compelling me to look away. When I turned to him again most of the cane had disappeared, only two small sections, the open ends of the U, protruding from the corners of his mouth.
>
> I have no idea how long he held this grotesque stance, his straining abdomen and chest racked with involuntary shudders. Already sickened by the display, I stiffened with shock as he raised his hands, grasped the ends of the cane and sawed it rapidly up and down, drawing it almost free of his mouth at the peak of every upward stroke. The fervor of the crowd mounted to a clamorous pitch, breaking in wave upon wave of pulsing cries, the final surge matching my own relief when he dropped the cane, bent from the waist, and vomited into the river.[17]

Examples of such uses of the body could be multiplied, but the very notion here of an example seems to miss the point. The performances are so shocking as to transcend their being examples of anything other than what Read calls "the Gahuku's exhausting tendency to seek excess." It would be a cold fish indeed who would not stand in awe of these ever more ingenious games with the body demanded to serve a sacred and supernatural purpose in which ritual gives way to theatricality, and the leading performer and most stunning prop is the human and all-too-profane body with its various appendages, fluids, undulating surfaces, folds, exits, and entrances.

Secrecy

A crucial conceptual point provided by Read's depiction of initiation here is the role of secrecy, or rather public secrecy, as with the secret sacred Nama flutes played only by initiated men. What is important is to realize how secrecy is intertwined with taboo (and hence transgression) to create a powerful yet invisible presence (indeed, the presence of presence itself), and how essential this seems to what we generally might mean by religion. For example, the circumcision lodge as described by Junod is taboo to women and the uninitiated, and a woman who has seen the dressing used for the penile wound must be killed. In their 1899 description of the sacred *churinga* objects of the Aranda of central Australia, Spencer and Gillen claimed that death or blinding by firestick awaited any woman or uninitiated man who saw such an object, and I would imagine that this sort of sanction and the fear and danger it articulates would have been found across much if not all of that continent. [18]

These dramatic examples give us insight into the strategic role of secrecy within the sacred propounded by the great world religions as well. "Not only is there no religion without secrecy," writes Kees W. Bolle, "but there is no human existence without it," and he is concerned to evoke a nonpositivist and self-reflexive view of the secret here at stake, as when he talks of limits, special mystery, caution, and self-restraint. He asks the pertinent question of the believer no less than of the scholar, "How do we become fully aware of [the secret] without distorting it?" [19]

Here we could say that the power of negation built into the secrecy depends upon the fearsome expectation of its transgression as indicated by the threatened penalties. Transgression, we could say, exerts its tremendous and tremendously creative force through its threat rather than its actualization. And this is more than sufficient. Yet there is an additional feature to consider, and that is that the anxiety illustrated in the two examples above with regard to *visual* manifestation of the mystery is of note, as it is the act of uncontrolled seeing that is prohibited in these and countless other examples, because the secret (and hence the transgression that has to break through it) has in fact to be not only concealed but revealed as well—in keeping with the logic of the negative in which transgression and taboo artfully play off one another in what I have described above as an endlessly discharging circuit. This negation of the negation is spectacularly illustrated by the unmasking of men masked as spirits in many societies across the globe, and in the showing of the sacred flutes or bull roarer as in central Amazonia, New Guinea, central Africa, and Australia.

To illustrate the importance of revelation in a studied back-and-forth movement between concealment *and* revelation as art forms generating a fund of power from taboo and transgression, let us first note that it is the drama involved in the revelation of the mysteries that ensures a person's initiation. In addition, such revelation ensures not disenchantment but further enchantment thanks to a mystical illumination. In this sense revelation leads to further concealment. Showing the secret leads to another if not deeper secret.

But there is even more to this. Let us turn our attention to the wider context, to the women and children left in the village and kept away from the sacred precinct of the circumcision lodge described by Junod, or to those who have to hide in their huts when the *molimo* trumpet plays among the Mbuti in central Africa,[20] when the sacred flutes play in central Amazonia and highland New Guinea,[21] or the masked figure of the *Shoort* spirit enters the camp of the Selk'nam in Tierra del Fuego (described for the early 1920s in vivid detail by Martin Gusinde).[22] Here too we find an exceedingly powerful but quite different expression of negation, because it is the task of the uninitiated persons (read generic woman) to form the *absent presence* and *active unknowing* as to what goes on in the lodge. Note how this absent presence and active unknowing is in itself, in its very makeup, a subtle expression of revelation and concealment, for the women know they must not know but in fact do "know" a good deal. In other words, while the powerful drama of revelation within the secrecy of the lodge can only be achieved by concealing it and all that goes on in the lodge from uninitiated others, such concealment is itself part of a larger scheme of revelation in that the secrecy at issue is strategically incomplete, being an open or public secret to some extent shared by all— once again displaying the artful play of negation as concealment *and* revelation, taboo *and* transgression.

"Secrecy lies at the very core of power" wrote Canetti, and to that we must add that this power very much includes the power of make-believe essential to religious force and without which there can be no religion.[23] Hence as Huizinga instructed in his work on play, the term "artful play" (as I deploy it for the work of negation) has to be seen as a precise characterization of transgression, as both utmost seriousness and gay abandon, thus making secrecy (that "lies at the very core of power") a potent stimulus to creativity, to what Simmel called "the magnification of reality" by means of the sensation that behind the appearance of things there is a deeper, mysterious reality that we may here call the sacred, if not religion.[24]

This same play with secrecy of things sacred and the controlled transgression of their revelation is forceful in discussions of medicine men and -women and of so-called *shamanism* (an essentializing term sanctioned more by conventional usage than the facts merit; see also pp. 129–30 above), it being repeatedly pointed out by anthropologists that, although it is widely suspected that such magic is fraudulent, it is nevertheless believed to be efficacious or potentially so. "It is perfectly well-known by all concerned," wrote Franz Boas towards the end of his long career, "that a great part of the shamanistic procedure [among the Kwakiutl] is based on fraud; still it is believed in by the shaman as well as by patients and their friends. Exposures do not weaken the belief in the 'true' power of shamanism. Owing to this peculiar state of mind, the shaman himself is doubtful in regard to his powers and is always ready to bolster them up by fraud."[25] What Boas refers to as a "peculiar state of mind" is this form wherein "fraud" and "belief" in "magic" are so many (inadequate) expressions not of skilled concealment but of skilled revelation of skilled concealment—this in atmospheres of expectation made dense by the seesawing contradictions built into the labyrinth that is the public secret of knowing what not to "know" about the practices in question. "Indeed, scepticism is included in the pattern of belief in witch-doctors. Faith and scepticism are alike traditional," wrote Evans-Pritchard in his 1937 book on Azande medicine men.[26]

Sound and Song as Invisible Presence That Has to Be Transgressed

Here is where *sound* as with bull roarers, sacred flutes, and singing, becomes important because, unlike the prohibition on the visual manifestation of the secret, the sound, whose whole purpose is to be public, evokes the secret's presence without otherwise manifesting it. Therefore, sound provides a perfect vehicle for absent presence. Sound is like a metasecret or the "skin" of the secret, announcing but concealing its content, and it is precisely this skin that represents the mysterious line of transgression that has to (yet must not) be breached.

With the sacred flutes of highland New Guinea or central Amazonia, the crucial mise-en-scène is men playing secret sacred flutes while the women and children must hide their eyes, secreted in their homes and gardens as an absent presence that augments the power of the invisible force of spirit manifested by the sound of the invisible flutes. Kenneth Read's description of human-made sounds during the three months' long Gahuku male initiation in New Guinea strikingly conveys this. For example, there was an overwhelming sense of noise in the initial stages of male initiation—the women's keening cries "stabbing into the din around me"; men ululating in synchrony with their chests thumped in counterpoint to the crashing of feet on the bare ground; "and rising above it all, . . . the cries of the flute, which I heard at close quarters for the first time, a sound like great wings beating at the ear drums, throbbing and flapping in the hollow portions of the skull." He notes the men's "ecstatic communion with an invisible force" at this point and states that although it was impossible for him to tell what they felt, "I was struck by the thought that they may have wanted to be seen [by the women]."[27]

In another sensitive and well-known account, *The Forest People,* which concerns the secret sacred *molimo* trumpet and its associated songs of the Mbuti "pygmies" of the Ituri Forest of central Africa, Colin Turnbull describes in unforgettable terms this same sort of invisible presence evoked by an instrument belonging to the men, seeing which, women are supposed to believe, will bring their death. With Turnbull, or should we say with the Mbuti, at that time at least, this is all the more exemplary in that it is this sound, this invisible musical instrument, that virtually is the religion providing comfort and beauty, mystery and efficacy, an ethical system and a sense of rootedness in "Being" in the forest. Above all, religion is the secret, carefully concealed *and* revealed.

> For a month I sat every evening at the kumamolimo [rite of the *molimo*]
> listening, watching, and feeling—above all, feeling. If I still had little idea of
> what was going on, at least I felt that air of importance and expectancy.
> Every evening, when the women shut themselves up, pretending that they
> were afraid to see "the animal of the forest"; every evening, when the men
> gathered around the fire, pretending they thought that the women thought
> the drainpipes were animals; every evening, when the trumpet drainpipes
> imitated leopards and elephants and buffalos—every evening, when all this
> make-believe was going on, I felt something very real and very great was
> going on beneath it, something everyone else took for granted, and about
> which only I was ignorant.[28]

In the Putumayo shamanism with which I was connected in the 1970s and 1980s in southwest Colombia, the shaman's singing is both his way of reaching out to and connecting with powerful spirits, just as it is those very same spirits that are singing through him, by means of the vehicle that is his body. He thus breaches the wall of the secret shrouded in taboos against spirit contact, and therewith presences them invisibly through a mystery of sound working dialectically between person and spirit.[29]

The hallucinogenic yage-inspired visions that follow give visual form to this sonically formed but otherwise invisible spiritual presence, it being precisely the point, however, that while enormously inspiring, hallucinogenic images are only precariously real. They are the epitome of what in modernity came to be called collage and montage. They come and go, they contradict one another, they are emotionally polarized, they may be sent by another, hostile shaman, and they may be deliberately misleading—in this form is created, thus, another mode of revelation and concealment and of concealment through revelation. In addition to recognizing the curative function of visual exposure, we should be mindful of how the danger and intensity of feelings associated with the taking of drugs such as yage indicate the depth of the transgression involved in breaking through into the otherwise forbidden domain of spirits. (And we might note, inter alia, the overarching taboos here against women, menstrual blood, and pregnancy as fearsome states that can physically destroy the shaman when he is engaged in his work.)

Along with this presencing of the invisible through song and music is the way the human body serves as a philosophical "device," theatricalizing and pondering innerness and veiling as the inviolable element of truth. Here I am thinking not only of the aforementioned use of the body as a sacred staging ground of religious rituals such as initiation but of the worldwide use of the human body for the staging of insidedness / outsidedness, of penetration and retrieval, and hence of evisceration and exposure of hidden depth in often spectacular performances of concealment and revelation. Healing someone of sorcery, for instance, generally involves the extraction of an object, a splinter or a worm or an animal, from the inside of the body, just as sorcery—an intrinsic part of religion and perhaps its most "transgressive" part—involves the placing of these things in that body. (Christian notions of exorcism, confession, catharsis, and purgation, as well as the ready use of Christian concepts to translate key elements of so-called primitive religions, the soul, for instance, are parallel phenomena energized by insidedness/ outsidedness.) Also of note here is the play with being and nothingness, as exemplified by the skill with which objects appear and disappear in and from the body in remarkable changes of pace, together with the often ontologically un-definable nature of the substances involved.

In many societies in Asia, Africa, and Latin America it is not a sorcery sub-stance but the spirit of a dead human through which notions of insidedness/outsidedness are staged. Powerful traces of this enormously widespread phenom-enon, often categorized as "spirit possession," underlie the Christian liturgy, specifically the Holy Spirit and the cult of the saints. Similarly, this use of the body to mark the drama and mystery of concealment has been called *physiog-nomy*—the ancient science of reading insides from outsides, character and soul, no less than the future, from external bodily features—and as such became a ba-sis for theorizing the (magical) power of film, especially the close-up of the face. The point to dwell upon with embodied insidedness/outsidedness is not, how-ever, the triumph of a catharsis with the eventual bringing to light of hiddenness, but rather the performance of hiddenness itself in an eternal and unstable move-ment with a continuously discharging circuit of taboo and transgression, con-cealment and revelation.

Negation and the Exhausting Tendency to Seek Excess

In drawing attention to the "exhausting tendency to seek excess," Kenneth Read unintentionally and hence all the more convincingly underscores Georges Bataille's 1933 theory of *dépense* or "expenditure,"[30] which is no less relevant for religion than for economics and which later became more fully elaborated in Bataille's three-volume work, *The Accursed Share* (1988).[31] Postulating a built-in need in all human societies for going over the top, for wasteful and lavish spend-ing for the hell of it, for a "toomuchness" (in the phrasing of Norman O. Brown)[32] and hence for expenditure without motive of gain other than sheer loss, Bataille suggested a way of reading world history that was especially relevant to sacrifice, a most important feature of many religions whose defining features are (1) the presence of an intermediary as victim between the sacrificer and the god, and (2) the destruction of the intermediary. "Sacrifice destroys that which it conse-crates," emphasizes Bataille searching for a formula that in negating utility and profit would give rise to the sacred quality of *dépense* in intimate relation to trans-gression.[33]

This view of sacrifice is intimately bound to a philosophical dispute Bataille had with Hegel over the meaning of the death space in Hegel's famous operation of *Aufhebung*, in which a concept or event is transcended by its negation yet preserved within it. In Bataille's view Hegel did not know to what extent he was right in his emphasis on death and dismemberment, as in the famous passage in the latter's preface to *Phenomenology of Spirit* wherein Spirit "attains its truth only by finding itself in absolute dismemberment. It is not that prodigious power by being the Positive that turns away from the negative. . . . Spirit is that power only to the degree in which it contemplates the Negative face to face and dwells with it. This prolonged sojourn is the magical force which transposes the negative into given-Being."[34] Against this sort of magic, Bataille sees the negation at work in human history and Spirit as a sort of derailed *Aufhebung* neither achieving redemptive closure nor interested in it. To close the dialectical would in fact be nondialectical. To the contrary, negation is a sacrifice of the very idea of closure in a continuous face-to-facedness with death and dismemberment.[35]

Automutilation and the Killing of the God

Death and dismemberment return us to the human body as a privileged theater of sacred activity in a way that makes it hard to avoid the topics of automutilation, of the killing of the god, and of the god killing himself. As the basis of Christianity, implicating extraordinary degrees of transgression at the core of that religion, these actions bear heavily on Nietzsche's famous concept of enlightenment as synonymous with the death of the god in which the god killing himself is taken to new heights, actually defining the place, character, and meaning of transgression in modernity.

This god did not die from senescence. Murder is how Nietzsche sees it. And it is murder by society as a whole, by the era in an act of such enormity that he asks in *The Gay Science,* "How did we do this?" "How could we drink up the sea? Who gave us the sponge to wipe away the entire horizon?" Uncertainty reigns, the earth unchained from the sun. "Whither is it moving now? Whither are we moving?" Moreover the event is not recognized for what it is—perhaps the most telling feature of all as regards transgression. The bearer of the news throws his lantern to the ground, and it breaks into pieces. "I have come too early," he says. "My time is not yet. This tremendous event is still on its way, still wandering; it has not yet reached the ears of men. Lightning and thunder require time."[36]

So fundamental is this death of God that in "A Preface to Transgression" (1963), Michel Foucault defined modernity itself in terms of transgression as a prelude to his all-consuming project for a new philosophy built around the poetic logic of experience at the limit in a world evacuated of the sacred (the infinitude of the limit replacing the rule of God with his limit of infinity).[37] The key insight here as I understand it, and one of great significance for the study of religion, is that the sacred, itself a staging ground of transgression (as the aforementioned examples are intended to indicate), is not so much erased by modernity, as is suggested by the famous notion of the disenchantment of the world, but is instead itself transgressed. Paradoxically this transgression of transgression can be viewed as the ultimate sacred act but one in which sacrilege becomes the place where the sacred is most likely to be experienced in modernity, sacrilege being the inverse of sacrifice, a charged space of negative holiness characterized by the meeting of extremes *in unending waves of metonymic proliferation.* For Foucault this charged space of transgression in modernity is sex, or should we say sex and language, located not in God but in his absence. With this a unique twist is given to transgression, demanding a fundamentally new "nondialectical philosophy" bound to an effervescent, impossible language of the limit reminiscent of Bataille's death space of excess and of laughter tracing, as Foucault puts it in terms no less lyrical than forlorn, "the line of foam showing just how far speech may advance upon the sands of silence." Everything here rests on language, this language-as-philosophy, language-as-being, language-as-transgression (taking us back to the issue of surrealism, Benjamin, and representational pathos): it is the "product of fissures, abrupt descents, and broken contours, this misshapen and craglike language describes a circle; it refers to itself and is folded back on a questioning of its limits."[38]

A leading but rarely acknowledged motif in Foucault's final project on the history of sexuality is that this sacred force of transgression bound to sexuality is intimately bound not only to language at the limit, but to secrecy, and in particular, to the play of concealment and revelation. "What is peculiar to modern societies," he repeatedly wrote in *The History of Sexuality* fourteen years later, "is not that they consigned sex to a shadow existence, but that they dedicated themselves to speaking of it *ad infinitum,* while exploiting it as *the* secret."[39] That this is the crossroads where surrealism comes to bear on the new mix modernity makes of religion and transgression, image and body, was one of Benjamin's insights, evident in his advice, in speaking for profane illumination, that "we penetrate the mystery only to the degree that we recognise it in the everyday world, by virtue of a dialectical optic that perceives the everyday as impenetrable, the impenetrable as everyday."[40]

Intoxication

Benjamin's sagacious recommendation, written in 1928, was inspired by the issue of intoxication as a mystical force all too ready at hand in the anarcho-communist class struggle: intoxication as the realm in which the maker of images may thus work, explosively dislocating and reconfiguring body and image; and intoxication in its more literal meaning of inspiration through drugs, which Benjamin regarded as weakening the profane element in profane illumination. This is dangerous territory but one we cannot avoid in discussing transgression and modernity at the end of the twentieth century, with drugs as much if not more than sex occupying a strategic position in politics, revolution, counterrevolution, and the sacred, in modern times canonized in the extensive writing and painting of William Burroughs (for whom the taking of yage with Indian shamans in Colombia and Peru was a formative experience). In referring to religion as the opiate of the masses, Karl Marx could not have known how literally correct his assessment would become, only that the equation could be read backwards as well as forwards. It is the early Foucault, in the wake of Nietzsche and Bataille, who has opened eyes to what a religion/philosophy of transgression would be like without an obvious church or priesthood and who thus allows us to understand the concepts of the sacred and the marvellous in modernity to which drugs may provide (or are thought to provide) access, complete with all the trappings of automutilation and self-sacrifice. This is obvious enough in Burroughs, whose work, beginning with *Naked Lunch*, problematizes image and word in obscene and transgressive forms, together with flights of great lyrical beauty, brings religion, sex, drugs, and montage together. That such transgressive phenomena are mistakenly seen as the antitheses of religion is testimony to the narrow moralism of organized religions today. Such organization finds its counterpart in the fact that modern societies and especially the United States, having made drugs illegal and attached extraordinary penalties to their use and sale, bring to terrible perfection the fearsome logic of taboo and transgression underlying the sacred.

When George W. Bush came to town for the Republican National Convention in 2004, the New York City Police Department—known as the NYPD, or "New York's Finest (and now, Bravest)"—swept thousands of protesters off the streets day after day in giant dragnets using plastic netting even thought the vast majority of the protesters were doing nothing illegal. This has been further confirmed by extensive video evidence, some of which was tampered with by the police or the prosecutor's office. The protesters were "processed" in chemically polluted "holding cells" hastily set up on Pier 57 by the Hudson River, known now as Guantánamo-on-the-Hudson, a procedure that normally should take at the most a few hours. Instead for most of the 1,800 arrested it took up to three days with little food and water. Many developed alarming skin rashes from the chemical waste on the floors on which they had to sleep. Others acquired systemic bodily disturbances. But the streets of New York City were maintained free of protest for the duration of the convention. That was the point. New York had been converted into a Potemkin Village, like a stage set, a fake place with happy smiling people greeting their gun-toting liberators with roses, as had been expected earlier when they rode into Baghdad.

An earlier version of this chapter was published as "The Injustice of Policing" in Austin Sarat and Thomas R. Kearns, eds., *Justice and Injustice in Law and Legal Theory* (Ann Arbor: University of Michigan Press, 1996).

These Potemkin Villages are created wherever the forty-third president and his cavalcade descend on a third world city. New York was no exception. Policing is not only a question of material force but of what the novelist J. M. Coetzee, in a story about CIA activity in the Vietnam War, referred to as "mythological warfare."[1] Such warfare comes easily to the police, suggested the young Walter Benjamin in Germany in 1920, because of their ghostly being, a suspended sort of violent nothingness.[2]

What Benjamin meant was that the police occupied a sort of no-man's-land indispensable to the maintenance of law. The "law" of the police, he said, is *independent* of the rest of the law. It "really marks the point at which the state . . . can no longer guarantee through the legal system the empirical ends it desires at any price to attain."[3] This terrifying assertion means that the people we pay to maintain the law are free of it so as to be able get on with their job. In a time of Homeland Security could this be any clearer, now that the exception is so blatantly the rule, now when people are tortured and left to rot in holding cells in sites such as Guantánamo Bay in Cuba (a country reviled by the United States for its lack of democracy), and when evidence is withheld on the grounds of "national security." Lest one thinks this state of exception is post 9/11, let us examine the record prior to that event, remembering that Benjamin wrote down his ideas on policing a decade before the Nazis took power.

From Benjamin's perspective as well as the record of the NYPD, it appears that no matter how much we may want to weed out corruption among the police, we do so with a certain "optimism of the will, pessimism of the intellect," understanding our task as endless in its necessity. As for our task, what exactly is it? Are we not in our way trying to police the police? Or, mindful of that trap, should we police ourselves as well? Perhaps there is a third alternative, that of a critique that succumbs to its own critique as a source of wisdom.

Policing the police concerns what since Benjamin's time has been referred to as "human rights," the monitors of which form a cultural and bureaucratic movement across the globe, especially in third world countries. It is hard to imagine human rights being raised in New York City or in the United States in general, although that does increasingly occur. What distinguishes Benjamin's analysis of the police from such organizations, however, as from liberalism in general, is his argument that the police are not and never can be subject to law.[4] What, then, are they subject to? With this question in mind, Coetzee's notion of "mythological warfare" takes on unsuspected power when hauled back from wars executed in poor, third world countries such as Vietnam or Iraq and applied right here in the homeland.

"Tough Cops, Not Brutal Cops," appealed a *New York Times* editorial around the time when I first drafted these thoughts, an editorial that, in trying to separate toughness from brutality, found itself awash in contradictions, reduced to pious finger-wagging in lieu of reasoned argument. The police commissioner of New York is cited as saying that "police officers are 'between a rock and hard place' because there is no way they can attempt to reclaim drug-ridden neighborhoods without being tough." "True," continues the editorial writer, "but as the Commissioner also notes, there is a 'right way to do it and a wrong way to do it' [and] no police officer worthy of his or her shield can fail to know the difference between aggressive policing and brutality."[5] The point however is that the difference is illusory, the contradiction insuperable, same as with notions like "unnecessary violence" or "irrational violence." And this is why the editorial writer follows in the rhetorical wake of commissioner, invoking in conclusion the magical talisman of the shield, that is, the shield-shaped police badge.

Let me recall the scene-of-the-shield several years back in the NYPD's Thirtieth Precinct in northwest Harlem, New York City, an area which my university, Columbia, is about to acquire in one of the more spectacular displacements of black people in the history of the city of New York. Several years ago in that precinct, police accused of corruption had their shields solemnly removed by the commissioner in a deft enactment of castration and beheading of one George Nova who, ever since he was a little boy, so they say, had wanted to be a cop. Here was a superb police officer. "It's mind-boggling how someone could be so good. He just had the knack," said a supervisor at the Thirtieth Precinct. Nova had an uncanny sense of crime. But at the same time, now it is revealed, he turns out to have been the most crooked of the lot. The best was the worst. Such are the ways of policing. Be it noted that throughout his brilliant career, until apprehended, he had but one "command discipline," a minor infraction—lending his shield to a friend to use with a Halloween costume.[6] Then one remembers not the policeman who became a thief but the thief who became not only one of France's great writers but also a saint, Saint Jean Genet, crushed at the bar by Bernadino's huskiness and self-assurance: "I was excited chiefly by the invisible presence of his inspector's badge. The metal object had for me the power of a cigarette lighter in the fingers of a workman, or the buckle of an army belt, of a switchblade, of a caliper, objects in which the quality of males is violently concentrated. Had I been alone with him in a dark corner, I might have been bold enough to graze the cloth, to slip my hand under the lapel where cops usually wear the badge, and I would have trembled just as if I had been opening his fly."[7]

It seems paradoxical that this thief could be so enamored of cops, their badges and their dicks. But maybe that's the point—the straining of contradiction within the what-we-all-know-anyway. It's not that cops are thieves, too. No! I insist on the difference! If they're thieves, then they're "cop-thieves," *double-men* as Elias Canetti refers to werewolves and magically endowed persons mystically identified with their totems.[8] The point is that that cops and thieves are erotically intertwined and that the thin blue line separating them is more like a veil in a striptease. Perhaps it's bad sex, when all is said and done, and perhaps Genet has a problem here, but that's another discussion. What should hold us are the curious properties of the distinction *uniting* the criminal with the policeman, something Nietzsche, for one, made clear when he argued that the police are worse than the criminal because they do the same things, but in the name of Law.

"All's fair in love and war." A 1994 *New Yorker* essay on the U.S. Attorney's Office, Northern District of Illinois, and its prosecution of the Blackstone Rangers brings this out in a startling manner. Drawing attention to a so-called "modern" trend in law enforcement toward prosecution of entire criminal organizations such as gangs and Mafia families in place of individuals, the article notes that this trend relies heavily on an alliance between prosecutors and turncoats from such organizations. Fraught with hazards, however, the greatest danger to such reliance "is not that what seems to be polar opposites—prosecutors and criminals—might never find a way to work together," maintains the author. "Rather it is just the reverse—that the good guys and the bad guys may fall in love."[9]

Now, "falling in love" is one of those metaphorically capacious expressions perfect for the theatrical world of cops and crims—"good guys and bad guys"— where passion no less than ambivalence oozes from every pore. To fall—from the heights of law into the pit, into the desires of the criminal, into unholiness—is here preordained as in ancient mythology despite the "modernity" of it all, fax machines, automatic weapons, and tape recorders included. At one point a tape recording was secretly made of a telephone call between the chief prosecutor's assistant and one of the "turncoats" in jail, a nice example of the police policing the police. The tape was played in court as evidence against the prosecutor. It was, to say the least, embarrassing: a matter of phone sex on the line between the federal prosecutor's office in downtown Chicago and the Metropolitan Correctional Center and nobody able to say who was sexing whom, the prosecutor's assistant or the admitted murderer.

She laughed. "Ten minutes in a locked room. That's all it would take." "All right, Rindy," Hunter said, changing the subject. "We done had enough business for the day. You have to tell me bedtime stories for the night."

"Tell you a bed time story? Gee." "Yeah, I have tension, too. You know." "You poor thing."

"And you help me release my tension." "I don't know, Eugene," Luchetta said. "Oh, let me see, what kind of story can I tell you . . . What would you have me do first?" "I just want to look." "Look but don't touch," Luchetta said. "I don't think so."[10]

And so it went on, in gathering waves of telephonic tumescence binding captor to prisoner, prosecutor to murderer cum informant.

The courtroom was very quiet when this tape was played. "Actually," comments the author, "it is not clear precisely what rule if any was broken by this conversation . . . It was inappropriate, bizarre, and embarrassing, but not, perhaps, illegal." The erotic and spectral effect of the ambiguity is reinforced by the author's choice of figurative language with his surmise that, for the presiding judge, this taped conversation must have been the last straw, the final and clear indication that the prosecution and the criminals had "ceased operating at some distance from one another and that their alliance was an unholy one."[11] Genet would be the first to testify to the inherent necessity, let alone unholiness, of this alliance.

In their demand for a "sacred sociology" of the modern world after the death of God, Georges Bataille and Michel Leiris had summed up just such an unholy alliance as is here presented between criminals and police. Searching for a notion of the sacred in a profane world, Leiris suggested it was anything characterized by ambiguity, danger, excitement, and prohibition. Bataille added disgust, fear, and attraction. Even more defining was the flip-flop between the negative and positive poles of the sacred in a profane world, there being every reason to include the diabolical, the nasty, and evil itself as no less sacred than the nice things we prefer to designate with that label. The modern world had drained holiness of this other fearsome meaning and had done its best to sanitize the church, repressing the unwholesome nature of religious power. But primitive societies knew better, and so do the police.

No less spectral is the elaborate charade played out between the cops and the courts, policing in the rough and tumble of the streets, on one side, and the calm adjudication of justice before the bench, on the other. Where does one end and the other begin? Where does the law of force give way to the force of law? What is one to make of the "emperor's new clothes" type of situation in which judges and prosecutors in New York City, for instance, give tacit approval to cops perjuring themselves in court? The head of the Legal Aid Society of New York's criminal defense division is cited recently as saying that "the police regularly invent witnesses, tailor their testimony to meet constitutional objections, and alter arrest records." What's more, "prosecutors and judges wink at it."[12]

Theatrical performance is crucial to the success of this public secret, which sets the stage for the recurring drama of force and fraud at the heart of the U.S. system of justice. The courtroom serves as the play within the play. As was said at the trial for perjury of a police officer, John Rossi, who beat up a prisoner named Luis Mora in order to force a false confession that would exonerate the officer from having committed a minor infraction: "This perjury is monstrous because the lie seems like the truth. Luis Mora looked guilty to John Rossi. He dressed guilty. He had a record of guilt. Luis Mora is the perfect fall guy. John Rossi knew after all those years of working with assistant district attorneys, of testifying before a grand jury, testifying before judges, that he would have no trouble selling a guy like Luis Mora up the river."[13] But to the police community, the prosecution of Officer Rossi was "wrongheaded and overzealous." It failed to take into account the dangers and difficulties of policing.

Strangest of all, to Officer Rossi it didn't seem to have happened at all. He didn't even believe the case had been brought against him. "From the second I realized they were going to prosecute me to this second right now," he said after being sentenced, "it's been beyond me. It seems fictional."[14]

And well he might be dazed at the hallucinatory haze at work on his fictions. After all, an attorney writing a month before this news report stated that in her sixteen years working in the city she had neither seen nor heard of a New York City prosecutor bringing a cop to court for perjury. What's more, she says that while it's routine in court to hear police give evidence that would strain the credulity of a seven-year-old, judges rarely reject such testimony as false.[15]

But does not the very same system let us know of its corruption? Is this not its saving grace? Yet what if these confessions change nothing, as seems likely? More than likely. How can we understand this? Is this then the ultimate in theater and ritual—confessions and commissions of inquiry, witnesses in black ski masks and a whole supporting cast performing a public ritual of purgation undertaken with each new mayor or every decade, a forced confession to the gods of the city? Farewell to the land of absolutes no less than absolution; the best you can hope for is a "minimal level" of badness achieved through frequent and regular reamings, like cleaning the toilet bowl. Is this the ultimate sign of the divine, revealing how scarce, indeed how miraculous, justice is?

Here's one such reaming. The Commission on Corruption is told . . . Two policemen ride the patrol car cruising the Thirtieth Precinct in northwest Harlem.

The report reads that "a drug crazed individual" was firing at another man. The two policemen "scrambled" out of their cars as other drug dealers joined in. "It was like Vietnam out there," a police officer said. Officer Vasquez shot one man down but as he was reloading, the downed man staggered to his knees, despite severe wounds, aiming his gun at Vasquez. Without hesitation Vasquez's partner, Jorge Alvarez, dived in front of him and killed the would-be killer. A few months later, as in a Greek tragedy, Alvarez turned in his partner for corruption as a way of mitigating his own involvement in crime. Yes! Maybe it was like Vietnam "out there." Alvarez's heroism haunted the minds of the other officers. "You have to look back and wonder whether Jorge did Vasquez a favor or not," commented one officer. "Maybe the best thing would have been if Vasquez had died right there. He would have been a hero. His family would have received a pension. Now his family is disgraced. The man is looking at life in prison. Who would want to be him?" Investigators policing the police "remain uncertain of just when and why any went bad." It is pointed out that the best cover is to do your job not just well but extremely well. The best way to be the worst is to be the best. The report speaks of cops "being like the beach"—what a strange metaphor!—subject to continuous erosion by the temptations thrown their way by crime.[16] You can see the waves pounding in from the surging sea, waves of money, waves of drugs, waves of secrets rolling in from the polluted ocean.

The report speaks of men "unraveling," overwhelmed by the size of the monthly mortgage payments; the unpaid taxes; the Datsun they own with over 200,000 miles on it; the house foreclosed; separations; divorces; the deprived backgrounds. Then there are the brown paper bags picked up at the bodega with tens of thousands of dollars. Who could resist?

But would any of that explain diving in front of your partner to save his life?

The drama is plain and absorbing: honest men slowly sucked into not just crime but treason. After all, they are police and for them to stoop to crime is to double the crime. Not thieves, but "cop-thieves." Double-men. The art of transformation: might there not be seduction in just that? Is this not Genet's pleasure of betrayal, the "eternal return" of the first of the great transgressions as the path to sanctity? And the report speaks of gaining a partial understanding of "the road to the dark side of the law." We stand appalled—yet intrigued—by the horrendous inevitability invoked by the notion here of a "road" to the storming depths. What road is this? Spellbound by the human drama, however, the report fails to follow up on this insight—that the law itself no less than human beings depends on, yet must deny, this "dark side" as part of its very being.

As policing strides along the "road to the dark side," so it creates a hierarchy of invisible layers of other police—perhaps "better" and more "noble" police—whose function it is to police the police. Note the time-honored practice of using a thief to catch a thief as with the now-routine practice of "the wire" in which a cop is wired to a tape recorder by a tiny microphone, like an animal of prey, trapping a fellow cop into an incriminating chat at the Policeman's Benevolent Society's barbecue. This practice has led to the further practice of police now secretly wearing wire detectors available at "spy shops" in New York City. Let us not forget the role of the FBI in conducting "sting" operations with patience and guile over many months, involving (once again) these notorious brown paper bags with $10,000 in them on kitchen countertops under the surveillance of a hidden video camera set to capture the police who are unable to resist the bait as they search apartments for drugs. All of which leads to other questions concerning mythological warfare, which, as with spy thrillers in art and real life, entails worlds within worlds of mutual suspicion, disguise, and deception. Can the law be dependent on something as fluid and eerie as policing through infinite regress? Who polices the police policing the police? It's like the shamans as Plato describes them in *Ion*, as I discerned them in the southwest of Colombia, each one dependent on a more powerful one—and the one at the end, at the headwaters of the river lost in the forest, what would he look like? What language would he speak? Who could he turn to in his moments of insight and weakness? It's said that the infamous head of the FBI, J. Edgar Hoover, had thirty-five file drawers and six filing cabinets that nobody but his personal secretary had access to, with dirt on presidents and important politicians and officials (including FBI officials). Is that the end point? When he died it caused a panic. His secretary, Helen Gandy, had to hide the files in Hoover's home and then destroyed an unspecified number of them. But did she destroy all? And why is this mysterious lode of dirt on the rich and powerful referred to sometimes as "gold" and other times as "a bucket of worms"?[17]

But the most intriguing feature in the theater of visibility and invisibility is the frequent attention paid in the press to the off-duty cop out of uniform who apprehends a criminal—as in a hairdressing salon or in a speeding car. These stories never fail to impress me although I am not sure why. Is it because that policing—as with the ministry of religion or a medical doctor, for instance—is more than just a job, so that even off duty one is still on duty? Is it because you are made suddenly to realize that you never know if the person beside you is an off-duty cop and that the line between the police and the public is not uniformly well defined when all along you thought it was and should be? Is it because there is something almost supernatural and certainly Hollywoodesque about the quicksilver transformation from the Clark Kent figure into Superman? Or is it because of the joy one feels that the tables were so unexpectedly turned on a criminal unexpectedly taking advantage of an unsuspecting public?

Here I cannot stop from wondering about the rather pathetic displays of rebellion involved in my switching back and forth from *police* to *cop*. This word *cop*, no less than *police,* seems to have the wondrous ambivalent power of those strange "primal" words that Freud brought to our attention.[18] But the term *cop* is doubly curious in that as the underside or left-handed term, not only does it have its official counterpart in *police,* but it has crept into if not the official then certainly the quasi-official and respectable U.S. lexicon. Its usage conveys not only critical distance from the "police" but a peculiar mix of insult and endearment, and much the same applies to the litany of cop appellations such as *dick, fuzz, flatfoot, sleuth, gumshoe,* and so forth. (It should be a cause for concern that the proliferation of such names seems to be tapering off. Perhaps they are too playful? Perhaps there is no longer the mythic space for such names and the police have achieved the ultimate perfection which is namelessness.)

If the swinging back and forth between *cop* and *police* provides linguistic evidence as to the doubleness at the heart of policing, the folkloric observation of the "good cop, bad cop" routine, offers *testimony* (now I too find the language of law irresistible!) to the fact that policing so easily lends itself to theatrical representation. This point is that the threat posed by the "bad cop" is even less important than the shocking duplicity of the "good cop." It is also testimony (!) to the sacred-making ambivalence of an authority whose corruption manifests a specific constellation of attraction and equally great repulsion.[19]

Let us emphasize at this point, therefore, Freud's rendition of extant ethnography and classical reference where he noted the following salient features of the taboo. "The meaning of 'taboo' as we see it," he wrote (in 1913), "diverges in two contrary directions. To us it means, on the one hand, 'sacred,' 'consecrated,' and on the other 'uncanny,' 'dangerous,' 'forbidden,' 'unclean.'" Moreover, contact with the tabooed person or object, he noted (as the strangest fact of all), leads to contagion by the same power such that that person in turn acquires the property of being tabooed.[20]

It is this very same sacred purity-and-impurity of policing that seems to me to underlie Benjamin's figure of police-as-ghosts. Sure, the magical power of the dead is a well-nigh universal phenomenon. But for Benjamin this magical power is greatly enhanced by a disturbing decay, an effervescent rottenness, at the heart of policing. Let me explain.

Their power is formless, Benjamin wrote of the police, like their "nowhere tangible, all-pervasive, ghostly presence in the life of civilized states."[21] In an age of revolution and counter-revolution rife with the implications violence holds for reason, no less than for law, Benjamin (all of twenty-eight years old) strove in 1920 to define rights of violence—as in the proletarian general strike, and with what he called the "divine justice of destruction," which was opposed to the "mythic violence that founds law."[22] He was especially interested in phenomena destabilizing the boundary between might and right, and he singled out capital punishment, for instance, as that act of law preservation which, through its exercising the highest violence possible within the legal system, the power over life and death, irresistibly brings forth the violent origins of law at the same time as it acts to maintain law and hence reveals what he called "rottenness" within the law. "Rottenness" meant the mystifications separating but also joining violence to reason—nowhere more so than in the role fulfilled by the police who, through violence or the threat of violence, daily *make* law as much as they *maintain* it. Policing goes beyond the "rottenness" implicated by capital punishment, to what Benjamin sees as "ignominy," a "far more monstrous combination" of law-preserving and law-founding violence.

This unabashed disgust exhibited by Benjamin toward our boys in blue strikes me as strange in what is otherwise an essay remarkable for its lofty and somber tone poised on the edge of incantation. It's as if the mixture of categories upsets him more than the violent reality it is meant to illuminate. Hence, in his attempts to pin down what is at the core of policing, he uses a variety of terms in quick succession, moving from the *rottenness* within the law as revealed by capital punishment to the far more *unnatural and monstrous combination,* the *spectral mixture,* the *ignominy* that arises from the *suspension of the separation,* and finally to the *emancipation* from conditions of both law making and law maintaining.[23]

My point is simple. It is the word *rottenness* that makes me sit up. As with Bataille:

What is sacred undoubtedly corresponds to the object of horror I have spoken of, a fetid, sticky object without boundaries, which teem with life and yet is a sign of death. It is nature at the point where its effervescence closely joins life and death, where it is death gorging life with decomposed substance.[24]

What then binds "rottenness" and "monstrous combinations" to "spectrality"? And if it is this magnified rottenness of the police that accounts for the spectral nature of policing haunting democratic states, then it not only behooves us to consider to what degree and in what ways the violence founding law in any particular society may continue to "inhabit" contemporary law keeping, but what else this monstrosity might signify other than the "monstrous combination" of ends and means, law making and law maintaining.

Here Benjamin's effort to theologically frame the discussion of police violence in democracies can be restaged by taking into account the sacred sociology of taboo and transgression, it being understood that the spectral nature of police is due *not to unclear boundaries but to the incessant demand for transgression by the boundary itself*.[25] Let us not forget that it's the police who "man" this thin blue line. They are the line. It does not exist independent of them, and it turns out to be not a line at all but porous and exists only in so far as it is transgressed. In the final analysis—but of course there never is one—the ethnography is clear: for the police, life is a beach.

Between earth and water, the beach is the prehistoric zone where life began. This prehistoricity—so Benjamin could be seen as arguing in his essay on Kafka[26]—is reactivated by the modern state, and the police are foremost in this primordial endeavor. Where might this put Thomas Hobbes's theory of power, Hobbes the materialist, with his mystical theory of the "awe" intrinsic to that infamous sword "without which covenants are but words"? Where does this put Leviathan, crawling out of the mud onto the very same beach?

The sword, which upholds the power of words, lies *outside* the circle of words. Its "meaning" draws on quite other realms of reference and bodies of feeling. These are not easy to talk about. Words are lacking. In this very otherness in the object world of bodies and weapons, the awe of Hobbes's sword allows for the mystical perfection of Leviathan—the point being that the awe, as the force necessary for law, is a mystical product of *defilement;* the radiance created when the aloof nobility of the law stoops to brutality. This is the movement. This is the moment. Leviathan, that mortal god, is a monster, after all, the great enemy of God, whose sublime status rests upon the metamorphosis of brutality into sacred force.

Added to this sacred quality of brutality is the sheer inexplicability that *must* define terror—especially the terror that underpins reason as a world historical mythological movement. Consider the prevalence and importance of violence to which Benjamin's essay alerts us in the law-founding acts and mythologies of modern states. We have already hinted at Freud's allegory of patricide at the formation of (the incest) taboo, hence law, but let us note also the law-founding violence in the great bourgeois as much as the great communist revolution. Consider also the violence in so many of the great anticolonial struggles. Finally, consider these Western mythologies: the expulsion from the Garden of Eden (I can see the angel with her fiery sword as I write); the violence necessary to rescue the enchained in Plato's cave dragging them kicking and screaming to the beauty of the sun's fiery light and therewith the founding of the Republic based on pure Law; Hegel's mysterious violence that out of nowhere kicks off the phenomenology with the life-and-death struggle of master and slave—"Therefore," writes Kojève with reference to the phenomenology, "to speak of the 'origin' of Self-Consciousness it is necessary to speak of a fight to the death for 'recognition.'" In this scheme "it is in the Terror that the State is realized."[27] What is so unnerving with all this is that the terror is what paves the way for the rule of reason yet lies beyond reason. It is a given, an absolute of some sort, where explanation ceases. It belongs to the gods.

In a move that coincided with a general shift of interest in social science toward culture and symbols, Louis Althusser turned what he considered a vulgar marxism on its head, teaching that the state was a cultural force and not simply a "body of armed men." Yet what seems overlooked here is precisely the culture of armed men, meaning the culture of force, brute force and uncontained violence *with meaning none other than itself.*[28] Althusser's break into culture was predicated on what now must surely seem a woefully impoverished vision of culture as a constraining, external force of ritual that he also called "material practises," but it was one of his students, Nicos Poulantzas who, not too long before killing himself, set forth the theory of the theatrical nature of state violence, thus combining the "materialism" of his master, at least as regards the human body and the technology of weapons, with the fantastic—theatrical—figures and emotional surges accompanying violence. It was like a confession about a vague something that had always been present yet denied, in that vast system of modern sociology and political theory but that now, thanks to May '68 and the Vietnam War, kindled an appreciation of statecraft as stagecraft. "Repression," he wrote, "is never pure negativity, and it is not exhausted either in the actual exercise of physical violence or in its internalization. There is something else to repression, something about which people seldom talk; namely the mechanisms of fear." I have referred to these mechanisms, he continues, "as the theatricals of that truly Kafkaesque castle of the modern state. They are inscribed in the labyrinths where modern law becomes a practical reality."[29]

What is fascinating is the lack of talk that Poulantzas strives to talk to, and what such silence concerning the mechanisms of fear implies with regards to the theatrical power of the castle as, with alarming vigor, the call went out when I first wrote this essay in 1995 here in New York, as elsewhere, for more police, more prisons, and more capital punishment. How innocent even that appears now, post 9/11, where the fear of which Poulantzas speaks, and the "impure sacred" of policing, which I address, has become so apparent yet at the same time so silencing.

For where the silence finds an outlet is in that decidedly other theater, the "negative sacred" fantasy theater par excellence of the underworld, the Mafia, the street gangs, the child molesters, the crack dealers, the Oklahoma bombers and now "the enemy" ever vigilant on all sides and in all homes whose name is terrorist. On this desperate image of evil the castle sustains itself. And while the theater of the castle needs this other theater, and vice versa, such that the mystical powers of the one are transformed into the mystical powers of the other, it would seem that it is always the negative sacred—hell and the underworld—that provides the most compelling scenario and performative power for the mystical foundations of authority. This is why the fear that *can* be spoken is displaced elsewhere.

Benjamin felt that the prehistoricity of the state world in Kafka was incomparably older than the world of myth. He felt that redemption—for we cannot conclude these pessimistic ruminations on the inevitability of corruption without at least a nod in that direction—could be imagined, if not sought, somewhere between myth and fairy tale. And surely it is the living theater of kitsch where the mythology of the sacred, pure or evil, is suddenly evacuated from policing and the Three Stooges take over as in Kafka's trial in the always possible comic displacement of the tragic that is crime. The truly corrupt policeman is not the one who, beachlike, is eroded by the waves of crime washing over him. Rather, he is the one who maladroitly stands in the way of the smooth functioning of the taboo and instead of allowing free passage for the conversion of crime into righteousness, lends his badge for a Halloween party.

The Language of Flowers

Asked on a radio interview a couple of years back why he drew animals and not people, the great cartoonist Chuck Jones of Bugs Bunny and Road Runner fame replied: "It's easier to humanize animals than humanize humans."[1] Recently the Colombian artist Juan Manuel Echavarría gave this a twist. Reacting against the stupendous violence in his country, he humanized flowers by photographing them like botanical specimens, replacing the stems, leaves, flowers, and berries with what look like human bones. He called this series of thirty-two black-and-white photographs Corte de Florero (The flower vase cut), referring to the name of one of the mutilations practiced in the Colombian *violencia* of the 1940s and 1950s in which the amputated limbs were stuffed, so it is said, into the thorax via the neck of the decapitated corpse.

In cartoons we laugh at distortions of the body, suggesting just how close violence is to humor. Indeed the human face when crying can seem very close if not identical to that same face laughing. It is, moreover, almost trite to observe that great comedians and clowns bear the burden of great tragedy as well. As for the cartoon quality in violence, hearken to Michael Herr's reference to his experience in the Vietnam War; he goes to considerable effort to deny these two elements have anything in common: "No jive cartoon," he says, "where the characters get

An earlier version of this article can be found in *Critical Inquiry* 30, no. 1 (fall 2003): 98–131.

smacked around and electrocuted and dropped from heights, flattened out and frizzed back and broken like a dish, then up again and whole and back in the game."[2]

No jive cartoon—indeed! So why bother to raise that specter, only to deny it? Why bother to come so close, only to draw back? Is it because the resemblance is too, too troubling, true but troubling, and by this maneuver we do precisely what is necessary, which is to catch a glimpse of the impossible unthinkable and then close it over again? Well, then, what is this impossible unthinkable that in equating war with a cartoon simultaneously heightens their stupendous difference?

Did I say *heighten,* as does Herr when he refers us to the cartoonish move of being dropped from heights, flattened out, "then up again and whole and back in the game"? What emotional register, what law of aesthetics and logic is being transgressed by this heightened drop and even steeper fall into . . . well, into what? Not redemption. That's for sure. Back into war, that's what—"up again and whole and back in the game." Is this not also what occurs when Echavarría humanizes not animals but flowers, meticulously duplicating the exactness and whimsy of botanical drawings with his bleached-out photographs of human bones?

At one point in an interview, Echavarría says, "My purpose was to create something so beautiful that people would be attracted to it. The spectator would come near it, look at it, and then when he or she realizes that it is not a flower as it seemed, but actually a flower made of human bones—something must click in the head, or in the heart, I hope."[3]

I myself do not see it that way. The flowers are so obviously not flowers. Instead it is the very clumsiness, the deliberateness of the artifice of posing bones as flowers, that perturbs one—and this is of the same order of artifice that makes the actual mutilation of the Corte de Florero so powerful, too.

The flowers in Echavarría's photographs have stems made of curving ribs or of the decayed long bones of arms. The petals are formed from what appear to be the human pelvis or spinal vertebrae. In some photographs, small bones like teeth or chips of bones lie to one side, thereby disturbing pretensions to symmetry or completeness. A vertebra hangs delicately off a rib, five of which are bunched together like plant stems emerging from a column of three vertebrae glued together, not as in the human spine, but separated from that, like a child's building blocks, then stuck front to back, one on top of the other.

Lying on their bleached-out background, the flowers appear fragile, suspended in midair and ungrounded. They could be flying. The law of gravity no longer holds. There is a sense of a world on hold, a painful absence of sound. What we see is silence, the silence of something gone awfully wrong with the human world in which we are all, God included, holding our breath, which is probably what happens when you fall a long, long way.

To add to their strangeness, each photograph bears a title like the Latin names used in the plant illustrations of the famous botanical expedition to Colombia organized by the Spanish crown and led by José Celestino Mutis at the end of the eighteenth century. Echavarría is very conscious of this genealogy. In fact he sees his flowers as its latest expression. The difference is that Echavarría's Latinate names are hybrids suggesting the grotesque, one pelvic bone flower being named *Dracula Nosferatu,* while another flower made of a curved rib with a bunch of metacarpals at one end, suggestive of petals, is called *Dionaea Misera.* Although these names are in small, discreet letters, names are of consuming importance to this work, beginning with the name of the mutilation—the flower vase cut. The name is crucial because on viewing the mutilated body without the name, I doubt whether an observer would get the point—as we say of a joke—without the name. All the observer would see would be a bloody morass of hacked-off limbs and a limbless trunk.

The mutilation would be incomplete, by which I mean it would lack the meaning that destroys meaning. I do not understand this. Perhaps I am not meant to. But what I do know is that what mutilation registers, what all mutilation registers, is this wave, this continuous wavelike motion of autosacrifice of meaning heightened then dissipated by the name in conjunction with the corpse as a work of art. I think it goes like this: that in attaching a commonplace name to a transgressive act the act is somehow completed, dignified with a meaning, we could say, only to shatter that name and that meaning. Herr's story of the necklace made of amputated ears in Vietnam comes to mind. Love beads they were called.[4]

Art Forms in Nature

The striking plant illustrations of the eighteenth-century Mutis expedition, many in color, are well known today both inside and outside of Colombia, where they are now virtually icons of the nation, all the more powerful for being natural symbols. They stand for something at once modest and sublime, the humble plant on the one hand, the greatness that is the nation on the other. They capture the wonder the New World had for the savants of Europe as a truly new world in which scientific curiosity and conquest existed side by side. How much of their beauty is due to this conflation of colonialism and botanical novelty?

Dionaea Viscosa

Lam. 33

From Juan Manuel Echavarría, Corte de Florero: Flower Vase Cut, *exhibition catalog (B & B Gallery, New York, n.d..), 5, 7, and 9.*

Mutis provokes another question as well: Is there an art in nature as well as an art of nature? This is the same question implicit in Ernst Haeckel's 1904 *Art Forms in Nature* as well as in the plant photography of a celebrated modernist, Karl Blossfeldt (1865–1932), who "believed that the best human art was modeled on forms preexisting in nature."[5] How curious it is, then, that Blossfeldt's images, faithfully reproducing nature but on an enlarged scale and with carefully controlled lighting, should illuminate the pages of that great sur/realist magazine, *Documents,* edited by Georges Bataille and used by him to illustrate his essay "The Language of Flowers."

When I first look at Mutis I see what I take to be an art in nature and am thrilled by what I call the book of nature opening before my eyes. But then a little later I become self-conscious and aware of the artist arranging the flowers and stems so they conform to an aesthetic as much as a need on the part of the botanist for vi-

From Juan Manuel Echavarría, Corte de Florero: Flower Vase Cut, *exhibition catalog (B & B Gallery, New York, n.d.), 5, 7, and 9.*

sual information. I had the same sensation as a medical student studying human anatomy. There was the corpse spread-eagled on its table in various shades of gray and blue with shards of yellowing fat and an insufferable odor of formalde-hyde; by its side was my textbook displaying the body in shimmering symmetries of reds and blues and all the more accurate, not to mention beautiful, for being thus rendered. So what has happened? The art in nature turns out to be an art of nature! It is like treason, the same as when a child realizes Santa Claus is a man dressed up. But who is to blame, myself for being so naive or the artist for being so clever? What is so silly is that every time I go back to look at these plant paint-ings of Mutis, which now strike me as pure kitsch, I run through the same se-quence of delight and disappointment, of concealment and revelation, as the en-gagement with the art in nature is followed by its conversion into an art of nature.

Why would this be, this now-you-see-it now-you-don't phenomenon? Is this what lies behind the *sur* of surrealism as in Bataille's use of Blossfeldt? For while Blossfeldt with his magnifying lenses was pursuing the art in nature, Bataille was enchanted by the rupture his images thereby created. Bataille's point, surely, was not the elementary one that representation trumps nature, but rather that Bloss-feldt's images are like magic tricks in which you suspect sleight of hand but are nevertheless filled with wonder as the rabbit is extracted from the top hat. You are left suspended, unable to decide what is art and what is nature, temporarily

Images from José Celestino Mutis's expedition to Colombia.

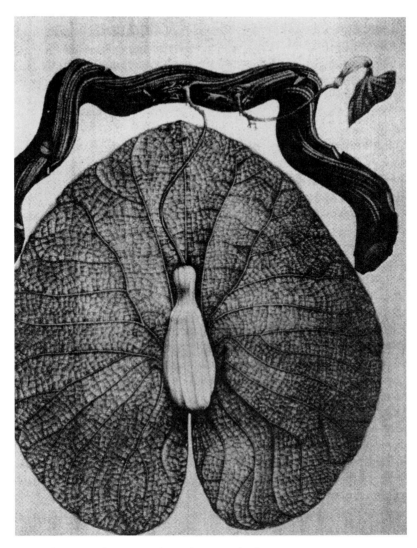

Images from José Celestino Mutis's expedition to Colombia.

stripped of your common sense with its assumptions as to the nature of nature let alone the nature of art. When it comes to the human body, that arbiter of the nature / culture divide, this becomes all the more pronounced. It is this that underlies all mutilation, whether of the corpse or the living body.

Bone Art

What is fascinating to me is the absence of the human skull, that wicked, grinning fellow centering death in the baroque and our various childhood fantasies of death, but nowhere to be found in Echavarría's work nor, apparently, in the mutilation itself. What did those mutilating Colombians do with the head, you wonder? Why can't we see the face of death? "Alas, poor Yorick." Certainly in other forms of human bone art—to designate a category—the skull takes pride of place, its hollow eyes a dark reminder of what once was. In the pirate flag of skull and crossbones, loved by children of all ages and many nations, it is the idea that is paramount, the actual execution of the design often woefully imperfect—but who cares so long as the wind is up and the flag flutters, bringing the animating force of nature into play. There is another reason for not caring: this pirate flag is also an antiflag—not merely a sign of belonging to no nation but a sign of refusal of all signs and hence of representation, too, as nature unfurls its own nation.[6] Miles removed from this anarchic sign are the images Bataille displayed in *Documents* (August 1930) of Capuchin catacombs in Rome with their skulls and bones from more than four thousand brothers who died between 1528 and 1870. What jaw-dropping images! Skulls are carefully arranged one next to the other yet in numbers so vast they lose all individuality to become like white dimples on seawalls in underworlds at the far edge of dreams. No doubt about it, this is art. With its mix of showbiz and heartfelt religious sentiments, Sedlec Ossuary in the Czech Republic carries this bone art a stage further, converting it into pure kitsch, draining the bones of whatever reverential and religious potential they might possess and completely evacuating the effect that so fascinated Bataille, namely, the oscillation from repulsion to attraction, the movement that I think lies behind mutilation, in general, and the flower vase cut, taken up by Echavarría, specifically. As with cartoons and violence, the Sedlec kitsch demonstrates how fine the line is between the somber face of death and its comic qualities, a line that Bataille crossed again and again in his investigations into the sacred surplus harvested by the transformation of saints' bones from the vile status of the corpse to their glowing destination under the stones of church or altar, a transformation enacted on a lesser scale with every body buried in the church cemetery. Mutilation is this same movement, in reverse, yet no less religious.

But the headlessness?

Flowers and Death

Might it be that flowers are in effect human bones? For what the mutilation of the flower vase cut draws upon is that flowers and death go together in the Christian world, with a long history of use on graves and in funerals.[7] Yet flowers salute not only death but also life, as with birthdays. Could it be that flowers frequent death because they are seen as bearers of life and that this "mix" is what enters so naturally into our everyday life rituals as something superbly sardonic, savage, cruel, and uplifting—like the fall into nothingness expressed by the disturbing collusion of cartoons and violence. "There are no black flowers," writes Jean Genet in reference to transgression, "yet at the end of his crushed finger, that black fingernail looked like nothing so much as a flower."[8] This intertwinement of life in death in flowers is what Herr is getting at when he describes Saigon during the Vietnam War: "Sitting in Saigon was like sitting inside the folded petals of a poisonous flower, the poison history, fucked in its root no matter how far back you wanted to run your trace."[9]

Like life, only more so, flowers are beautiful and fragile, and this may be why many people consider them appropriate for death and even more so for disaster. This message comes across strongly in an article in the *New York Times* by Barbara Stewart on 22 September 2001 with reference to the attack on the World Trade Center. She notes the abundance of flowers, bunches of them, four and five layers deep, laid at the doorsteps of fire stations, churches, and impromptu shrines on park lawns, stoops, windows, and sidewalks. This turns her attention to the presence of flowers cultivated in little gardens throughout the city during the past decade. Against the backdrop of the city, these flowers strike her as incongruous: "heartbreakingly bright and fragile."

"What's more fragile than a flower?" asks her informant, the aptly named Michael Pollan, whom she describes as a writer on botany and a philosopher, who goes on to describe the value of flowers as lying with their uselessness. "'Flowers are a luxury,' Mr. Pollan said. 'They're not useful. . . . You don't worry about flowers until you've solved a lot of other problems in life.'" Even his question—"What's more fragile than a flower?"—can be thought of as a flower, a rhetorical question, we say.

But, when disaster strikes, the useless becomes useful.

Mandrake, the Magician

There is one flowering plant that stands out with regard to life and death in the same way as do Echavarría's flowers, a plant that perturbs the pious platitudes of life and death. It is known as the mandrake or mandragora, said to be the most important hallucinogen in western Europe and the Near East over two millennia.[10] Hugo Rahner of the Society of Jesus says it can be "the herb of life or of death, a symbol of both sensual love, the bringer of death, or of divine love, the restorer of life."[11] Note, not just life, but love; not just life or death, but restorer of life. Mircea Eliade, the professor and virtual founder of the history of religions calls it "a miraculous plant, far stronger than any other . . . which can multiply life or strike dead."[12] Miraculous indeed, it serves to cure infertility, arouse the organs of regeneration, accrue wealth, stave off accidents, and—in what we like to call the Dark Ages—was an indispensable element in the witch's cauldron. Some say it is the plant Hermes gave Odysseus to resist the magic of Circe. It appears in the Old Testament in Genesis and in the Song of Songs and is said by scholars to be associated with witchcraft into modern times. Mandrakes were being sold in many herbalists' shops in the poorer part of London even in the early twentieth century.[13] One of the charges against Joan of Arc was that she carried a mandrake on her breast. In her defense she denied that, but said she had heard of a mandrake near her town. Women were burnt by the Inquisition as witches because of alleged possession of mandrakes, which they fed and clothed. For the mandrake was like a human being. Extracted from the ground it would be bathed several times a year and dressed in costly cloth or clothes and sometimes even fed with food and drink twice a day.

Part plant, part human, the mandrake is an astonishingly precise instance of something hovering between an art of nature and an art in nature, and surely this is what accounts, in part, at least, for its magical powers. It is described as a plant of very peculiar appearance, a perennial with broad leaves, a prominent white, yellow, or purple flower, with fruit like a plum or small apple. Over all it exudes a peculiar, pronounced, and pleasant scent. But the below-ground part is even more crucial. This is the footlong blackish root, often forked, and said by many—but not all—to have a human form, even with a male sexual organ, which juts out as a subsidiary root. For this reason the mandrake is in many languages given a name suggesting man, or living being, from ancient Persia to ancient Greece, ancient Rome, and Asia Minor—parts of the ancient world from where it passed to northern Europe and east into Asia. In the Christian tradition it was said to be fashioned from the same earth whereof God formed Adam.[14]

The technique considered to achieve the best mandrakes, as used in what is now Syria and Asia Minor, was to extract the root, manipulate its shape with cutting and pressure, bandage it, and then replace it in the ground, giving it time to grow some more and thus, when extracted a second time, become—in the words of one source—"so natural in appearance as to make it difficult or impossible to discern where the artist shaped it."[15]

In 1891 von Luschan exhibited six mandrakes from Asia Minor, declaring that a "clever artist will thus produce these little figures which look entirely natural and whose genuineness no one would suspect. Such figures are not merely 'very rare and obtainable with great danger to life, but are considered costly and valuable talismans.'"[16] By the sixteenth century this composite little fellow, art in nature / of nature, was being shipped over much of the world, from Persia to northern India, from Germany to France and England, and being imported into Egypt as well.[17]

What about the bizarre ritual required to extract the mandrake from the ground? It shrieks as it is being pulled out. It shrieks like a person. That is why a dog, a black dog, at that, is required to pull it out and why, when the mandrake shrieks the dog falls dead. The point, as I see it, is this: coming out of the ground, the semihuman mandrake is in a classic liminal space betwixt and between an art in nature / of nature. This is precisely what ensures it will become more than human—that is, superhuman—and why at the point of transition from an art in nature to an art of nature it is too dangerous to be handled by a human.

And here, once again, in this most curious of all states between nature and art, lies the issue of the head. According to at least one Christian commentator—Rahner—the mandrake sadly lacks a head, thus making it a ripe subject for redemption to a heady state, while ancient and medieval illustrations depict it as both headless and with a head. In this regard, the illustrations I have found are really quite startling, for not only are some with, others without, a head, but they vary greatly in their degree of dignified, soulful sanctity. Some have a marked iconlike look about them, resembling religious paintings used in the Church, while others look like cartoons (for example, the drawing of the mandrake being pulled by a dog chasing a ball). In either case it is the anthropomorphism that is eye-catching, disturbing, and fun (figs 3a–e).

Above, the coronation of Queen Mandragora (mandrake). Twelfth-century miniature, Munich MS clm 5118 (Honorius's Commentary on the Song of Songs).

In keeping with its ambiguous status, the mandrake has perplexing pharmacological effects, being credited with powerful pain-killing and sleep-inducing properties, as well as with erotic stimulation. One reads of "mandrake narcosis" no less than of its capacity to excite voluptuousness. The Christian bible tells me that "the Arabs call it 'devil's apple,' from its power to excite voluptuousness."[18] It is a "poison" that calms; it is "'half-way between poison and sleep.'"[19] Experts on hallucinogenic plants claim mandrake's reputation is due to its "bizarre

Mandrake, from the Herbal of Pseudo-Apuleius, *seventh-century* A.D. *Based on a fourth-century* A.D *Greek source.*

Above, mandrake, from a fifteenth-century Italian Herbal.

psychoactivity," which includes hallucinations that occur during the transition between consciousness and sleep.[20]

Who would have guessed it? In "The Language of Flowers," published in the magazine *Documents* in 1929, a magazine that despite its short tenure appears today as the crucible for much of what was intellectually audacious in the European avant-garde, Bataille, the magazine's editor, singled out the mandrake as an example of what the plant world might teach us about the relation of beauty to sex and death.[21]

He was looking for processes in nature that, when framed in a particular manner, made you realize how models drawn from nature surreptitiously formed our thinking. Bataille's title, "The Language of Flowers," which I have borrowed, is itself borrowed from an eighteenth- and nineteenth-century Western European tradition similar to the Renaissance assumption of Egyptian hieroglyphs as a universal language uniting God with nature. We could say that as the hieroglyph was to the Renaissance magicians, such as Ficino and Bruno, so flowers were to those people in later centuries excited by the idea that flowers possessed a secret language. One book published in this tradition in 1867 begins with the statement:

"I said to the flowers, Tell me what God told you to tell me.'" According to Goody this language had roots in eighteenth-century orientalism's notion that there was an esoteric language of the harem. It was the conclusion of one Austrian savant that this was the secret language for lesbian attachments.[22] Be that as it may, the French language of flowers seems to have been more concerned with tabulation, calling to mind the later structuralism of Claude Lévi-Strauss, as in his famous work, *The Savage Mind* (La Pensée sauvage), which puns as the "wild pansy." In its late nineteenth-century emphasis on classificatory tables of smells and colors, as part of such system building, the tradition of the language of flowers also recalls the early nineteenth-century work of the French visionary and communist Charles Fourier, beloved by both Karl Marx and Walter Benjamin. Although he nowhere makes mention of the fact, Bataille's language of flowers thus emerges from two centuries of tradition with its roots in secrecy, the occult, orientalist fantasies, and an appeal to a logic of nature that makes divine wisdom accessible. Yet at the same time his essay marks a radical departure from this tradition.

Like the French ethnologist Robert Hertz, Bataille was excited by the way the patterns of symmetries and differences in the human body served for modeling culture. Hertz had focused on the role given to the hands and the division of the body into left and right. To the right hand go all the honors: justice, good, the sun, maleness, the hand of writing, and conservative politics. To the left there was sorcery, the moon, women, and communists. Twenty years later Bataille focused not on the vertical but the horizontal division of the human body into an upper, dignified half and a lower unmentionable one.

A keen student of Hegel's dialectic and the unity of opposites, Bataille brought a surrealist sensibility and love of the absurd to bear on the way the upper and lower parts of the body related to cosmic schemes of reconciliation and redemption. It was Bataille's contention that a true dialectic could never come to rest. Hence not only could there be no truce to the war raging between the superior and the inferior, but thought itself was set permanently ajar and out of sorts because thought relied on these categories read into nature. Therefore as regards the language of flowers, and especially with the fearsome mandrake, Bataille had a field day.

Bataille's point overlaps with the *New York Times* article on the function of flowers following the World Trade Center attack. Yet the differences are instructive, for Bataille sees flowers as sexual metaphors that bring death and eroticism into conjunction with beauty. He compares flowers to human sex organs, stamens and petals directed towards the sun, and the essence of their beauty owes much to the fragility of their life. Doomed to die almost as soon as they bloom, they wither sadly on the stem in rank disorder, eventually falling to the ground from which they came. Hence, his conclusion to "The Language of Flowers": "Don't all these beautiful things run the risk of being reduced to a strange *mise en scène*?" he asks. "Are not they destined to make sacrilege more impure?"[23]

If Hertz had seen a complementarity in the woeful asymmetry between the right and left hands, Bataille sees a similar imbalance between the good and evil in making up the sacred sphere. They not only feed off one another and are complementary, as in the Christian scheme of heaven and hell, but their asymmetry ensures an excess that cannot be contained by the play of opposites. This is Bataille's signature idea, and this is what is implied in his question concerning flowers: "Are not they destined to make sacrilege even more impure?" And to sharpen his point, to bring his cascading thoughts to their highest head of pressure, he then focuses on the mandrake.

The mandrake expresses the passage from the sacred to sacrilege with astonishing clarity. In its very shape it can be said to express the cosmic architecture of heaven and hell and its analogue in the human body. For Christians the headlessness is a sign of possible future redemption from sin. But for Bataille this headlessness is nature's *acéphale* the name his group applied to their sacred, secret society in the late 1930s, emblematized by André Masson's drawing of a headless man, naked with arms outstretched, a dagger in one hand, a flaming heart like a hand grenade in the other, stars as nipples, and a skull in place of genitalia. "I saw him immediately as headless, as becomes him," said Masson. "But what to do with this cumbersome and doubting head?—Irresistibly it finds itself displaced to the sex, which it masks with a 'death's head.'" [24]

Acéphale was not only a secret society. It was scary. One of its members, Patrick Waldberg, relates that at Bataille's urging some of its members arranged to meet at a lonely forest outside of Paris near the railway station of Saint-Norn to perform a human sacrifice, but decided against it at the last moment. Bataille described the site for these meetings as follows: "On a marshy soil, in the centre of a forest, where turmoil seems to have intervened in the usual order of things, stands a tree struck by lightning. One can recognize in this tree the mute presence of that which assumed the name Acéphale, expressed here by arms without a head.'" [25]

Likewise, do we not discern the mute presence of Acéphale in the mandrake?

Another meeting place for Acéphale was the Place de la Concorde where Louis XVI was "acephalised" (as the editors of the *Encyclopaedia Acephalica* put it) by the revolutionary guillotine. A few years later Napoleon installed the famous

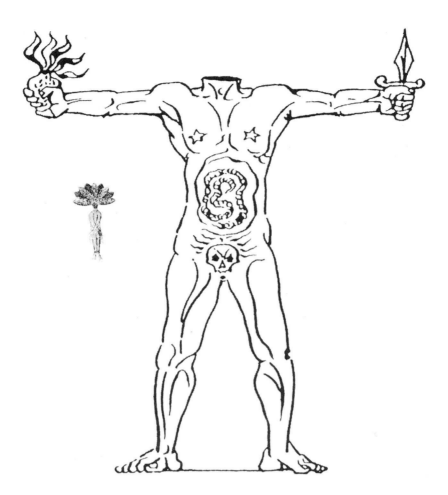

The acéphale.

obelisk stolen from Egypt on this spot. The phallus, so to speak, that drew down the sun, replaced the head.

After he cut off the head and used it to displace the male genitalia, André Masson contemplated his work and said: "'Well, fine so far, but what to make of the stomach? That empty container will be the receptacle for the Labyrinth that elsewhere had become our rallying sign.'"[26]

This labyrinth of coiled intestines is the anatomical no less than pictorial register of the excess that exceeds oppositions. Hence its name, "the labyrinth": a crazy-quilt maze from which there is no escape, no enlightenment, one could say, other than by some miraculous thread, as in Greek mythology, not given in the oppositions themselves.

Bataille had found this same labyrinth of the intestines in his hilarious three-page study of "The Big Toe" published in *Documents* five months after "The Language of Flowers." Opposing the head to the big toe in a series of delightful forays invoking the eagle of state, Enlightenment reason, and Hegel's dialectic no less than bunions and the sexual draw of foot fetishism, Bataille displayed the dependence of the lofty heights on the humble toe that they looked down upon. The text was accompanied by alarming full-page photographic enlargements of a big toe that effectively estranged this part of our anatomy. It looked fearsome yet silly at the same time, a thoroughly vexed dialectic, you could say, once again the Mutis / Echavarría conundrum: an art in nature or an art of nature?

But more than that—and here is where the irreducible excess comes in—was *tone* and *stomach*. Tone meant in this case the tone of the absurd and the tone of laughing, not exactly ideas but something else. But what is this something else? Likewise the stomach, not just the Rabelaisian belly laugh of carnival, but the stomach of the motile intestine, smooth muscle irregularly pulsing with the echoes of a distant pinging as with a stone hurled into a mine shaft full of water, and the whole unholy morass of circular motion displaced by quiverings and unsteady forward motion of chyme. It was to this swampland of the *informe* that all roads led, Bataille's Rome no less than his Big Toe, and it is this same swamp he had in mind when he envisaged a headless man unaware of prohibition—"He is not a man. He is not a God either. He is not me but he is more than me: his stomach is the labyrinth in which he has lost himself, loses me with him, and in which I discover myself as him, in other words as a monster."[27]

In conclusion, therefore, like the mandrake, this image of the *acéphale* does not simply invert heaven and hell, but deranges their interdependence such that there is little possibility of dialectical recuperation or, for that matter, of redemption. It is as if the dialectic consumes itself, reminding us that self-sacrifice is the mark of divinity as when the god takes his own life. Behind this lurks both the joy and despair of the realization that, like language, reason is at best an approximation of reality and that reality exceeds the terms and schemes by which we organize it. Similarly with the mandrake we are propelled into a world of "bizarre psycho-activity"—midway between sleep and consciousness—a rhizomic mass of roots, according to Bataille, "swarming under the surface of the soil, nauseating and naked like vermin."[28]

But why is it that the most magically powerful mandrake is to be found under the gallows?

The Little Gallows Man

Fact: For centuries in Europe it was said that where a man was hanged by the state a white flower might sprout from his ejaculated semen or urine. That flower was none other than mandrake, and it came to be called "the little gallows man."[29] However it is not the innocent white flower that attracts attention here. In fact the flower is merely the sign, beautiful and striking in its own right, for the marvels of the black root twisting itself into the soil in its efforts to acquire a human form.

This is nicely set forth for England as early as 1587 in *An Herbal to the Bible*, which provides a separate chapter for each plant of importance. The first chapter is dedicated to mandrake, the second to manna. The mandrake is described as having a strong scent and taste, provoking sleep, pleasant and delightsome. Cloven into branches or limbs, like legs, folding and wrapped one about another, the root is covered with fine threads or small hairs—such that makeshifts and deceitful peddlers derive shapes of humans, male or female, and persuade the simple ignorant people that they grow naturally out of the earth and are magically empowered.[30]

> Some of this lewd rabble of shifting mates and shameless deceivers, impudently and boldly announce and constantly affirm, that this is a creature, having life, and engendered under the earth of the seed of some dead person, that has been convicted and put to death for some felony or murder.[31]

It was said in the sixteenth century that for mandrake to be effective it must be gathered from under the scaffold, and that is why it was so expensive.[32] Others held that mandrake only grew next to the scaffold.[33] Still others opined that it was the most potent form that was to be found under a gallows.[34]

Folklore: Carefully extracted from the soil by bizarre and magical means, washed in red wine and wrapped in precious silks, red and white, this little gallows man will answer any question put to him about future or about secret matters. "Would you be rich"? Put money beside him at night and in the morning it will be doubled.[35]

Fact: The German poet Rist (1607–1667) described a mandrake over one hundred years old. It lived in a coffin over which was placed a tapestry depicting a thief on the gallows, underneath which grew a mandrake. It would pass from father to youngest son.[36]

Fiction: Early on in Genet's novel *Querelle,* first published in 1947, the character Gil walks through the foggy streets of the naval port of Brest, northern France, with his buddy, Querelle. They are talking about sex and through his pocket Gil flattens his penis against his belly. "Indeed, it had the stature of a tree," writes Genet, "a mossy-boled oak with lamenting mandrakes being born among its roots. (Sometimes, when he woke up with a hard-on, Gil would address his prick as 'my hanged man.')"[37]

Fact: Audiences of up to 100,000 were claimed to have attended hangings in London in the latter half of the eighteenth and early nineteenth centuries. Crowds of three to seven thousand were standard.[38] In the mighty spectacle that was the public hanging (as many as eight a day during one year in the second half of the eighteenth century), the London mob fought the authorities at the scaffold for possession of the corpse, and this for a variety of motives: to ensure a Christian burial; to prevent the corpse being sold to surgeons and medical schools; and because of what that ingenious advocate of free market capitalism, Bernard de Mandeville, described in 1725 as the "superstitious Reverence of the Vulgar for a Corpse, even of a Malefactor."[39]

Fact: But the corpse of a person hanged by the state is no ordinary corpse. The social historians rightly hesitate to entertain the macabre worlds opened up by these weird varieties of necrophilia that challenge all propriety, including intellectual propriety. That threshold can only be crossed by the novelists, as we see in the works of Genet or William S. Burroughs. Yet is not something of the order of that imagination necessary if we are to even begin to relate to the state's investment in capital punishment—not to mention the public's investment, in the United States today, as well? How else are we going to connect to what seems so outrageously indecent, the magic of the corpse, let alone its erotic potential, once it is pointed out to us that not so long ago in decent, wholesome Western society the state-hanged corpse was an especially wondrous entity, capable of restoring life and health in sick people?

In a recent essay on crowds, carnival, and the state in English executions, Thomas Laqueur designates the hanged body as "the magic body." He cites James Boswell in 1776 describing the "superstition" he witnessed at a London hanging whereby "no less than four diseased persons had themselves rubbed with the sweaty hands of malefactors in the agonies of death, and believed this would cure them."[40] It was said that a withered limb could be made whole by placing it on the neck of a recently hanged man and that women visited the gallows to be stroked by a just-dead hand so as to become fertile. Nurses brought children in their care to be touched to ensure the health of their young charges. And just before Murphy the coal heaver was cut down from the gallows at Tyburn in 1768, a well-dressed woman appeared with a child aged three to pass his right hand three times over "the child's left hand which had four holes in it from the King's Evil" (scrofula).[41]

The name tells it all. The King's Evil. For just as the corpse of the state-executed criminal could cure this disease, so the king with the mere passing of his hand could also cure this horrific, lingering, and often fatal illness. Thanks to state execution, king and corpse of the malefactor are made magically equivalent.

Fiction:

"You must touch with the limb the neck of the man who's been hanged."

She started a little at the image he had raised.

"Before he's cold—just after he's cut down," continued the conjuror impassively.

"How can that do good?"

"It will turn the blood and change the constitution. But, as I say, to do it is hard. You must go to the jail when there's a hanging, and wait for him when he's brought off the gallows. Lots have done it, though perhaps not such pretty women as you. I used to send dozens for skin complaints."

This is a conjuror speaking in the southwest of mid-nineteenth-century England in Thomas Hardy's tale, "The Withered Arm."[42] The young woman he is addressing has an incurable disease withering her arm, a disease that bears the marks of sorcery.

The day before the hanging she sees the harness maker fashioning the rope for the hanging. "''Tis sold by the inch afterwards,'" he tells her. "I could get you a bit, miss, for nothing, if you'd like?'" (49).

Later at night she makes a surreptitious visit to the hangman whose normal occupation—this being a country town—is that of a gardener. "''Tis no use to come here about the knot," he tells her before she can explain that what she wants is to touch the neck as soon as the man has been hung. Examining her withered arm he exclaims: "That is the class o' subject, I'm bound to admit! I like the look of the wound; it is as suitable for the cure as any I ever saw. 'Twas a knowing-man that sent 'ee, whoever he was" (50, 51).

Interpolation: Why such emphasis on the knot? Because if death was due to strangling, rather than breaking the neck by the fall of the body, then the knot could be adjusted so as to give the victim a chance of surviving, which is why Peter Linebaugh in his essay on hanging in London wryly refers to the public's great interest in knot lore.

The next day she approaches the corpse supported on two trestles. She feels a gray mist floating before her and can barely discern anything. "It was as though she had nearly died," writes Hardy, "but was held up by a sort of galvanism" (53).

Interpolation: Somewhere between dying and galvanism. Could this be equivalent to the "bizarre psychoactivity" attributed to the mandrake by our ethnobotanical experts Schultes and Hofmann?

The hangman took her poor cur'st arm, uncovered the face of the corpse, and laid her arm across the dead man's neck, "upon a line the colour of an unripe blackberry, which surrounded it" (53). She shrieked. The "turn o' the blood" predicted by the conjuror had taken place.

Hanging as Sex as the Magic of the State

Hanging not only turns the blood of those able to touch the neck but may turn on the person being hung. At least this is part of the folklore of sexual excitement, testimony to Bataille's coupling of sexual pleasure with death.[43] Knud Romer Joergensen reminds us of erotic hanging in the Marquis de Sade's *Justine* (1791) and informs us of an infamous case that went to trial in London that same year on account of a prostitute, Susannah Hill, assisting a composer, and one of the greatest double bass players in Europe, Frantz Kotzwara, to hang himself for sexual pleasure with fatal results.[44]

Hanged bodies jerking at the end of a rope in orgasm appear often in the span of Burroughs's life's work, from *Naked Lunch* to *Cities of the Red Night*. In the latter book, Kelley killed the quartermaster of his ship while at anchor in Tangier and was sentenced to death by hanging but some pirates come, cut him down, and revive him. "It was thought," writes Burroughs, "that a man who had been hanged and brought back to life would not only bring luck to their venture but also ensure protection against the fate from which he had been rescued."[45]

The pirates rubbed red ink into the hemp marks around Kelley's neck to keep their magic visible. Kelley claimed he had learned the secrets of death on the gallows such that he was endowed with unbeatable skill as a swordsman and with such sexual prowess that no man or woman could resist him. When asked what it was like being hung, Kelley responded:

At first I was sensible of a very great pain due to the weight of my body and felt my spirits in a strange commotion violently pressed upwards. After they reached my head, I saw a bright blaze of light which seemed to go out at my eyes with a flash. Then I lost all sense of pain. But after I was cut down, I felt such indescribable pain from the pricking and shooting as my blood and spirits returned that I wish those who had cut me down could have been hanged.

Actually these words are credited to "Half-Hanged Smith," a former soldier hanged for burglary in 1705. Burroughs found them in Daniel P. Mannix's *The History of Torture.*[46] It appears that Smith had been hanging for fifteen minutes before he was cut down following a reprieve on account of his military record. Hanging at that time rarely meant snapping the neck with instantaneous death. Instead the victim was slowly choked to death, dancing at the end of the rope (which might later be sold for high sums in small lengths). Hence Smith was still living when cut down and from that point on, as Half-Hanged Smith, he led a miraculous career being repeatedly arrested for burglary, yet always freed. At one point the prosecutor dropped dead during the trial. The law no longer had any hold over this half-hanged individual.

At the same time in Burroughs's cities of the red night, hanging has become a nightclub act, reminding us once again of the uncanny relationship between cartoons and violence. Take the club called the Double Gallows where there is a hanging show every night, and one night in particular, Flasher Night, is especially wonderful as chic clients make unexpected entrances in extravagant gear. Some pop up through the floor in green drag, "screaming like mandrakes," Burroughs says. Others arrive through mirrors with ropes already around their necks while "noose peddlers circulate among the clients" who feel the quality of the nooses. There are silk ones, "in all colors, hemp cured and softened in rare unguents, tingle nooses burning with a soft blue flame, leather nooses made from sniff-hound hide." Led in by a red demon comes the star of the show, a dummy called Whitey who stands with the noose around his neck, cock almost hard, pupils pinpointed. "The platform falls and he hangs there ejaculating and a blaze of light flashes out of his eyes."

"'A Flasher! a Flasher!' The clients throw up their arms and wriggle . . . ecstatically."[47]

To my mind, being cut down in the nick of time is equivalent to what I wish to call the *mandrake state-execution magical complex,* a mouthful, to be sure, but then this is a hard row to hoe. In my opinion, the magic Burroughs invokes, magic that permeates his entire body of work, comes not from hanging per se but from state execution carried over into other spheres where the hanging bears the "shadow" of state executions. This is the same magic gathered together by the little gallows man, taken a stage further by Burroughs to release his intimate familiars: color, smell, and a train of unearthly memories sweeping back and forth through time and space as transhistorical unconscious.

Take the handsome young Captain Strobe being hung for piracy in 1702 in front of the courthouse of Panama City. There is a curious smile on his face, and a yellow green aura surrounds his body. Rescued dangling on the gibbet in the hot sun by a hit squad and fed opium, he awakens with a throbbing erection. He knows where he is: forty miles south of Panama City. "He could see the low coastline of mangrove swamps laced with inlets, the shark fins, the stagnant seawater."[48]

Captain Strobe is hung; Captain Strobe returns to the living. He awakes not in heaven but in the swamp, in the equatorial third world swamp where anything could happen in a headless world where God is dead. He awakens with his body intact, indeed more than intact, afloat on opium and with a throbbing erection. Acéphale.

Remember: "It was thought," writes Burroughs, "that a man who had been hanged and brought back to life would not only bring luck to their venture but also ensure protection against the fate from which he had been rescued."

The question then is this: What is this mysterious power that is snatched from the jaws of the state? Nietzsche condemns the police for practicing the same deceits as the criminals they apprehend. In his eyes this makes them worse than the criminals. Is this why judicial murder is a good deal more mystical than other sorts of murder? It not only kills and eliminates a person. It seems to release an energy into the world.

Is Captain Strobe the Little Gallows Man?

Ever-sensitive to Christian allegory, Rahner tells us that just as Christ, "like one who is poisoned, fell asleep in death and yet awoke to life as the wondrous root from the earth of Adam, so too the Christian who wishes to free himself from Adam's poisoning and numbness, must take the cup of mandrake in his hand."[49] Rahner wants us to see Christ's mutilated body as a body readied for redemption, as if so much pain must, by some law, be rewarded as the harmonious meshing of opposites resulting in a transcendental payoff. But could we not equally well argue that the power of Jesus lies in the Roman colonial state's use of capital punishment and that what is found in Tyburn with Murphy the coal heaver and with all those just-dead hands wiped across the bodies of sick children in eighteenth-century London, that all of these practices as well as those presented by Genet and Burroughs are but the expression of the magic of the little gallows man—not Jesus—sprouting under the scaffold? The little gallows man, our mystical mandrake, with its reputation for hallucinogenic effects, voluptuousness, and occult power speaks to this fantastic process of state execution as the founding moment of a religion repeated with each state hanging. The magic of the little gallows man is nothing less than the magic of the state.

To this we might add the fearsome thesis that the Enlightenment expresses the domination of nature to such an extent that nature returns as a prehistoric and magical force within the rule of law.[50] Nowhere does the famous dialectic of Enlightenment occur with greater élan than with capital punishment for nowhere does the prehistoric surface in modernity with greater alarm. And nowhere else, therefore, would we expect the mandrake plant to surge more appropriately than under the hanging tree. Just as the gallows reverts to nature as the "hanging tree," as the speech of time would have it, so the mandrake plant becomes a socialized human being, the little gallows man.

Emergent from the seed of the judicially murdered criminal, mandrake is preeminently contradictory—poisonous, soporific, and voluptuous—in a word, miasmatic, derived from the ancient Greek μίασμα, meaning polluted, a contagious spiritual condition of considerable danger such as that surrounding the corpse or the murderer.[51] Mandrake contains and focuses this contagion, as its powerful scent gives testimony. Mandrake is proof of the continuity of life at the precise moment when life is being taken by the state; it is the life—the excess, if you will—that escapes death as the noose tightens; it is the life that is created by death—the perverse, magical, turned-around life that only state violence could create. If we are to follow custom and define the state as that which has the monopoly of the legitimate use of violence, would it not be equally true to say that the mandrake springing from underneath the gallows expresses the mystical foundations of authority on which that violence, and the law, rest?

Postscript

Despite many visits to Colombia since 1969, I myself had never once heard of the flower vase cut until Echavarría's artwork, and I found myself wondering about

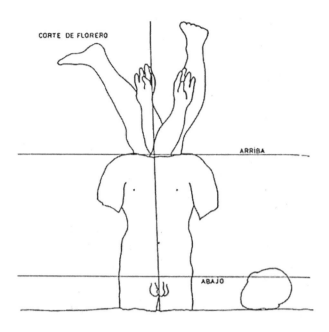

its frequency. Echavarría cites as his source a 1978 book concerned with massacres during the *violencia* of 1948–1964 in just one, albeit heavily afflicted, region, that of Tolima.[52] To ensure that the reader understands the different mutilations, this book presents eleven full-page diagrams of the human form like those used in target practice, providing what at first sight seems like a cross between the egg-and-sausage figures that children draw and diagrams meant to exude clinical detachment. I imagine police or people responsible for autopsy reports may have diagrams similar to these, which I find frightening and destabilizing indeed. Could it be that just as cartoons have a vexed and alarming connection to violence, so adults' appropriation of children's drawings of the human form has a similarly disturbing overlap with the police and autopsies? Or is it because these forms are so detached from reality, so clearly, so strenuously unreal, yet nevertheless terribly real—as in their use in clinical settings—that they acquire the haunting power of ghosts? Being so utterly without life, these diagrams of the outline of the human form create an emptiness that no mutilation or cartoon ever did. Here the art in nature and the art of nature coalesce and collapse the one in the other with a final phut.

Thomas Hobbes presents us with the same conundrum. He claimed that vio-

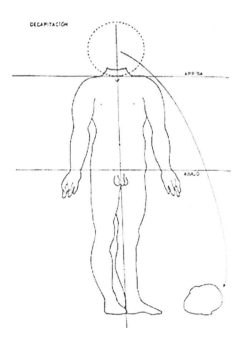

lence was the state of nature and, thanks to the famous contract, violence became the nature of the state. When I look at Mutis and see the flowers metamorphose from an art in nature to an art of nature, I am in my way replaying Hobbes's metamorphosis, too. Hobbes's contract is a fiction. It never happened as such. Yet everything conspires to occur as if it happened, and it is the mighty reed from which the rule of law is suspended (as I read Rawls), which is why we call it not a fiction but a necessary fiction, the realm, after all, of great art. Thus what might be called one of humanity's greatest inventions and institutions, namely, the state, can honestly lay claim to being great art, too, precisely where the art in nature and the art of nature coalesce in the permanent threat of violence against the person.

What then is capital punishment? Is it not exemplary of the law of mutilation? In his critique of violence, Walter Benjamin said it was the reenactment of the state's "founding violence." Actually the title of this essay, "Kritik der Gewalt," can mean both a critique of violence and a critique of authority, the one word, *Gewalt,* collapsing the two meanings into the one unsteady mix like Mutis / Echavarría. In other words we can think of this founding violence as an actual physical human conflict, of which there was much in Hobbes's time, including bloody violence against the king. But we can also think more precisely of founding violence as this unsteady mix of an art in nature with an art of nature wherein violence becomes authority. Thus is the mystery solved—how might becomes right. A singular, if not exactly solid, achievement.

This is what Echavarría's flowers mean to me and why Chuck Jones finds it easier to humanize animals than humanize humans.

Acknowledgments

I thank these people: Steve Poellet for his formidable intellectual sleuthing; David Gordon for running his eye over the author's note; Mark Taylor for inviting me to write "Transgression" for his *Critical Terms in Religion;* Clara Llano for co-reading the poetry of Don Tomás Zapata with me to that frighteningly large audience in Bogotá in 1992 where the lights went out; Vicky de Grazia for inviting me to her seminar at Rutgers on consumption where "The Sun Gives without Receiving" was born; Tom Mitchell and *Critical Inquiry* for enthusiasm for "The Beach" and "The Language of Flowers"; the curator Rosa Pera and the artist Federico Guzmán for inviting me to the "Revolutionary Plants" conference at the Antoni Tapies Foundation gallery in Barcelona, 2001, for which I wrote the first draft of "The Language of Flowers" and met Anxo Rabinal who took me to the lighthouse off Santiago de Compostela, which appears in my essay on the beach; the Bogotá-based artist Juan Manuel Echavarría for his Flower Vase Cut images and conversations concerning them; Mary Crane in Barcelona for arranging my trip to Walter Benjamin's grave at Port Bou; Xavi Hurtado in Barcelona for looking after me in many ways and supplying me with the names of the winds that whistle past that grave; Stephen Muecke at the University of Technology at Sydney for his nomadology, his vision for fictocriticism, and for giving me the chance to present the essay that grew out of my visit to Port Bou; Stephen Pascher for art and art theory advice; Chris Lamping for his breadth of knowledge encompassing mandrakes and eighteenth-century British hanging; Laurie Mona-han for her work on Masson and *Acephale;* Adam Ashforth and the Mfete family for their hospitality in Soweto; the Shawangunks School of Art and Philosophy, Anarchy and Mysticism, located off exit 18 off interstate 87 in upstate New York between New Paltz and High Falls, including Carolee Schneemann, Peter Lam-born Wilson, David Levi Strauss, and Nancy Goldring as an honorary member, as well as Elizabeth Branch Dyson of the University of Chicago Press for her quiet genius in bringing this book into being as an artifact; David Brent of the Univer-sity of Chicago Press for his counsel and continued faith in me over the decades; Lucy Kenyon for love, laughter, and suspicion of academical prose; and my old-est friend in the world, Clive Buhrich of Sydney, who drew the sketches of Syd-ney harbor with the explicit intention of preserving, on paper, at least, those rem-nants of harbor life we enjoyed so much, as children, together.

Author's Note

1. Michael Taussig, *My Cocaine Museum* (Chicago: University of Chicago Press, 2004).

2. Michael Taussig, *The Nervous System* (New York: Routledge, 1992).

Chapter 1

1. Cited in Gershom Scholem, *Walter Benjamin: The Story of a Friendship,* translated by Harry Zohn (Philadelphia: Jewish Publication Society, 1981 [1975]), 226.

2. Scholem, *Walter Benjamin,* 226.

3. Walter Benjamin, "Theses on the Philosophy of History," in *Illuminations,* edited and with an introduction by Hannah Arendt, translated by Harry Zohn (New York: Schocken, 1968), 255.

4. Walter Benjamin Museum, Port Bou.

5. Ingrid and Konrad Scheurmann, eds., *For Walter Benjamin* (Bonn: AsKI, 1993), 140.

6. Cited in Lisa Fittko, *Escape through the Pyrenees,* translated by David Koblick (1985; Evanston, IL: Northwestern University Press, 1991), 11.

7. Fittko, *Escape,* 108,

8. Hans Sahl, "Benjamin in the Internment Camp," in *On Walter Benjamin: Critical Essays and Recollections,* edited by Gary Smith (Cambridge, MA: MIT Press, 1988), 350–51.

9. Sahl, "Benjamin in the Internment Camp," 349, 351.

10. Fittko, *Escape,* 113, 114.

11. Varian Fry, *Surrender on Demand* (New York: Random House, 1945), 31.

12. Arthur Koestler, in his book *Scum of the Earth,* with commentary in Momme

Brodersen, *Walter Benjamin: A Biography*, translated by Malcolm R. Green and Ingrida Ligers (1990; London and New York: Verso, 1996), 258, 309–10. Brodersen's book is a gold mine of clearly presented and fascinating information.

13. Fry, *Surrender on Demand*, 16.

14. Jean Selz, "Benjamin in Ibiza," in *On Walter Benjamin: Critical Essays and Recollections*, edited by Gary Smith, 352–66 (Cambridge, MA: MIT Press, 1988), photograph on 356. See also Brodersen, *Walter Benjamin*, 196; and Vicente Valero, *Experiencia y pobreza: Walter Benjamin en Ibiza, 1932–1933* (Barcelona: Ediciones Peninsula, 2001), photographs between pages 128–129, especially valuable because of captions identifying the persons photographed.

15. Valero, *Experiencia y pobreza*, between pages 128–29, photograph no. 19.

16. Walter Benjamin, "In the Sun," in *Walter Benjamin: Selected Writings*, edited by Michael W. Jennings (Cambridge, MA: Harvard University Press, 1927–34), 2: 662.

17. Benjamin, "Spain, 1932," in *Walter Benjamin: Selected Writings*, edited by Michael W. Jennings (Cambridge, MA: Harvard University Press, 1927–34), 2: 648.

18. Benjamin, "Spain, 1932," 2: 651.

19. Theodor W. Adorno, "A Portrait of Walter Benjamin," 227–42 in *Prisms*, translated by Samuel and Shierry Weber (1967; Cambridge, MA: MIT Press, 1986), 240.

20. Walter Benjamin, "A Berlin Chronicle," in *Reflections*, edited and with an introduction by Peter Demetz (New York: Schocken, 1978), 25–26.

21. Jane Mayer, "Outsourcing Torture: The Secret History of America's 'Extraordinary Rendition' Program," *New Yorker*, February 14 and 21, 2005, 106–123.

22. Benjamin, "Theses on the Philosophy of History," 253–64, theses, 255.

23. Adorno, "Portrait of Walter Benjamin," 233.

24. Adorno, "Portrait of Walter Benjamin," 233.

25. Fittko, *Escape*, 101.

26. Fittko, *Escape*, 110.

27. Fittko, *Escape*, 127.

28. Benjamin, "Spain, 1932."

Chapter 2

1. Walter Benjamin, "The Storyteller: Reflections on the Works of Nikolai Leskov," in *Illuminations*, edited and with an introduction by Hannah Arendt, translated by Harry Zohn (New York: Schocken, 1968), 83–109.

2. "Esto existía pero estaba en privado, pero cuando ya Colón vino, entonces ya pasó a la historia, ya esto no quedó en privado; esto ya pasó a la historia. Eso mismo viene haciendo Miguel; sacando unas cosas que están en privado para llevarlcs a la historia. Esto era lo que yo quería decir de Colon."

3. The War of One Thousand Days (1899–1901).

4. *Chulavitas* was a name given to the paramilitary assassins recruited by the Conservative Party. Chulavita is the name of a neighborhood (*vereda*) in the department of Boyacá from where initially many such assassins were recruited. "The most terrible came from Boavita and Chulavita," wrote Eduardo Franco Isaza in his memoir, *Las guerrillas del llano*,

2nd ed. (Bogotá: Librería Mundial, 1959), 2, "so that this latter neighborhood [*vereda*] earned the horrific honor of bestowing its name on the horde." The Recorder's notes state that his informants remember that the *chulavitas* were generally "indios" or "mestizos," recruited from the highlands of Narino, certainly not blacks. They were more commonly referred to in this area as *pajaros* (birds) and have been seen as forerunners of the *sicarios* or hired assassins said to be frequently employed by the cocaine cartels (and other interests) in Cali and Medellín today. Dario Betancourt and Martha L. García, *Matones y cuadrilleros: Origen y evolución de la violencia en el occidente colombiano, 1946–1965* (Bogotá: Tercer Mundo, 1990), 20–22.

5. Gómez was the notoriously authoritarian and bloody-minded Conservative Party president of Colombia, eventually expelled to Spain because of the nature of his involvement in the *La Violencia*.

6. John Willett, "The Case of Kipling," in *Brecht in Context: Comparative Approaches* (London and New York: Methuen, 1984), 44–58.

7. Ibid., 50.

8. Georges Bataille, *The Accursed Share*, translated by Robert Hurley, 3 vols. (New York: Zone, 1988).

9. Friedrich Nietzsche, *The Use and Abuse of History*, translated by Adrian Collins (Indianapolis: Bobbs Merrill, 1981), 7.

10. The government national census for 1918 shows there being no more than 655 day laborers and 1,077 landholders for the whole municipality of Puerto Tejada. The figures for the town would be less. The same census reported for 1918 the population of the five adjoining municipios, Caloto, Santander, Puerto Tejada, Corinto, and Miranda, as 32,963.

11. Homer, *The Odyssey*, translated Robert Fitzgerald (Garden City and New York: Doubleday Anchor, 1963), 497.

12. Walter Benjamin, "On Some Motifs in Baudelaire," in *Illuminations*, edited and with an introduction by Hannah Arendt, translated by Harry Zohn (New York: Schocken, 1968), 147–200, see 194.

13. Nietzsche, *Use and Abuse of History*, 40.

14. Ibid.

15. Hayden White, *Metahistory: The Historical Imagination in Nineteenth-Century Europe* (Baltimore: Johns Hopkins University Press, 1973), 4.

16. Sigmund Freud, *Beyond the Pleasure Principle*, in *The Standard Edition of the Complete Psychological Works of Sigmund Freud*, edited and translated by James Strachey, vol. 18 (London: Hogarth, 1968), 19.

17. Francesco Balilla Pratella, "Futurist Music: Technical Manifesto," in *Futurist Performance*, edited by Michael Kirby and Victoria Nes Kirby (New York: PAJ Publications, 1971), 160–65.

18. Charles Baudelaire, "To Arsene Hcussaye," *Paris Spleen*, translated by Louise Varese (New York: New Directions, 1970), ix–x.

19. Benjamin, "On Some Motifs in Baudelaire," 194.

20. Alfredo Molano, *Los años del tropel: Relatos de la violencia* (Bogotá: Fondo Editorial CEREC, 1985).

21. Sigmund Freud, "Remembering, Repeating and Working Through," in *The Standard Edition of the Complete Psychological Works of Sigmund Freud*, edited and translated by James Strachey, vol. 12 (London: Hogarth, 1958), 154.

22. Walter Benjamin, "Theses on the Philosophy of History," in *Illuminations*, edited and with an introduction by Hannah Arendt, translate by Harry Zohn (New York: Schocken, 1969), 253–64, quotation on 261.

Chapter 3

1. This essay was first written in March 1993, as a contribution to the weekly seminar on "Consumer Culture in Historical Perspective" organized by Victoria de Grazia in the Center for Historical Analysis at Rutgers University, of which I was a fellow for one semester. Without her intellectual sympathy and the center's support, this essay would not have been written. I am grateful to all the members of the seminar, mainly historians, who infused the seminar with life and grace, especially to Jim Livingston and Elin Diamond for their commentaries and interest.

2. Walter Benjamin, "Some Motifs in Baudelaire," in *Charles Baudelaire: A Lyric Poet in the Era of High Capitalism* (London: New Left Books, 1973), 107–54, quotation on 113.

3. Georges Bataille, "The Notion of Expenditure," in *Visions of Excess: Selected Writings, 1927–1939*, edited by Alan Stoekel (Minneapolis: University of Minnesota Press, 1985), 116–29, quotation on 118 (first published in *La Critique Saddle* 7 [January 1933]).

4. Georges Bataille, *The Accursed Share*, translated by Robert Hurley (New York: Zone Books, 1988; first published; Paris, Éditions de Minuit, 1967), vol. 1.

5. A more detailed description with bibliographic information can be found in Michael Taussig, *The Devil and Commodity Fetishism in South America* (Chapel Hill: University of North Carolina Press, 1980).

6. Benjamin, "Some Motifs in Baudelaire," 141.

7. Walter Benjamin, "Theoretics of Knowledge, Theory of Progress," in *The Philosophical Forum* 15 (fall–winter 1983–84): 1–40, quotation on 6 (Convolut N in *Das Passagen-Werk*, Frankfurt am Main: Suhrkamp, 1982, Band 2, 571–611).

8. Compare with Jeffrey Mehlman's recent work, *Walter Benjamin for Children: An Essay on His Radio Years* (Chicago: University of Chicago Press, 1993), 28–30, in which Mehlman draws attention to Benjamin's radio story for children concerning the 1755 earthquake of Lisbon—Benjamin disputed the older theory that earthquakes are due to pressure from the earth's fiery core and favored the theory that the earth's surface is constantly shifting, the result of tension from permanently unstable tectonic plates.

9. Benjamin, "Theses on the Philosophy of History," in *Illuminations*, edited and with an introduction by Hannah Arendt, translate by Harry Zohn (New York: Schocken, 1968), 253–64, at 255.

10. Benjamin, "Theses," 263.

11. Bataille, *Consumption*, vol. 1 *of The Accursed Share*, 21.

12. A liter in 1992 there cost 5,000 pesos (around six U.S. dollars) and covered around one and a half acres in two days of labor costing around 6,000 pesos, whereas working the

same land and area with a machete or *pala* could take twenty days of labor at a cost of around 60,000 pesos.

13. Benjamin, "Some Motifs in Baudelaire," 139–40.

14. Michael Taussig, "Coming Home: Ritual and Labor Migration in a Colombian Town" (Working Paper Series, 30, Centre for Developing Area Studies, McGill University, Montreal, 1982).

15. Michael Taussig, *The Magic of the State* (New York: Routledge, 1992).

16. Michael Taussig, *Shamanism, Colonialism, and the Wild Man: A Study in Terror and Healing* (Chicago: University of Chicago Press, 1987).

17. This article was largely written here. Thanks to the hospitality of the Mfete family and Adam Ashforth.

18. See the footnote at the beginning of this article.

19. Bataille, *Nietzsche and Communism*, in *Sovereignty,* vol. 3 of *The Accursed Share*, 365–71, quotation on 367. Friedrich Nietzsche, *Twilight of the Idols (or How to Philosophise with a Hammer)*, translated by R. J. Hollingdale (Middlesex: Penguin, 1990), 86.

20. Friedrich Nietzsche, *The Gay Science,* translated with commentary by Walter Kaufmann (New York: Vintage, 1974), 275. On the concept of "the eternal return," Bataille wrote early on in his life, in 1937: "Of all the dramatic representations that have given Nietzsche's life the character of a laceration and of the breathless combat of human existence, the idea of the eternal return is certainly the most inaccessible." This passage is in "Nietzsche and the Fascists," in *Visions of Excess,* edited by Alan Stoekel (Minnesota: University of Minnesota Press, 1985), 182-96, quotation on 191.

21. Bataille, "The Notion of Expenditure," 118.

22. Bataille, in *Consumption,* vol. 1 of *The Accursed Share*, 106.

23. Bataille, *Consumption,* 9.

24. When I write "economic," I have, of course, in mind the way that with modern capitalism *economic* has come to stand not simply for goods and prices, production, distribution, and exchange but for a totalizing way of thinking *reasonably,* as Lionel Robbins put it, defining *economics* as the science of the logical apportioning of scarce means to alternate ends—hence a definition of reason, no less than of efficiency. Bataille is fascinating because he, too, creates a totalizing definition of economics as a logic, only in this case the logic—to employ the language of Lord Robbins et al.—is of ends, not means, and is therefore drastically opposed to the instrumental reason of capitalist schemata of means and ends. Here one sees, therefore, the radical possibilities opened up by a science of consumption that is true to consumption proper.

25. Bataille, in *Sovereignty,* vol. 3 of *The Accursed Share*, 209.

26. See Michael Taussig, "The Genesis of Capitalism amongst a South American Peasantry: Devil's Labor and the Baptism of Money," *Comparative Studies in Society and History* 19, no. 2 (1977): 130–55. See also Marc Edelman, "Landlords and the Devil: Class, Ethnic, and Gender Dimensions of Central American Peasant Narratives," *Cultural Anthropology* 9, no. 1 (1994): 58–93; and also Taussig, *Devil and Commodity Fetishism.* The terminology of use value and exchange value hearkens back to Aristotle's discussion of

oeconomia in *The Politics*. In building on this, Marx couples it to the very basis of Hegel's philosophy, the logical and historical problem of how the concrete particular can be coordinated with the universal (as with money and the modern state).

27. Marcel Mauss, *The Gift: Forms and Functions of Exchange in Archaic Societies* (New York: Norton, 1967; first published as *Essai sur le don, forme archaique de l'echange*, Paris, 1925).

28. Claude Lévi-Strauss, *The Elementary Structures of Kinship* (Boston; Beacon, 1969).

29. Derrida has expounded on this with great verve and insight in his *Counterfeit Money* (Chicago: University of Chicago Press, 1992).

30. Mauss, *The Gift*. 1.

31. Bataille, *Sovereignty*, vol. 3 of *The Accursed Share*, 347. Towards the end of his essay on the gift, Mauss makes two interesting moves in this respect. One is to point out that, except for the European Middle Ages, all his examples of the gift come from societies structured into symmetrical "segments" in which "individuals, even the most influential, were less serious, avaricious and selfish than we are; externally at least they were and are generous and more ready to give" (79). The next move is to relate the "exaggerated generosity" to the fragility of peace in such societies, to see, in other words, the gift as that which is composed by a peace forever fragile in the shadow of imminent violence. From this Mauss draws the lesson for the naturalness, if not the need, for socialism in modem Europe: the socialism of a gift being "wealth amassed and redistributed in the mutual respect and reciprocal generosity that education can impart" (81). Karl Polanyi's anthropologically informed distinction between reciprocity, redistribution, and markets as the three basic forms of economy comes to mind, especially since it regards Polanyi's equation of socialism with redistribution (the model for which are Trobriand chiefdoms!). See, for example, Karl Polanyi, *The Great Transformation: The Political and Economic Origins of Our Time* (Boston: Beacon Press, 1944), chap. 4; and also Marshall Sahlins on the gift and war in *Stone Age Economics* (Chicago: Aldine-Atherton, 1972). Like Mauss and Polanyi, Bataille saw the solution to the crucial problems of the world economic order as requiring the capitalist states to consider "the gift in a rational manner" (in *Sovereignty*, vol. 3 of *Accursed Share*, 429).

32. The political repressions involved come across strongly in Bataille's articles in the late 1930s on Nietzsche reprinted in *Visions of Excess* (see note 19).

33. Georges Bataille, *The Impossible* (1962, first published as *The Hatred of Poetry*).

34. "Too-muchness" is a term I take from Norman O. Brown's essay, "Dionysus in 1990," in his *Apocalypse and/or Metamorphoses* (Berkeley: University of California Press, 1990), 179–200, quotation on 183.

35. Bataille, *The History of Eroticism*, vol. 2 of *The Accursed Share*, 94.

36. G.W. F. Hegel, *Phenomenology of Mind* (New York: Harper & Row, 1967), 93; Alexandre Kojève, *Introduction to the Reading of Hegel: Lectures on the Phenomenology of Spirit,* assembled by Raymond Queneau, edited by Allan Bloom (Ithaca: Cornell University Press, 1969)

37. Bataille, *The History of Eroticism*, vol. 2 of *Accursed Share*, 101.

38. Nietzsche, *The Gay Science*, no. 125, "The madman," 181.

226

39. Nietzsche, *The Gay Science*, no. 342, "Incipit Tragoedia," 275 (end of book 4, introduction to the concept of "the eternal return").

40. Roger Caillois, "Mimicry and Legendary Psychaesthenia," *October* 31 (winter 1984): 17–32, quotation on 30 (originally published in Paris as "Mimetisme et psychasthenie legendaire," in *Minotaure* 7 [1935]). For a wide-ranging discussion of this, see Taussig, *Mimesis and Alterity: A Particular History of the Senses* (New York: Routledge, 1993).

41. Nietzsche, *Twilight of the Idols*, 84.

42. Nietzsche argues in *Twilight of the Idols*, 87, and throughout his works, that mimicry is no less the essential weapon of power throughout history than it is of thinking and the cultural construction of reality itself. Moreover, he sets up two kinds of mimicry: on the one hand, the Dionysian and, on the other, that of calculation, dissimulation, self-control, and lying. Thus is raised the fascinating problem: How do these two forms interrelate through history, and what are the implications thereof for understanding the gift in relation to capitalism? This question can now be seen as what guides one of the most significant contributions to social theory in the twentieth century, namely, *Dialectic of Enlightenment* by Max Horkheimer and Theodor W. Adorno (New York: Continuum, 1987). As to the identity of the devil, Nietzsche had a swift response: that Christianity distilled the Evil One out of Dionysus—a point explored in *The Anti-Christ*, 123–99, at 129, in *Twilight of the Idols and The Anti-Christ* (Harmondsworth, Middlesex: Penguin, 1990).

43. Nietzsche, "The madman," in *The Gay Science*, 182.

Chapter 4

1. Sigmund Freud to Wilhelm Fliess, 2 May 1897, in *The Complete Letters of Sigmund Freud to Wilhelm Fliess, 1897–1904*, translated and edited by Jeffrey Moussaieff Masson (Cambridge, MA: Belknap, 1985), 239.

2. William S. Burroughs, "The Literary Techniques of Lady Sutton-Smith," *Times Literary Supplement*, 6 Aug. 1964, 682.

3. See Charles Olson, *Call Me Ishmael* (San Francisco: City Light Books, 1947).

4. This theme is evoked and explored with originality and great insight by Allan Sekula in his *Fish Story*, a 240-page catalog of text and photographs to accompany a traveling exhibit (Dusseldorf: Richter, 1995). Reminiscent of John Berger's work with photographs by Jean Mohr, Sekula writes terse, telegraphic, echoing prose alongside his photographs that, through a wide-ranging Marxist sensibility, knits together political with art historical interests concerning the awesome mix of business and romance that is the sea and the ships that cross it. (Thanks to Tom Mitchell and Antony Gormley for reminding me of this work, and Michael Watts for giving me a copy of it as the deluge descended over San Francisco.)

5. James Joyce, *Ulysses*, annotated student's edition, with an introduction and notes by Declan Kiberd (London: Penguin, 1992), quotations on 3, 1, 4.

6. Joyce, *Ulysses*, 55, 56, 57.

7. Joyce, *Ulysses*, 57.

8. Joyce, *Ulysses*, 58.

9. Joyce, *Ulysses*, 62.

10. Joyce, *Ulysses*, 64.

11. Quoted in Walter Benjamin, "N [Theoretics of Knowledge; Theory of Progress]," *Philosophical Forum* 15 (fall–winter 1983): quotations on 12.

12. Theodor W. Adorno, "A Portrait of Walter Benjamin," *Prisms*, translated by Samuel and Shierry Weber (Cambridge, MA: MIT Press, 1981), 233.

13. Olson, *Call Me Ishmael*, 13.

14. Benjamin, "The Storyteller: Reflections on the Works of Nikolai Leskov," in *Illuminations*, edited and with an introduction by Hannah Arendt, translated by Harry Zohn (New York: Schocken, 1969), 87. B. Traven, *The Death Ship* (New York: Alfred Knopf, 1934).

15. André Breton, *Mad Love*, translated by Mary Ann Caws (1937; Lincoln: University of Nebraska Press, 1987), 19.

16. Benjamin, "N," 10.

17. Klaus Theweleit, *Male Fantasies*, translated by Stephen Conway, Erica Carter, and Chris Turner, 2 vols. (Minneapolis: University of Minnesota Press, 1987–89), 1: xviii–xix.

18. See Hakim Bey, *T. A. Z.: The Temporary Autonomous Zone, Ontological Anarchy, Poetic Terrorism* (New York: Autonomedia, 1985). See also Peter Lamborn Wilson [Hakim Bey], *Pirate Utopias: Moorish Corsairs and European Renegadoes* (New York: Autonomedia, 1995).

19. William S. Burroughs, *Cities of the Red Night* (New York: Holt, Rinehart, and Winston, 1981), 332.

20. Her father was German, born in Grabow, in the Polish Corridor, and a professor of entomology. See Anne Stevenson, *Bitter Fame: A Life of Sylvia Plath* (Boston: Houghton Mifflin, 1989), 4–5.

21. Ted Hughes, "Dream Life," *Birthday Letters* (New York: Farrar, Straus, Giroux, 1998), 141.

22. Sylvia Plath, "Daddy," *Ariel* (New York: Harper & Row, 1966), 49.

23. Ibid., 49–50.

24. See Peter Linebaugh, "'All the Atlantic Mountains Shook,'" *Journal of Canadian Labour Studies* 10 (fall 1982): 87–121.

25. "I have settled on the image of ships in motion across the spaces between Europe, America, Africa, and the Caribbean as a central organizing symbol for this enterprise and as my starting point" (Paul Gilroy, *The Black Atlantic: Modernity and Double Consciousness* [Cambridge, MA: Harvard University Press, 1993], 4). This helps him get away from nationalistic and ethnically rooted analyses, in favor of "rhizomorphic, fractal structure of the transcultural, international formation I call the black Atlantic" (4).

26. Jones, *The Formative Years and the Great Discoveries, 1856–1900*, vol. 1 of *The Life and Work of Sigmund Freud* (New York: Basic Books, 1953), 331. Freud's letter to Fliess are a gold mine for such Italian references.

27. W. H. Auden and Elizabeth Mayer, introduction to J. W. Goethe, *Italian Journey, 1786–1788*, translated by W. H. Auden and Elizabeth Mayer (San Francisco: North Point Press, 1962), xvii.

28. Karl Marx, "The So-Called Primitive Accumulation," *Capital: A Critique of Political Economy*, translated by Samuel Moore and Edward Aveling, edited by Friedrich Engels, 3 vols. (New York: International Publishers, 1967), 1: 755–56.

29. Goethe, *Italian Journey,* 82.

30. Richard Sennett, *Flesh and Stone: The Body and the City in Western Civilization* (New York: W. W. Norton, 1994), 223.

31. See Sennett, *Flesh and Stone,* and Jan Morris, *The Venetian Empire: A Sea Voyage* (New York: Harcourt Brace Jovanovich, 1980), 148.

32. Thomas Mann, *Death in Venice,* 201.

33. Mann, *Death in Venice,* 263.

34. Michael Taussig, *The Nervous System* (New York: Routledge, 1992).

35. Friedrich Nietzsche, *The Gay Science,* translated with commentary by Walter Kaufmann (New York: Vintage, 1974), 247–48.

36. Nietzsche, *The Gay Science,* 248, n. 38.

37. Nietzsche, *On the Genealogy of Morality and Other Writings,* translated by Carol Diethe, edited by Keith Ansell-Pearson (Cambridge: Cambridge University Press, 1994), 61, 70.

38. Sylvia Plath, *The Journals of Sylvia Plath,* edited by Ted Hughes and Frances McCullough (New York: Dial Press, 1982), 182.

39. Ibid.

Chapter 5

1. Marcel Mauss, "Les techniques du corps," lecture 17 May, 1934, translated by Ben Brewster as "Body Techniques," in Marcel Mauss, *Sociology and Psychology* (London: Routledge, 1979), 95–123.

2. Laurie Goodstein and Juan Forero, "Robertson Suggests U.S. Kill Venezuela's Leader," *New York Times,* 24 August, 2005, A10.

3. Leo Steinberg, *The Sexuality of Christ in Renaissance Art and in Modern Oblivion* (1983; Chicago: University of Chicago Press, 1996).

4. Edward Burnett Tylor, *Primitive Culture* (New York, 1871).

5. E. Lucas Bridges, *Uttermost Part of the Earth* (London: Hodder and Stoughton, 1951), 406.

6. Bridges, *Uttermost Part of the Earth,* 262. Note that Bridges spoke the Ona (Selk'nam is the native term) language, and when he describes speech as guttural he is not necessarily mistaken. *Joon* is the word for shaman or native doctor.

7. Bridges, *Uttermost Part of the Earth,* 263.

8. Bridges, *Uttermost Part of the Earth,* 264. And note the story in Gusinde's more than one thousand pages of ethnography on the Selk'nam (based on fieldwork undertaken over four trips between 1918 and 1924) of how in 1919 a group of medicine men had been offered presents by Bridges's brother, Guillermo, if they could kill one of his dogs with magic. The medicine men refused, as they believed their magic to be of no use against white men or their dogs. Martin Gusinde, *Los Selk'nam,* vol. 1 of *Los indios del Tierra del Fuego,* translated by Werner Hoffman (Buenos Aires: Centro Argentina de Etnología Americano, 1982), 698–99.

9. Gusinde, *Los Selk'nam,* 18.

10. Bridges, *Uttermost Part of the Earth,* 285.

11. Bridges, *Uttermost Part of the Earth*, 286.

12. Bridges, *Uttermost Part of the Earth*, 286.

13. Franz Kafka, "Cares of a Family Man."

14. Friedrich Nietzsche, *The Birth of Tragedy*, translated with commentary by Walter Kaufmann (New York: Vintage, 1968), 23. Max Horkheimer and Theodor W. Adorno, *Dialectic of Enlightenment*, translated by John Cumming (New York: Continuum, 1969), 3–43.

15. Friedrich Nietzsche, *The Gay Science*, translated with commentary by Walter Kaufmann (New York: Vintage, 1974), 37. See also Michael Taussig, "Why the Nervous System?" in *The Nervous System* (New York: Routledge, 1992), 1–10.

16. On the importance of the eighteenth-century explorations in Siberia for the dissemination of the very notion of shamanism, see Gloria Flaherty, *Shamanism and the Eighteenth Century* (Princeton: Princeton University Press, 1992). These terms are splendid examples of hybrids emitting much cultural and historical mischief. "Totemism," for example, was brought to European attention by a whisky-peddling fur trader on the late eighteenth-century North American frontier and then professionalized by certified anthropologists in the twentieth century as a worldwide institution by which clans were thought to identify with a particular plant or animal species or other natural phenomenon such as lightning. Later it was easy for Claude Lévi-Strauss to disassemble it for his purposes of demonstrating his thesis that culture is like a language. But the story does not end there, as this essay demonstrates.

17. Waldemar Bogoras, *The Chukchee*, edited by Franz Boas, American Museum of Natural History, Memoirs, 11 (1904–9; New York: New York: Johnson, 1969), 433–67.

18. Bogoras, *Chukchee*, 447.

19. Bogoras, *Chukchee*, 447.

20. Franz Boas, "Religion of the Kwakiutl Indians," in *Kwakiutal Ethnography*, edited by Helen Codere (Chicago: University of Chicago Press, 1966), 121.

21. Irving Goldman, *The Mouth of Heaven* (New York: John Wiley, 1975), 102.

22. Stanley Walens, *Feasting with Cannibals: An Essay on Kwakiutl Cosmology* (Princeton: Princeton University Press, 1981), 24–25.

23. Walens, *Feasting with Cannibals*, 7.

24. Walens, *Feasting with Cannibals*, 9.

25. Goldman, *Mouth of Heaven*, vii .

26. Hunt, "I Desired to Learn the Ways of the Shaman," in Franz Boas, *The Religion of the Kwakiutal Indians*, part 2, *Translations* (New York: Columbia University Press, 1930), 1–41.

27. Claude Lévi-Strauss, "The Sorcerer and His Magic," in *Structural Anthropology* (Garden City, N.Y.: Doubleday, 1967), 161–80.

28. Boas, "Religion of the Kwakiutal Indians," 121.

29. This is hardly the place to make an extended analysis, but it needs to be observed that Hunt's mode of ethnography contains enormous problems for the interpretation of Kwakiutl culture precisely because the character of the relationship between Hunt and Boas is not opened to analysis. Why did Hunt write? How did he see his task? What instructions

did Boas give him? What did Hunt think he was doing telling a white man about the secrets of shamanism? How could Boas publish a text under his name that was one hundred percent written by Hunt? Only when we get a better understanding of their relationship will we be able to understand the subtleties of the culture being investigated.

30. I acquired this terminology of intercultural autoethnography from Mary Louise Pratt.

31. Goldman, *Mouth of Heaven*, 86–7.

32. Hunt, "I Desired to Learn the Ways of the Shaman," 5.

33. Hunt, "I Desired to Learn the Ways of the Shaman," 5.

34. Hunt, "I Desired to Learn the Ways of the Shaman," 31.

35. Hunt, "I Desired to Learn the Ways of the Shaman," 30.

36. Hunt, "I Desired to Learn the Ways of the Shaman," 31–32.

37. I am tempted by this to overturn the distinction essential to Michel Foucault's discussion of transgression and confession—where he contrasts the transmission of bodily knowledge through a premodern master-apprentice system he calls *ars erotica*, versus *confession* which he sees as part of modern Western sexuality, confession here amounting to the secret that has to be spoken in order to remain secret! It is the latter, the so-called "modern" mode, which fits perfectly with the Kwakiutal shamanism! See Michel Foucault, *The History of Sexuality*, vol. 1, *An Introduction*, translated by Robert Hurley (New York: Vintage, 1980).

38. Hunt, "I Desired to Learn the Ways of the Shaman," 32.

39. In his first major monograph Boas described this double-headed serpent, the Sisiul, as perhaps the most important of the fabulous monsters whose help was obtained by the ancestors and had therefore become the crest of a clan. To eat, touch, or see it was to have one's joints dislocated, to have one's head turned backward, and to meet with eventual death. But to those persons who had supernatural help, it may instead bring power. Franz Boas, *The Social Organization and the Secret Societies of the Kwakiutal Indians* (Washington, D.C.: United States National Museum Report, 1895), 371–72.

40. Hunt, "I Desired to Learn the Ways of the Shaman," 35.

41. Walens, *Feasting with Cannibals*, 24.

42. Walens, *Feasting with Cannibals*, 25. Claude Lévi-Strauss makes the mistake of omitting this native understanding from both of his famous essays on magic, "The Effectiveness of Symbols," concerned with Cuna shamanism in the San Blas Archipelago off Panama, and "A Sorcerer and His Magic," most of which works through George Hunt's 1925 account of his shamanic experiences that I discuss in this essay. In the Cuna case, Lévi-Strauss assumes that the sick person understands the curing song sung in a specialized shamanic language—a dubious proposition because the ethnography indicates that ordinary Cuna do not understand such language and because the song is *intended not for the patient but for the spirits,* providing, through words, the same sort of simulacrum Walens describes for the performances practiced by the Kwakiutl shamans. It is curious how this error is made in both of Lévi-Strauss's essays and through which he is able thereby to supplant the *mimetic* (a form of bodily knowing through empathy) with the *semiotic* (a form of intellectual knowing).

43. Hunt, "I Desired to Learn the Ways of the Shaman," 27–28.

44. Walens, *Feasting with Cannibals*, 25.

45. Ibid., 25.

46. Ibid., 24.

47. Ibid., 25; Boas, *Social Society*, 433–34.

48. Joseph Masco, "'It's a Strict Law which Bids Us Dance': Cosmologies, Colonialism, Death and Ritual Authority in the Kwakwaka'wakw Potlatch, 1849 to 1922," *Comparative Studies in Society and History* (1995): 55–56.

49. "Talk about the Great Shaman of the Nak!waxdax Called Fool," in Franz Boas, *The Religion of the Kwakiutal Indians,* part 2, *Translations* (New York: Columbia University Press, 1930), 41ff.

50. Hunt, "I Desired to Learn the Ways of the Shaman," 41.

51. Walens, *Feasting with Cannibals*, 26.

52. Goldman, *Mouth of Heaven*, gives a figure of fifty-three from Boas's report of 1895, and sixty-three from Edward S. Curtis, *The North American Indian*, vol. 10 (New York: Johnson reprint, 1915).

53. Hunt, "I Desired to Learn the Ways of the Shaman," 172.

54. Goldman, *Mouth of Heaven*, 102.

55. Hunt, "I Desired to Learn the Ways of the Shaman," 4.

56. Goldman, *Mouth of Heaven*, 102.

57. E. E. Evans-Pritchard, *Witchcraft, Oracles, and Magic among the Azande* (Oxford: Clarendon Press, 1937), 193.

58. Clifford Geertz, "Slide Show: Evans Pritchard's African Transparencies," *Raritan* 3, no. 2 (fall 1983): 62–80.

59. In this regard Evans-Pritchard was unlike Frank Hamilton Cushing, who through bluff and trickery forced himself into the priesthood of the Bow Lodge of the Zuni. See "My Adventures in Zuni," in *Zuni: Selected Writings of Frank Hamilton Cushing,* edited by Jesse Green (Lincoln: University of Nebraska Press, 1979), 99–101.

60. Evans-Pritchard, *Witchcraft, Oracles, and Magic,* 152.

61. Nietzsche, *Gay Science,* 38.

62. Evans-Pritchard, *Witchcraft, Oracles, and Magic,* 151 (emphasis added).

63. Evans-Pritchard, *Witchcraft, Oracles, and Magic,* 186.

64. Ibid., 230.

65. Ibid., 231.

66. Ibid.

67. Ibid. (emphasis added).

68. Ibid., 191–92.

69. Here, the word *leech* is an archaic English term for a folk healer. Like other terms used by Evans-Pritchard, such as *ensorcell* and *knave*, this term creates its own mystique combined with an implicit notion that African medicine occupies a stage on an evolutionary line of development that British society superseded. This is unfortunate and probably far from the author's intention.

70. Evans-Pritchard, *Witchcraft, Oracles, and Magic,* 232–33.

71. I have not here analyzed the deceit wherein the witch doctor is supposed to cut a deal

with the witch who caused the disease so that both will share in the fee for curing (see Evans-Pritchard, *Witchcraft, Oracles, and Magic*, 191–93). Here the skepticism in the magical powers of the witch doctor is balanced by faith in those of the witch to cause and withdraw misfortune by mystical means and that these means reside in mangu substance inherited at birth in the body of the witch. The question begged by this account is, Why would there be a need for the elaborate performance of the witch doctor? Why can't the doctor act more like a lawyer or peacemaker? Why the art? In the healing practiced by the people indigenous to the New World (if I may be so bold as to generalize), the answer lies readily at hand: the art is essential as the mode of establishing a mimetic model with the spirits. I know too little about Africa to comment, but I suspect the New World notion is applicable there, too, raising a totally different approach to the one of rationality and philosophy of science that has dogged British commentary on magic.

72. Evans-Pritchard, *Witchcraft, Oracles, and Magic*, 184.

73. Ibid., 210–11.

74. Ibid., 209.

75. Ibid., 213–14.

76. Maya Deren, *Divine Horsemen: The Living Gods of Haiti* (New Paltz, NY.: McPherson, 1983); Evans-Pritchard, *Witchcraft, Oracles, and Magic*, 154–82.

77. Evans-Pritchard, *Witchcraft, Oracles, and Magic*, 162.

78. Walter Benjamin, *The Paris Arcades*, Convolut o, "Prostitution and Gambling."

Chapter 6

1. Sigmund Freud, *Totem and Taboo: Some Points of Agreement between the Mental Lives of Savages and Neurotics*, vol. 13 of *The Standard Edition of the Complete Psychological Works of Sigmund Freud*, edited and translated by James Strachey (London: Hogarth, 1913), 20.

2. Emile Durkheim, "The Negative Cult and Its Functions," in *The Elementary Forms of the Religious Life* (New York: Free Press, 1965).

3. Mary Douglas, *Purity and Danger: An Analysis of the Concepts of Pollution and Taboo* (London: Routledge, 1966), 4.

4. Henri Junod, *The Life of a South African Tribe*, 2 vols. (New Hyde Park, N.Y.: University Books, 1962).

5. Victor Turner, "Betwixt and Between: The Liminal Period in Rites de Passage," in *The Forest of Symbols: Aspects of Ndembu Ritual* (Ithaca, N.Y.: Cornell University Press, 1966); Arnold van Gennep, *The Rites of Passage* (London: Routledge, 1960).

6. E. E. Evans-Pritchard, "Some Collective Expressions of Obscenity in Africa," *Journal of the Royal Anthropological Institute* (1929): 59; and Roger Caillois, *L'Homme et le sacre* (Paris: Gallimard, 1950), translated by Meyer Barash as *Man and the Sacred* (Urbana: University of Illinois Press, 2001).

7. Max Gluckman, "The Licence in Ritual," in *Custom and Conflict in Africa* (Oxford: Blackwell, 1960).

8. Mikhail Bakhtin, *Rabelais and His World*, translated by Helene Iswolsky (Bloomington: University of Indiana Press, 1984).

9. André Breton, *Mad Love*, translated by Mary Ann Caws (Lincoln: University of Nebraska Press, 1987).

10. Walter Benjamin, "Surrealism," in *Reflections*, edited and with an introduction by Peter Demetz (New York: Schocken, 1978).

11. Benjamin, "Surrealism," 178–79.

12. William S. Burroughs, *Naked Lunch* (London: Calder, 1964).

13. Georges Bataille, "Sacrificial Mutilation and the Severed Ear of Vincent van Gogh," in *Visions of Excess: Selected Writings, 1927–1939*, edited by Allan Stoekl, translated by Allan Stoekl with Carl R. Lovitt and Donald M. Leslie, Jr. (Minneapolis: University of Minnesota Press, 1985).

14. Robert Lowie, *Primitive Religion* (New York: Liveright, 1948).

15. George Catlin, *Letters and Notes on the Manners, Customs, and Conditions of the North American Indians*, 2 vols. (New York: Dover. 1973), 1: 173.

16. Kenneth Read, *The High Valley* (New York: Scribners, 1965), 131.

17. Read, *High Valley*, 133–34.

18. Baldwin Spencer and F. J. Gillen, *The Native Tribes of Central Australia* (New York: Dover, 1968).

19. Kees W. Bolle, "Secrecy in Religion," in *Secrecy in Religions*, edited by Kees W. Bolle (Leiden: Brill, 1987).

20. Colin Turnbull, *The Forest People* (New York: Simon and Schuster, 1962).

21. Joan Bamberger, "The Myth of Matriarchy: Why Men Rule in Primitive Society," in *Woman, Culture, and Society*, edited by Michelle Z. Rosaldo and Louise Lamphere (Stanford: Stanford University Press, 1974); Christopher Crocker, "Being and Essence: Totemic Representation among the Eastern Bororo," in *The Power of Symbols: Masks and Masquerade in the Americas*, edited by N. Ross Crumrine and Marjorie Halpin (Vancouver: University of British Columbia Press, 1983); Gillian Gillison, "Images of Nature in Gimi Thought," in *Nature, Culture, and Gender*, edited by Carol P. MacCormack and Marilyn Strathern (Cambridge: Cambridge University Press, 1980); Ronald Berndt, *Excess and Restraint: Social Control among a New Guinea Mountain People* (Chicago: University of Chicago Press, 1962); Terence Hays, "'Myths of Matriarchy' and the Sacred Flute Complex of the Papua New Guinea Highlands," in *Myths of Matriarchy Reconsidered*, edited by Deborah Gwertz, Oceania Monographs, 33 (Sydney: University of Sydney, 1988); and Thomas Gregor, *Anxious Pleasures: The Sexual Lives of an Amazonian People* (Chicago: University of Chicago Press, 1985).

22. Martin Gusinde, *Los Indios de Tierra del Fuego*, vol. 1, *Los Selk'nam* (Buenos Aires: Centro Argentino de Etnología Américana, 1982).

23. Elias Canetti, *Crowds and Power*, translated by Carol Stewart (New York: Farrar Straus Giroux, 1962), 290.

24. Johannes Huizinga, *Howo Ludens: A Study of the Play-Element in Culture* (Boston: Beacon, 1955); and Georg Simmel, "Secrecy," in *The Sociology of Georg Simmel*, translated and edited by Kurt H. Wolff (New York: Free Press, 1950).

25. Franz Boas, *Religion of the Kwakiutal Indians* [1930], in *Kwakiutal Ethnography*, edited by Helen Codere (Chicago: University of Chicago Press, 1966), 121.

26. E. E. Evans-Pritchard, *Witchcraft, Oracles, and Magic among the Azand* (Oxford: Clarendon Press, 1937), 193.

27. Read, *High Valley*, quotations on 126, 117.

28. Turnbull, *Forest People*, 88.

29. Michael Taussig, *Shamanism, Colonialism, and the Wild Man: A Study in Terror and Healing* (Chicago: University of Chicago Press, 1987).

30. Georges Bataille, "The Notion of Expenditure," in *Visions of Excess: Selected Writings, 1927–1939*, edited by Allan Stoekl, translated by Allan Stoekl with Carl R. Lovitt and Donald M. Leslie, Jr. (Minneapolis: University of Minnesota Press, 1985).

31. Georges Bataille, *The Accursed Share*, translated by Robert Hurley, 3 vols. (New York: Zone, 1988).

32. Norman O. Brown, "Dionysus in 1990," in *Apocalypse and/or Metamorphoses* (Berkeley and Los Angeles: University of California Press, 1991).

33. Bataille, *Accursed Share*, 1: 58.

34. G. W. F. Hegel, preface to *Phenomenology of Spirit*, translated by A. V. Miller (Oxford: Oxford University Press, 1977), 19.

35. Georges Bataille, "Hegel, Death, and Sacrifice," translated by Christopher Carsten, in *Yale French Studies* 78 (1990): 9–28.

36. Friedrich Nietzsche, *The Gay Science*, translated by Walter Kaufmann (New York: Vintage, 1974), 181–82.

37. Michel Foucault, "A Preface to Transgression," in *Language, Counter-Memory, Practice: Selected Essays and Interviews* (Ithaca, NY: Cornell University Press, 1977).

38. Michel Foucault, "A Preface to Transgression," 44.

39. Foucault, *History of Sexuality*, 35.

40. Benjamin, "Surrealism," 189–90.

Chapter 7

1. J. M. Coetzee, "The Vietnam Project," in *Dusklands* (Harmondsworth: Penguin Books, 1974), 1–49.

2. Walter Benjamin, "Zur Kritik der Gewalt" [1920–21], translated as "Critique of Violence," in *Reflections*, edited by Peter Demetz (New York: Harcourt Brace Jovanovich, 1978), 277–301, quotation on 286–87.

3. Benjamin, "Critique of Violence," 287.

4. He writes that the police are suspended from both the law-making and law-founding forms of violence.

5. Editorial, *New York Times*, 5 May 1994, A6.

6. N. R. Kleinfield and James McKinley Jr., "Lives of Courage and Sacrifices, Corruption and Betrayals in Blue," *New York Times*, 25 April 1994, A64.

7. Jean Genet, *The Thief's Journal* (Harmondsworth: Penguin, 1976), 157.

8. Elias Canetti, *Crowds and Power*, translated by Carol Stewart (New York: Viking Press, 1962).

9. Jeffrey Toobin, "Capone's Revenge," *New Yorker*, 23 May 1994, 46–59, quotation on 47.

10. Toobin, "Capone's Revenge," 55.

11. Toobin, "Capone's Revenge," 56.

12. Robert Baum as cited by Joe Sexton, "Testilying," *New York Times*, 4 May 1994, A26.

13. Sexton, "Testilying," A26.

14. Sexton, "Testilying," A26.

15. Jane B. Freidson, letter to the editor, *New York Times*, 6 May 1994. Also see letter of rebuttal by H. Morgenthau of Freidson's allegation that police are not prosecuted for perjury, *New York Times*, 13 May 1994.

16. Kleinfield and McKinley, "Lives of Courage," 64.

17. Curt Gentry, *Edgar Hoover: The Man and the Secrets* (New York: Norton, 1991), 728.

18. Sigmund Freud, "The Antithetical Meaning of Primal Words," in *The Standard Edition of the Complete Psychological Works of Sigmund Freud*, edited and translated by James Strachey, vol. 11 (London: Hogarth, 1957), 153–61.

19. Cf. Georges Bataille's work on the sacred, the abject, and power as in "Attraction and Repulsion II" in *The College of Sociology (1937–39)*, edited by Denis Hollier (Minneapolis: University of Minnesota Press, 1988), 113–24; and in Bataille, *The Accursed Share*, 2 vols. (New York: Zone Books, 1988, 1991). Also Roger Caillois, "Power," in Hollier, *College of Sociology*, 125–36. This last essay seems to be a composite Bataille-Caillois product.

20. Sigmund Freud, *Totem and Taboo*, in *The Standard Edition of the Complete Psychological Works of Sigmund Freud*, edited and translated by James Strachey, vol. 13 (London: Hogarth, 1957), 1–161, quotations on 18, 22.

21. Benjamin, "Critique of Violence," 287.

22. Of importance here was Georges Sorel's eclectic and fascinating work, *Reflections on Violence*, first published in 1915. Sorel has separate chapters on "The Proletarian Strike" and "The Political General Strike." His disposition to see "the big picture," to see violence no less than the general strike in terms of apocalyptic Christian mythology, makes this essay germane to Benjamin's similarly philosophical and religious concerns with violence. Furthermore, it seems to me that this work of Sorel's is the basis of Benjamin's strange gestures toward "pessimism" at the end of the latter's essay on surrealism—a pessimism that fuses eloquently with Benjamin's refiguration of Blanqui.

23. Benjamin, "Critique of Violence," 286.

24. Bataille, *Accursed Share*, 2: 95.

25. Bataille, see note 19. Roger Caillois, "The Sociology of the Executioner," in *The College of Sociology (1937–39)*, edited by Denis Hollier (Minneapolis: University of Minnesota Press, 1988).

26. Walter Benjamin, "Franz Kafka: On the Tenth Anniversary of His Death," in *Illuminations*, edited by Hannah Arendt (New York: Schocken, 1969), 111–40.

27. Alexandre Kojève, *Introduction to the Reading of Hegel: Lectures on "The Phenomenology of Spirit,"* assembled by Raymond Queneau, edited by Allan Bloom (Ithaca: Cornell University Press, 1980), 7.

28. Louis Althusser, *"Lenin and Philosophy," and Other Essays*, trans. Ben Brewster (New York: Monthly Review, 1971). Widely read and cited for a decade or more in this collection was the essay "Ideology and Ideological State Apparatuses," 127–86.

29. Nicos Poulantzas, *State, Power, Socialism,* translated by Patrick Camiller (New Left Books: London, 1978), 83.

Chapter 8

1. This is also how he begins his book, Chuck Jones, *Chuck Amuck: The Life and Times of an Animated Cartoonist* (New York: Farrar Straus Giroux, 1989), 13.

2. Michael Herr, *Dispatches* (New York: Knopf, 1977), 46.

3. Calvin Reid, "Juan Manuel Echavarria," *Bomb* 70 (winter 2000): 25.

4. See Herr, *Dispatches,* 199.

5. Editorial note to Walter Benjamin, "News about Flowers," translated by Michael Jennings, in Walter Benjamin, *Selected Writings,* trans. Rodney Livingstone et al., edited by Michael Jennings, Howard Eiland, and Gary Smith (Cambridge, MA: Belknap Press, 1994–2003), 2: 157 n. 1. See also Hans-Christian Adam, *Karl Blossfeldt, 1865–1932* (Cologne: Taschen, 1999).

6. Their rotten hulk seemed more inviting

That ship without a flag at all

Oh heavenly sky of streaming blue!

Enormous wind, the sails blow free!

Let wind and heaven go hang! But oh

Sweet Mary, let us keep the sea!

Bertolt Brecht, "Ballad of the Pirates," *Poems, 1913–1956,* translated by Edith Andersen et al., edited by John Willett and Ralph Manheim (New York: Meuthen, 1976), 18.

7. And not only in the Christian world. In the index to Jack Goody, *The Culture of Flowers* (Cambridge: Cambridge University Press, 1993), page 459, funerals are one of the major entries, with many subcategories referring us to "ancient Egypt, ancient Greece, ancient Rome, Asante, Confucian, contemporary Europe, contemporary Hong Kong, contemporary India . . . [ending with] Socialist Europe." "Flowers are particularly associated with rites to the dead," he writes with regards to China, Taiwan, and Hong Kong. Even in Africa, where he finds, in comparison to Eurasia, little interest in flowers, he notes the planting of red and green leafed bushes in Asante cemeteries. Yet Christianity has not wholeheartedly endorsed the sacramental use of flowers. In fact there seems to be a decided ambivalence. The Protestant churches are generally opposed to their use in ritual, and there have been long stretches of time, such as the Middle Ages, when the church as a whole prohibited their sacramental use. Could this ambivalence be a sign, however, of whatever it is that makes flowers seem appropriate for death?

8. Jean Genet, *Querelle,* translated by Anselm Hollo (1952; New York: Grove Press, 1974), 37.

9. Herr, *Dispatches,* 43.

10. See Richard Evans Schultes and Albert Hofmann, *Plants of the Gods: Their Sacred, Healing, and Hallucinogenic Powers* (Rochester, VT: Healing Arts Press, 1992).

11. Hugo Rahner, *Greek Myths and Christian Mystery* (New York: Harper & Row, 1963), 258.

12. Quoted in Frederick J. Simoons, *Plants of Life, Plants of Death* (Madison: University

of Wisconsin Press, 1998), 101. I thank Jenny Davidson of the English department of Columbia University for this reference as well as for her comments on my approach to hanging, mandrakes, and the language of flowers

13. See Schultes and Hofmann, *Plants of the Gods*, 86–91; and Simoon, *Plants of Life*, 103.

14. See C. J. S. Thompson, *The Mystic Mandrake* (1934; New Hyde Park, NY: University Books, 1968).

15. Simoons, *Plants of Life*, 104; emphasis added.

16. Quoted in Frederick Starr, "Notes upon the Mandrake," *American Antiquarian and Oriental Journal* 23 (July–Aug. 1901): 259–60.

17. As if to accentuate the metaphysical dilemma such a potent creature presents, either counterfeiting nature or counterfeiting art, there was deep concern in early modern Europe concerning counterfeit mandrakes being sold for great sums.

18. *Handy Bible Encyclopedia*, in *The Holy Bible and International Bible Encyclopaedia and Concordance* (New York, 1940), s.v. "mandrake." See also Rahner, *Greek Myths and Christian Mystery*, 224–77.

19. Rahner, *Greek Myths and Christian Mystery*, 258.

20. Schultes and Hoffman, *Plants of the Gods*, 86.

21. See Georges Bataille, "The Language of Flowers" (1929), in *Visions of Excess: Selected Writings, 1927–1939*, edited and with an introduction by Allan Stoekl, translated by Allan Stoekl with Carl R. Lovitt and Donald M. Leslie, Jr. (Minneapolis: University of Minnesota Press, 1985), 10–14.

22. Goody, *Culture of Flowers*, 244, 234.

23. Bataille, "The Language of Flowers," 14. In this respect I think also of the rainbow. Like the flower, the rainbow is remarkable for its mysterious effulgence of color and its ephemerality. Once "picked," it too withers to yield not debris and dirt, but a sex change or a pot of gold—just out of reach. So let us anticipate what fun it would be to write another essay entitled "The Language of Rainbows."

24. Quoted in Alastair Brotchie, introduction to *Encyclopaedia Acephalica*, edited by Georges Bataille (London: Atlas Press, 1995), 12. On Masson, about whom little is written, I am greatly indebted to Laurie J. Monahan, "Violence in Paradise: André Masson's Massacres," *Art History* 24 (Nov. 2001): 707–24, as well as to her essay "'Printing Paradoxes': André Masson's Early Graphic Works," in *André Masson inside/outside Surrealism*, exhibition catalog (Toronto: Art Gallery of Ontario, 2001), 53–78.

25. Brotchie, introduction, quotations on 15–16, 15.

26. Brotchie, introduction, 12.

27. Brotchie, introduction, 14.

28. Bataille, "The Language of Flowers," 13.

29. "Little gallows man," from the German *Galgenmannlein*. See Thompson, *Mystic Mandrake*, 166. According to one source the little gallows man could also arise from the froth that fell to the ground from the choking mouth of a hanged woman. I thank Christopher Lamping for this reference as well as the reference to Peter Linebaugh's essay on hanging (see below). I have only come across this one reference to mandrake and hanged

women. The issue seems to me to revolve around male seed. On the other hand, woman's part in this gallows/mandrake scheme has ever so much to do with capturing fertility.

30. See Thomas Newton, *An Herbal for the Bible* (London, 1587), 10–12. I am paraphrasing and to a slight extent transcribing or translating archaic words in this sixteenth-century text.

31. Newton, *An Herbal for the Bible,* 11.

32. See Starr, "Notes upon the Mandrake," 262.

33. See Marie Trevelyan, *Folk-Lore and Folk-Stories of Wales* (London: E. Stock, 1909), 92–93.

34. See Starr, "Notes upon the Mandrake," 262.

35. Thompson, *Mystic Mandrake,* 169.

36. See Simoons, *Plants of Life,* 127.

37. Genet, *Querelle,* 20.

38. See V. A. C. Gatrell, *The Hanging Tree: Execution and the English People, 1770–1868* (Oxford: Oxford University Press, 1994).

39. Quoted in Peter Linebaugh, "The Tyburn Riot against the Surgeons," in *Albion's Fatal Tree: Crime and Society in Eighteenth-Century England,* edited by Douglas Hay et al. (New York: Pantheon Books, 1975), 72.

40. Quoted in Thomas W. Laqueur, "Crowds, Carnival, and the State in English Executions, 1604–1868," in *The First Modern Society: Essays in English History in Honour of Lawrence Stone,* edited by A. L. Beier, David Cannadine, and James M. Rosenheim (Cambridge: Cambridge University Press, 1989), 346.

41. Linebaugh, "The Tyburn Riot," 110.

42. Thomas Hardy, "The Withered Arm," in *Selected Short Stories and Poems,* edited by James Gibson (London: J. M. Dent, 1992), 44. Again my thanks to Christopher Lamping of the anthropology department of Columbia University for this invaluable reference.

43. Known in some circles as autoerotic asphyxiation or asphyxophilia, hanging has been used as a treatment for erectile dysfunction and impotence in Europe since at least the early 1600s. A French psychiatrist reported in 1856 that 30 percent of men who died from hanging had erections or ejaculations. In a survey of ninety-seven suicides among young people in the Boston area during 1941–1950, one investigator found twenty-seven of them to be possibly due to autoerotic hanging gone wrong. See "The Autoerotic Asphyxiation Syndrome in Adolescent and Young Adult Males," found in 2002 at http://members.aol.com/bjo22038/.

44. See Knud Romer Joergensen, "Please Be Tender When You Cut Me Down," http://www.sexuality.org/l/fetish/aspydang.html. An anonymous pamphlet of 1792, the "Art of Strangeling, etc. . . .," states that it was one Jonathan Wild who first discovered, while examining the pockets of hanged felons, that "they evinced certain emotions and commotions, which . . . proved that all flesh must die to live again."

45. William S. Burroughs, *Cities of the Red Night* (New York: Holt, Rinehart, and Winston, 1981), 70.

46. Daniel P. Mannix, *The History of Torture* (New York: Dell, 1964).

47. Burroughs, *Cities of the Red Night,* quotations on 179, 180, 181.

48. Burroughs, *Cities of the Red Night,* 29.

49. Rahner, *Greek Myths and Christian Mystery,* 259–60.

50. See Max Horkheimer and T. W. Adorno, *Dialectic of Enlightenment,* translated by John Cumming (New York: Continuum, 1987).

51. See Robert Parker, *Miasma: Pollution and Purification in Early Greek Religion* (Oxford: Clarendon Press, 1983), 3.

52. See MaríaVictoria Uribe, *Matar, rematar y contramatar: Las masacres de la violencia en el Tolima, 1948–1964* (Bogotá: CINEP, 1990), 175.

magic, 151; and sorcerer as both dupe and believer, 121, 123